OBJECT ORIENTED ENVIRONS

OBJECT ORIENTED ENVIRONS

edited by Jeffrey Jerome Cohen
and Julian Yates

Ⓟ punctum books, earth

OBJECT ORIENTED ENVIRONS
© 2016 Jeffrey Jerome Cohen and Julian Yates

http://creativecommons.org/licenses/by-nc-sa/4.0/

This work carries a Creative Commons BY-NC-SA 4.0 International license, which means that you are free to copy and redistribute the material in any medium or format, and you may also remix, transform and build upon the material, as long as you clearly attribute the work to the authors (but not in a way that suggests the authors or punctum endorses you and your work), you do not use this work for commercial gain in any form whatsoever, and that for any remixing and transformation, you distribute your rebuild under the same license.

First published in 2016 by
punctum books
Earth
http://punctumbooks.com

punctum books is an independent, open-access publisher dedicated to radically creative modes of intellectual inquiry and writing across a whimsical para-humanities assemblage. We solicit and pimp quixotic, sagely mad engagements with textual thought-bodies. We provide shelters for intellectual vagabonds.

ISBN-13: 978-0692642030
ISBN-10: 069264203X

Cover image: Based on a volvelle that appears in Martín Cortés's *Breve compendio de la sphera y de la arte de navegar* (Seville, 1551), 20r, photographed by Sarah Werner.

Facing-page drawing: Heather Masciandaro.
Cover and book design: Chris Piuma.
Editorial assistance: Bert Fuller.

Before you start to read this book,

take this moment to think about making a donation
to **punctum books**, an independent non-profit press,

@ http://punctumbooks.com/about/

If you're reading the e-book, click on the image below
to go directly to our donations site.
Any amount, no matter the size, is appreciated
and will help us to keep our ship of fools afloat.
Contributions from dedicated readers will also help us
to keep our commons open and to cultivate new work
that can't find a welcoming port elsewhere.

Our adventure is not possible without your support.
Vive la open-access!

Fig. 1. Hieronymus Bosch,
Ship of Fools (detail; 1490–1500)

In Lieu of a Table of Contents
A Note to Readers about Navigating this Book

ALTHOUGH WE HAVE PROVIDED YOU WITH A PRINCIPLE OF ORGANIZATION for this volume, we hope you will ignore it. The essays are arranged alphabetically by author. The alphabet is a powerful ordering machine, but it is one of many and not any better than most. We encourage you to surrender the power to pilot the contents of this book to something else—perhaps, in honor of a theme of this volume, some object that you will allow to exert its aleatory agency over your reading. You might even create that object yourself: a spinner, perhaps, or a volvelle. A twenty sided die would work nicely, provided you also number the essays in a way that pleases you rather than allow the alphabet that power too. If you are reading the book as a PDF, use the word search function and group the essays according to which have the most letters of your favorite animal (Katherine Cohen's suggestion), or the least references to any word that irritates you. If the book exists for you as a material object that you hold open in your hand right now, keep in mind that sortilege and bibliomancy are ancient practices that might profitably be revived.

The essays that form *Object Oriented Environs* were a collective endeavor and therefore should feel like walking into a lively conversation. They possess no vectors towards culmination, no sense of progress towards a final goal or definitive revelation. You are the latest interlocutor. Surrender with some object to being with these pieces, and you will see that their authors were intensely with each other (as well as with their own objects) during the long processes of composition.

Introduction
(An Environing of this Book)
Jeffrey Jerome Cohen & Julian Yates

> The best television arguments and discussions are...those which open themselves towards people not assumed in advance to be already represented.... Some of the worst, for all their internal skills, are those that *simulate a representation by their own criteria*.
> —Raymond Williams, *Television*[1]

IN THE SPRING OF 2013, WE WERE INVITED TO PROPOSE A POSSIBLE session for the Shakespeare Association of America meeting in St. Louis for 2014. The SAA is an organization that, in addition to running paper panels at its annul conference, offers participants the opportunity to share work-in-progress through themed seminars. The two of us had been in conversation for some time about nonhumans, *things*, animal, vegetable, and mineral, medieval and renaissance, about questions of ecology, and how to craft nontraditional conversation and thinking spaces in which something unanticipated might unfold. We decided to collaborate to build a gathering that would bring together these interests, objects, and possibilities for eventuation. The title of the seminar we proposed was "Object-Oriented Environs in Early Modern England," which took its cue from the philosophical movement called Object-Oriented Ontology (frequently abbreviated to OOO) in the hope of provoking a conversation about how early modernists, or humanists in general, parse the question of matter, of *things*. We called the collocation OOE @ SAA.

---

1 Raymond Williams, *Television: Technology and Cultural Form* [1974/5] (Routledge: London and New York, 1990), 49–50.

Beyond or beside this thematic set of concerns, our hope was to have the seminar itself constitute an object of sorts, a *thing* in the word's etymological sense of a gathering that might become more than the sum of its papers and our parts. We wanted to create an experience akin to the open spaces that Raymond Williams imagines in *Television*, a conversation that unfolds not by fulfilling a set of criteria laid out in advance, simulating a sense of fullness, a sense of community or comprehension, but remaining open to the unexpected, comfortable with pauses, meandering, moments of silence, experiments that might fail, that might solicit still other sets of criteria, viewpoints, orientations than those we were able to imagine at the start. José Esteban Muñoz calls such unforeclosed expectancy *cruising utopia*: finding the openness where an unknown or queer futurity might start, a journey with companions and with a destination difficult to know in advance.[2] We wanted not a gathering that maps terrain already covered in the hope of attaining some certain prospect, but a seminar on the move. Or to adapt Williams a bit, we wanted to collaborate with the seminar participants and the gathering of objects they would make to create openings towards people and things "not assumed in advance to be already represented," towards strangers unknown and unanticipated, possibly even hostile to the unfolding project yet welcome all the same.

While it may seem odd to invoke a televisual signal and form as a model for face-to-face conversation, all communication occurs across gaps. We are all, however intimate, however habituated or oriented to one another, *tele*-friends or *tele*-beings, operating at a distance, bridging those divides and crossing the gaps by way of sound, vision, affect, touch, and forms of technical mediation. Like Williams, what we hoped for was something on the order of a community or "charity of production" as opposed to the frequently happy, even festive, "charity of consumption" that tends to characterize our shared spaces.[3] It seemed to us that this might be accomplished by calling attention to the distances between us, that we still endeavored to cross, distances rendered lively by the objects that oriented us, the objects that we threw in each other's way, and so came between us. The resulting book, *Object Oriented Environs*, archives

---

2   José Esteban Muñoz, *Cruising Utopia: The Then and There of Queer Futurity* (New York: New York University Press, 2009).
3   Raymond Williams, *The Country and the City* (Oxford and New York: Oxford University Press, 1975), 30–31.

INTRODUCTION (AN ENVIRONING OF THIS BOOK)   xiii

this endeavor. But it is a strange form of repository for its existence was mooted, projected, planned for, and announced to all-comers, to all members of our seminars in advance. Writing, compiling, this book began as a collective endeavor and putative product—some *thing* that everyone, seminar participants and their objects, and the turn to which their objects put them, helped to make, enables us to compose. OOE is an archive of hazard, an aleatory recording of things fleeting, perilous, embarrassing, embraced; of enthusiasms and reluctances; of objects and bodies that cross distances for a while to become an ephemeral gathering with a powerful trace.

RUBRICS

We began by publishing the following rubric in the notice of seminars disseminated by the Shakespeare Association's Fall 2013 Bulletin:

> This seminar will stage a confluence between two important trends in critical theory: the environmental turn so vigorous within early modern studies and object-oriented ontology (vibrant materialism, the new materialism and speculative realism). Our aim is to imagine a conversation that moves beyond anthropocentrism and examine nonhumans at every scale, their relations to each other, and the ethics of human enmeshment within an agentic material world. How does our apprehension of the inhuman change when texts become laboratories for probing the liveliness, mystery and potential autonomy of objects, in their alliances and in performance?

To this invitation we received thirty-five requests to participate and, at the request of the conference organizers, agreed to run two seminars. We agreed that these would be held back to back on the same day to engender continuity, intensity, and exhaustion. We also agreed that the two of us would share a hotel room and much conference time. The planning for the seminar's unfolding proceeded through the mediation of email, FaceTime chats, meals, and rambling walks.

This collection of essays archives the endeavor and offers its essays as the still remarkable, surprising fruits of the conversations we shared in

St. Louis in the course of a day of two-hour long seminars, the email conversations that preceded and post-dated them, and a collective feast at an Indian restaurant to end the event. Full of bees, bushes, laundry, crutches, lists, poems, plague, planks, chairs, rain, shoes, meat, body parts, books, and assorted humans (living and dead), these are the essays that those papers and conversation became. Each responds in its own particular way to the rubric we offered but also to this further prompting we sent in advance of the sessions as we invited participants to think expansively about the topic, and to bring an object or totem to St. Louis:

> Dear Object-Oriented Environers,
>
> Welcome to our seminar and collective adventure. We hope that you are as excited as we are by the prospect of our collaboration. We are delighted by the response to the topic, but in order to accommodate everyone who signed up, we have decided to run two parallel, independent seminars of roughly 15 people each. Obviously, you are all invited to attend both sessions as you are able—we should be delighted in fact if you did. In terms of format, we would like to imagine each two-hour seminar as an opportunity to stage an object-oriented event-space focused on the *things*/issues you are embarked on studying and writing about. Each seminar will take on its "feel" from the inventory of things you provide.
>
> To that end, in place of the usual 12-page (3000–4500 word) papers, we should like each participant to write a 6-page (1500 word max) position paper on his or her object and the environs it orients that names the importance of the *thing* in question, outlines what it enables you or prompts you to think/say, and so do. We will pre-circulate these papers as per SAA deadlines and then Jeffrey and Julian will work out a way of ebbing and flowing through them or setting the things into a cascade that opens things up to discussion for each seminar. We will provide a current that you can allow to take us, that you can buck, or dam, as the mood/orientation takes.
>
> To help anchor us in the "thingliness" that our papers will convoke, we ask also that on the day of each seminar, you bring some version/iteration of your object or a totem with you to the seminar.
>
> We realize that the words "object" and "thing" carry with them a range of philosophical and theoretical moorings anchored to a

INTRODUCTION (AN ENVIRONING OF THIS BOOK) xv

succession of names and movements (Martin Heidegger, Michel Serres, Bruno Latour, Object-Oriented Ontology, Affordance Theory, Lacanian psychoanalysis, the object relations theory of Winicott, as well a the rich and varied bibliography of material culture studies and preservation studies). We welcome all these orientations to the table as, in our view, each tends to emphasize some differing aspect or property of an object—its physicality, psychic life, finitude, function.

We are fortunate also, in the context of this impossible wealth of a bibliography, to have invited four respondents (Drew Daniel and Julia Reinhard Lupton and Eileen Joy and Vin Nardizzi) who have worked extensively with objects in different registers—and we have asked them to share with us a short excerpt from their work to serve as an example of some of the work that medievalists and early modernists have embarked upon. In addition, because the movement gives it name to our seminar, we recommend reading the following excerpt from Ian Bogost's *Alien Phenomenology* as an emblem for the broader development of an object-oriented ontology / speculative realism as developed by philosophers such as Quentin Meillasoux and Graham Harman. (Readings are attached at the end of this message in PDF).

In terms of imagining our flow of work, we provide a timetable below:

- December 1, 2013 please circulate a brief introduction and "hello" to the group from you and your object (4–5 sentences). Please also let us know at this point if it would be useful for us to have any particular kind of a / v help on site if that is necessary to staging your object.

- March 1, 2014 SAA requires that all participants pre-circulate their papers by this date to have their name included in the conference program. We ask that you do your very best to honor this date—especially given the number of participants involved.

Looking beyond SAA, we invite all who would like to do so, to turn their 1500 word position paper into a short essay of 3000–4000 words that we hope to include in a book (likely with Punctum

Books http://punctumbooks.com) that aims to archive the work of our two seminars along with responses from our respondents. Please feel free to write us both with any questions you may have.

Best, Excited wishes to All!

Jeffrey and Julian[4]

The book you now possess marks the end of a collective work cycle that aimed to allow a series of projects or object orientations to cohabit for a day, to cross-pollinate, and so provoke juxtapositions, quandaries, epiphanies, and frustrations. We think also that the mooting of a book project, a collective home but also moment of ending at which ideas become papers become essays, might be alienated in the form of publication, even as some of us continue to work with our objects, provided an important impetus and sense of shared endeavor, a sense that the time we spent together in St. Louis would lead to more than individual memories or remembered conversation — always partial, always fragmentary.

Reading over the essays these papers and our conversations became, we cannot help but still feel a welcome sense of surprise at the object-oriented environs together we crafted, environs that occurred in and around, anchored to and by the ligatures that formed between and among the contributors, the respondents, and the objects that oriented them, the seminar, and this resulting book.

---

[4] To the seminars we distributed as readings an excerpt from Ian Bogost, *Alien Phenomenology, or What It's Like to Be a Thing* (Minneapolis: University of Minnesota Press, 2012); the epilogue to Drew Daniel, *The Melancholy Assemblage: Affect and Epistemology in the English Renaissance* (New York: Fordham, 2013); Julia Reinhard Lupton, "The Renaissance *Res Publica* of Furniture," in *Animal, Vegetable, Mineral: Ethics and Objects*, ed. Jeffrey Cohen (Washington DC: Oliphaunt / punctum books, 2012), 211–36; Eileen Joy, "You Are Here: A Manifesto," in *Animal, Vegetable, Mineral*, 153–72; and an excerpt from Vin Nardizzi, *Wooden Os: Shakespeare's Theatres and England's Trees* (Toronto: University of Toronto Press, 2013).

INTRODUCTION (AN ENVIRONING OF THIS BOOK)   xvii

Figure 1.   Figure 2.

ARRIVAL

When a fountain runs red, an object enacts its etymology and throws itself (*obiacere*) into the world and in our way. We knew the local sports team was at the stadium, that the crimson of the city's fountains was offered to the Cardinals and not some record of sacrifice. Yet gathered in St. Louis to speak of Shakespeare, objects, and environing, it was difficult to look at the fountains and not see the joyful excess of early modern plays that revel in red. As civic architecture, fountains domesticate water into the soothing center of a park or the obligatory ornamentation of corporate plazas. Most function by remaining invisible. They are simply part of the mundane cityscape, below notice. Their mineral means of relaying water obey the seasons — or condense them to a binary on and off as they are "winterized" and then allowed to spring forth once more. Seasonal change registers in the human maintenance of an infrastructure that the weather might corrode. Stony desert become spring's new gush, the fountain testifies merely to the maintenance of a network against the changes that local environs might wreak. Yet the shift in the water's spectrum through the addition of some dye proves estranging. The cascade of red de-cloaks the fountain from obscurity (Figures 1 and 2).

As we walked around the city, pondering the shape of the seminars to come, we found ourselves drawn to the flowing red waters. One of us may have reached a hand into the liquid, performed a strange anointing. The other may have proved too shy, too timid. Red proves uncanny. And we wonder now if the fountain full of red is a story that offers a parable. Maybe no truth of the object inheres, only a tale of humans and dye, sports or academic meetings, and a desire for a world that is assertively nonhuman.

Objects throw themselves in the way of human (in)attention, as when the water of a public fountain runs crimson and triggers thoughts of blood, of Shakespeare. How disorienting, like a golden apple that tumbles the path and ruins the race. But the apple was tossed by human hand; it did not "throw itself in the way of" Atalanta's attention. Someone dyed those fountains and made of them a human story, not a tale of water. Or maybe the tale is too tangled to unloose its smaller strands, so that worrying about human versus object agency limits our expanse? And what about objects that abide, the apples and the streams and stones that enable cooking, transport, friendlier relations? Objects offer quiet environments most of the time. We are used to their compliance. And so that is why we walk. Peripatetic philosophizing traces some new routes, or follows familiar paths in the hope that something not so ordinary will surface. The anthropologist Tim Ingold calls the process "thinking with the feet." Rejecting the relegation of the pedestrian to mere "stepping machine," he advocates a process of unknowing quotidian environments by wandering them sensually, in bare feet if necessary, so that perambulation becomes a mode of cognition.[5]

To heighten attentiveness, environing is best done in company.

PLAYTIME

Tradition dictates that an SAA seminar remains in its assigned conference room for a two-hour span, perhaps with a very short break in the middle. With its nondescript chairs and tables, its hotel-meeting-room beige nonstyle, the space and its furnishings want to be invisible. We could be anywhere: St. Louis or Boston or New Orleans. Upon arrival then, or perhaps before, we decided that in seminar, Jacques Tatti-like, rather than let the table at which we sat rest as a given, we would seek to render it urgent by inviting all our participants to take a break mid-conversation, get up, and follow us on a perambulation through the hospitality confining space of

---

5   Tim Ingold, "Culture on the Ground: The World Perceived Through the Feet," in *Being Alive: Essays on Movement, Knowledge, and Description* (London and New York: Routledge, 2011), 33–50.

INTRODUCTION (AN ENVIRONING OF THIS BOOK) xix

Figure 3.

the hotel's infrastructure, up and down escalators, through doors, and back—changing our orientation, rendering the world that we take as a support, something now that we need to take cognizance of. Halfway through our conversation, we invited our participants to take a walk (or not), to spend the interval between talking on his or her or our own recognizance (Figure 3). The break, the walk, did us good; provided a necessary break to the flow of conversation (an on and off switch) that enabled us all to take our seats again and respond to what we had heard anew, as a group that now had walked together or clustered in corners around the table, refreshing coffee cups, water glasses, nipping in and out to the bathroom, devolving into smaller, serial, serendipitous polities.

Table, you have become urgent to us—that urgency tied to the mundane eventfulness of getting up and sitting back down, the becoming lively of the table as environing object. The course of the perambulation was left to the respondents (though we did give suggestions). In the first seminar we strolled as a group out the doors of the room and down the long escalator to the hotel lobby. On reaching that public space we made a U-turn and took the escalator heading back up, passing seminar members still descending. Some of them may have tried to reverse their own steps; resist the pointlessness of our way-finding but the downward drag of the escalator proved too much. They gave in and allowed the machine to do their walking for them. We confess that we enjoyed their looks of surprise when they realized that we had departed the confines of the room to wander together. We enjoyed as well the wonder of those who were not at the seminar, those just milling around outside to catch up with friends or gossip about the plenaries, witnessing their quiet space traversed. The second seminar wandered farther: through a door marked STAFF ONLY DO NOT ENTER and into the portion of the hotel where the labor that enables a meeting to unfold is hidden. Those who walked into the service area (and there were many who turned back to the conference room at this point) saw where the coffee is made, the tablecloths laundered, the dishes washed. We stopped and chatted with people at their interrupted tasks, who seemed pleased not to be invisible for a few moments (but we admit they may also have been annoyed beneath the contracted cheerfulness the hotel demands of its employees or hospitality technicians) and to guide us through the winding corridor and out a "secret" exit on the other side, the route they used to access our meeting space without walking among the visiting scholars. You will have guessed that a story about race, privilege, and access unfolded here and was carried into what followed when we returned to the beige room.

These walks fractured the group. That was also their purpose. There was no correct way to walk. The point was to enable this devolution of the group into smaller ones; chance decisions or demarcations; deliberate and accidental. It was not possible then or now to map all the routes we collectively described. And those who wandered, who left the room assigned to us, cannot begin to know what passed among those who stayed put with the table or chatted with the onlookers (these seminars have audiences) or took the elevator back to their room to retrieve this or that or snatch a moment alone. And this fracturing, which designated also a moment of formation, enables us to return to the table and begin a second time, bodies and minds registering the fact of the conversations we had had and attuned also to the urgency of the time that remained.

"STARSKY AND HUTCH"

Of course, memory idealizes, inoculates itself against the lapses or losses, the erasures. Our seminars were not utopian, or were precisely so in the sense that the only "end" they knew was provided by the clock. We begin now. We end now. Our time together unfolds between. Let's make the most of it. Still, St. Louis punctuated our conversations with its own strange writing, its own comprehending or environing of the bubble we sought collectively to blow. The Gateway Arch (Figure 4) at the Jefferson National Expansion Memorial framed our time together, proclaiming this river crossing an entrance, a gateway to an America that retrospectively re-articulates that crossing in stone and steel. You can still cross

INTRODUCTION (AN ENVIRONING OF THIS BOOK) xxi

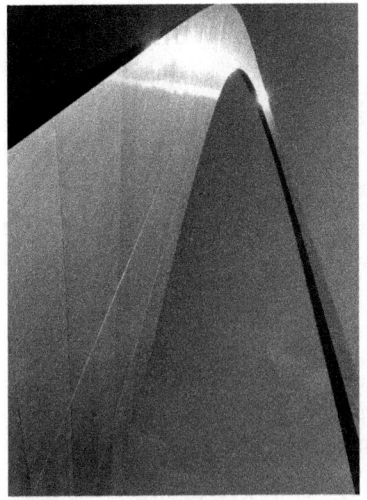
Figure 4.

Figure 5.

the river; drive coast to coast; plying the trails-become-freeways; but you can also ascend the arch from within by way of a tram of tiny capsules, and achieve a synoptic view of the land that travelers past lacked even as the trails and tracks their wagon wheels and trains left made today's view possible. (You will be warned as you enter the capsule that you may experience claustrophobia, and that these conveyance devices were designed for a time when Americans better fit their seats [Figure 5].) We enjoyed our space travels; enjoyed the social awkwardness that our newfound capsule friends and we finessed with time-honored scripts and hunched up knees. They thought we might have been in St. Louis for the skin-care-products exhibition at the city's convention center, a conference far better attended than the SAA. But what a short journey we had in comparison to those whose wagon-riders, whose collective writing enabled the translation of those tracks to stone, glass, steel — to the concrete, tar, and trade of the manifest destiny of the interstate below us, as though the road wanted to run that way, wanted to carve out a track through the land, obliterating or over-writing what came before. Of course, those wagon trails are themselves now idealized. In the nineteenth century, there were in fact lines and long waits at treacherous crossings, handbooks or how-to-do-it guidebooks as to when to set off; which trails to follow; and sites of mass

Figure 6.

Figure 7.

graffiti to memorialize the fact of the journey, fellow travelers who died en route, ephemeral traces of those human subjects whose destiny manifested precariously whatever the state or the nation claimed as its rights (Figure 6).[6]

Of course that imperative proves to be of shallow foundation. Outside of the city are giant mounds, the remains of a vast indigenous Mississippian settlement that vanished before pioneers built St. Louis and dubbed it the "Gateway to the West." These structures tell a deeper story about habitation, one in which cities rise and fall long before European-descended settlers colonize, one in which a variety of peoples come and go, build and abandon, one in which genocide and white agency do not yet dominate story, but unfold as merely one chapter within a larger structure of relation. No one is quite certain why they left, but the city was empty long before Europeans arrived. We rented a car to get there; joined the handful of tourists; a minor parade of elementary school children; tramped the curated walkways alongside city-dwelling joggers who drive out to experience the muscle burn these artificial mountains now afford in this place of flatness. Cahokia Mounds is located in Collinsville, Illinois, just off the interstate, fifteen minutes east of St. Louis. During the Middle Ages, the city dwarfed London. The people who dwelled there over the centuries were accomplished builders. They constructed ordinary houses, vast public monuments, roads and walkways. They planned their city. Not a

---

6   Signature Rock in Wyoming and Newspaper Rock in Utah are the two most famous sites of graffiti from the period of migration West. http://www.nationalparkstraveler.com/potw/historical-graffiti (Accessed May 21, 2015).

INTRODUCTION (AN ENVIRONING OF THIS BOOK) xxiii

Figure 8.

Figure 9.

gateway but a destination. Goodbye Old World. Goodbye New World (Figures 7–9).[7]

"St. Louis also spoke to us—called us out if not exactly to account. Out walking early one morning, we met almost no one, but turned the corner to be saluted by a glance and the wag of a finger and a voice that greeted us with the words "Starsky and Hutch," a phrase we processed, inevitably, instantaneously, for we knew the reference, had watched the show, maybe even owned or once upon a time played with the iconic car. *Starsky and Hutch* names the late 1970s police procedural set in "Bay City, California" (no such place has ever existed) starring Paul Michael Glaser and David Soul. At the time we were delighted; played the giddy game of academic tourists, who routinely make lemonade out of the bitter but not unsweet realities of the environs that host their presence. Environs bought and sold by municipalities and City Fathers, contracted for a certain period of time within the calendrical liturgy of the conference scene and circuit, bartered in terms of services offered and opportunity costs, but whose residents are never asked whether they might like to have the purveyors of the bard or skin care products set up their respective shops in their town, in their environs. We kept on walking; enjoyed our breakfasts; debated who of us was Starsky, and who might be Hutch?

---

7 You can visit the online, curated remains of Cahokia at http://cahokiamounds.org (Accessed May 20, 2015).

But, thinking back (or even at the time), it seems best that we own the fact that we did not know and do not know now what those words meant—"Starsky and Hutch"—even as they seemed to beckon to us, to address us with a televisual past, with the memory of one island in the "flow" of programming that, once upon a broadcast time, in Williams's sense of things, kept time.[8] Yes. The man's words, his naming of the show, formed a momentary relay between us that (despite our respective environs—when and where we were coming from and going) linked Jeffrey to Julian to this old man who seemed emphatically not to be passing through. What and how did this cry of the city mean? To whom was it addressed? To us, perhaps—or not—just a note to self, or an address to the environs: look who's coming now. It seems important also to admit that, while we might have smiled, both of us knew that we had been remarked and had acknowledged that remarking, been hailed, hallowed, named or maybe simply seen and designated as if Starsky and Hutch, a duo of white guys who do and do not belong, who move ghost-like along the sidewalk through neighborhoods that are not their own, and get into their car and drive off. And who, whatever their associations with the likes of Huggy Bear (who stole the show), bore guns, brought violence with them even as they might like to think of themselves as peace officers. In a city that everywhere bears the scars of racial violence both slow and sudden, we were hailed as if the police, addressable, stunt or touristic keystone cops whose exaggerated movements weren't funny any more, just evidence that we got to inhabit a different time and space even as we inhabited another's. We never met this man even as he remarked us. All we can recall is the impression he made on us and the way in which our turning of a blind corner accosted him in his environ.[9]

---

8   Williams, *Television*, 78.

9   In recalling this moment, we are alluding obviously to Louis Althusser's account of ideological interpellation or hailing in "Ideology and Ideological State Apparatuses (Notes towards an Investigation)," in *Lenin and Philosophy and Other Essays*, trans. Ben Brewster (New York: Monthly Review Press, 1971), 127–186. Crucially, however, the scene of nomination we describe functions a bit differently casting us in the guise of the police. The address calls our world into question. In this sense, our little street theater enacted something that Donna Haraway adds to Althusser's account of interpellation—that the moment of ideological hailing can function also as a calling of the question, a call for recognition or the recognition of a shared world. See Donna Haraway, *When Species Meet* (Minneapolis and London: University of Minnesota Press, 2008), 278.

INTRODUCTION (AN ENVIRONING OF THIS BOOK) xxv

Later in the summer of 2014, Michael Brown would be shot to death in nearby Ferguson. Thinking back to what had seemed a little theater of the street, it stops us now in our tracks, brings home to us that whatever we may have managed to do in our seminars—they were no community or charity of production, or if they were, then the price for them was paid by a host of others, who were there also even as they went unacknowledged. "There is," we know "no document of culture which is not at the same time a document of barbarism."[10]

This book entails its own erasures.

---

10 Thesis VII of Walter Benjamin's "Theses on the Philosophy of History," in *Illuminations: Essays and Reflections*, trans. Harry Zohn (New York: Schocken Books, 1968), 256.

Venus's Bush(es)
Lizz Angello

ON THE CORNER OF MY OFFICE LAPTOP PERCHES A SMALL SHRUBBERY made from extruded plastic: LEGO greenery, fashioned into a wedge of landscape to obscure the tiny LEGO TARDIS resting over the power button.

My young son has been here.

He clearly meant for his ersatz foliage to cover up the time machine, but it actually calls attention to it. It signals that *something* must be hiding there, something we are meant to find. "Look, look!" say the bushes, "but pretend you aren't looking." Real flora can function similarly, as when leaves in a bouquet direct our eyes away from unsightly stems and toward colorful blooms. But curious pedestrians also peer through hedges at the houses behind them. Does a bush conceal, then, or only pretend to conceal? Is a bush an actant or an alibi, like the pasties on Barthes' strippers, the conceit of privacy serving only to heighten the eroticism of the hidden?[1] Perhaps we can't even speak of "*a* bush" but rather "*bushes.*" Bushes are messy, insistently plural; yet they can be tended and tamed into the very embodiments of b/order, separation, and singularity. Shakespeare's *Venus and Adonis* bears witness to the multivalence of bushes, suggesting that they contain all of these possibilities — and more — within their interlace.

My consideration of the bushes in *Venus and Adonis* is thus appropriately both messy and linear, tracing a complex network but firmly rooted in questions of gender(ing). In much of his work, Shakespeare binds genitalia and identity, often along traditionally gendered lines (as when Lear strips naked to find that he has become "the thing itself")

---

1 Roland Barthes, *Mythologies*, trans. by Annette Lavers (New York: Hill and Wang, 1972), esp. 84–87.

but also occasionally along transgendered ones (as when Hamlet finds his masculine identity in his father's ring). Much of the critical attention paid to the poem justifiably argues that it reverses the expected gender dynamic, especially in Venus's usurpation of the masculine roles of wooer/hunter/objectifier and Adonis's occupation of the passive, reluctant position. However, Venus's "bush/es," both anatomical and floral, help us to see the goddess's abundant femininity throughout the poem and insist that we read her actions as not only acceptable but also desirable.

As Heather Dubrow has observed, *Venus and Adonis* departs from other Renaissance *epyllia* partially in its lack of engagement with the pastoral mode, especially in the poem's relative dearth of landscape description. The pastoral typically expends a great deal of energy creating its Arcadias, but Shakespeare picks up mid-conversation in a non-descript and non-specific location.[2] What we do know of the titular couple's surroundings is that they are lush with leafy things, from the grasses that support Venus's weight to the thickets skirting the forest. In other words, we don't see much, but what we do see is largely green—and all of it is in bloom, which accords with Venus's status as the embodiment of love and fertility. It turns out that the poem does not eschew the pastoral landscape so much as displace it onto Venus: we get more than one eyeful of *her* hills and valleys.

In the most famous of her linguistic peep-shows, Venus blazons herself, acting the early modern love poet since Adonis refuses. Playing on the homophones "dear" and "deer," she constructs herself as a "park" in which he should graze.[3] "If those hills be dry," she says of her lips, "Stray lower, where the pleasant fountains lie." If he continues this downward trend, she tells him, he will find her "sweet bottom-grass" and "brakes obscure and rough" (233-34, 235-36). Although "bush" as common parlance for female pubic hair would not take root for a couple of centuries, this passage clearly allies her nether-hairs with foliage.[4] Elsewhere, Shakespeare forges links between hair (if not specifically pubic hair),

---

2   Heather Dubrow, *Captive Victors: Shakespeare's Narrative Poems and Sonnets* (Ithaca, NY: Cornell University Press, 1987), esp. 52–54.

3   Quotations of Shakespeare's work follow Stephen Greenblatt, gen. ed., *The Norton Shakespeare, Based on the Oxford Edition* (New York: W.W. Norton, 1997).

4   "Bush, *n.*, 1," OED. Eric Partridge catalogs the many other euphemisms for female pubic hair and genitalia more generally (including this poem's "brakes" and "hill," plus "leaves," "flower" or "rose," "river" or "pond," and, once, "withered pear") in his encyclopedic *Shakespeare's Bawdy* (New York: Routledge, 1968), esp. 24–26.

flowers and leaves, and vitality, writes Edward J. Geisweidt, citing examples from *As You Like It* and *A Midsummer Night's Dream*. The association crops up all over early modern literature, philosophy, and medical discourse, and Geisweidt identifies its sources in the Aristotelian doctrine of the vegetative soul and the Galenic tradition of describing bodies as landscapes.[5] Thus, when Venus figures her pudendum as a "green world," we should understand such travel as natural and life-giving. And although she certainly behaves in ways traditionally coded in early modern poetry as "masculine" (the viewer, the poet, the hunter, and the aggressor), she does so only in order to focus Adonis's (and our) attentions on her female body: her hills, fountains, and especially her sweet bottom.

If Venus is a park, then the park is also Venus: all bushes are her bushes. The sympathy between living things and goddess means that even her massive form barely registers on the grass beneath her: "Witness this primrose band whereon I lie; / These forceless flowers like sturdy trees support me" (lines 1551–52). Despite her prodigious size, she trips like a fairy and dances like a nymph without making footprints in the sand (lines 146–48); she flies through the air pulled by "two strengthless doves" (line 153). Her form and weight cannot burden the plants and animals because she is consonant with them. Regardless of how we must cringe at her blindness to Adonis's terror during her campaign of seduction, the poem repeatedly invites us to think of all love and desire as natural.[6]

To illustrate this point, another of Venus's bushes (one *not* attached to her "ivory pale") parts to reveal "a breeding jennet, lusty, young, and proud" (260). She spots Adonis's courser, who immediately "breaketh his rein" to join her in an elaborate parody of Petrarchan courtship that even Venus pauses to admire. Capitalizing on the moment, Venus explains to Adonis that her union with him would be as natural as his courser's with the jennet: "Thy palfrey, as he *should*, / welcomes the warm approach of sweet desire. [...] Therefore *no marvel* though thy horse be gone" (lines 385–86, 390; emphases mine). The horses' "lesson is but plain," she says, and in this sense, we must understand Adonis's abstinence as unnatural.

---

5 "Horticulture of the Head: The Vegetable Life of Hair in Early Modern English Thought." EMLS Special Issue 19 (2009) 6.1–24. Web. 21 February 2015.

6 This invitation, however, conflicts with the unnatural, incestuous undercurrents of the love-relationship between Venus and Adonis. For an excellent examination of how Adonis's refusal enacts his vengeful reversal of his mother Myrrha's seduction of her own father, see Karen Newman, "Myrrha's Revenge: Ovid and Shakespeare's Reluctant Adonis," *Illinois Classical Studies* 9.2 (1984): 251–265.

Venus admits as much when she describes him as a "statue," and a "thing like a man, but of no woman bred" (line 214). We might be tempted to read this as sour grapes, were it not for the scene that we just witnessed emerging from a nearby bush. The greenery and the horses mating within it extend Venus's body to instruct the youth of his natural duty.

Tragically, of course, Adonis fails to heed the steed's instruction or Venus's warnings against hunting the boar, and we discover the most revealing bushes in a copse of myrtles that tear at Venus as she pursues her beloved into the forest. These brambles perform her growing sense of dread: "And as she runs, the bushes in the way / Some catch her by the neck, some kiss her face, / Some twine about her thigh to make her stay" (871–73).[7] As Lisa Starks-Estes explains, the bushes tread the same path of dominance and submission as Venus, caressing and kissing her face and neck like a lover and embracing her thighs in exactly the same tender-but-unbreakable "twining" that she earlier exercised on Adonis. The bushes delay her progress but ultimately cede to her passion, belying her inner conflict: like anyone en route to witness a horror they know exists, Venus is both desperate to confirm the atrocity with her own eyes and desperate to never see such a thing. Starks-Estes reads the myrtle as part of "an animated botanical world with bushes and trees that wish to ravish her."[8] I would add that, around Venus, *all* things wish to ravish something: she is the animating principle of this verdant world.

If we linger among these myrtles that are, like Venus, part lover and part attacker, and we perhaps practice the "slow looking" that some art historians currently advocate, they reveal all sorts of secrets, bound to one another in a dense copse of associations between Venus's vegetal and anatomical bushes.[9] Pliny the Elder explains that the Romans cel-

---

7   The phrase "to make her stay" also appears in *The Rape of Lucrece*, when a parallel group of agentive objects seeks to prevent an unnatural wrong. Lucrece's house comes to life to defend her against Tarquin, her would-be rapist, as he sneaks down the hallway toward her room. One of the agents, a gust of wind, "wars with his torch to make him stay" (311). For a more extended discussion of Lucrece's domestic agents, see my article "Moving Like a Ghost: Tarquin's Specter and Agentive Objects in *The Rape of Lucrece, Julius Caesar*, and *Macbeth*," *Forum* 7 (Autumn 2008).

8   *Violence, Trauma, and Virtus in Shakespeare's Roman Poems and Plays: Transforming Ovid* (London: Palgrave Macmillan, 2014), esp. 77.

9   See, for example, Jennifer L. Roberts, "The Power of Patience," *Harvard Magazine* (November–December 2013), 40–43 and Peter Clothier, *Slow Looking: The Art of Looking at Art* (Los Angeles: Toad Rampant Books, 2012).

ebrated Venus with myrtle crowns during pre-marriage ceremonies and with drinks meant to stimulate female desire. They also planted myrtle alongside shrines to Venus, especially the Etruscan-Roman hybrid goddess Venus Cloacina; one chapel, dedicated to the lesser-known Venus Murcia, stood behind an entire grove of the bushes.[10] In her guise as Venus Cloacina, she presided over Rome's Great Sewer, the Cloaca—a term which became synonymous with "vagina," as an opening for drainage and cleansing. Biologists still use the term when speaking of reptiles and birds, who have a single orifice for evacuation and reproduction. The Greeks employed various forms of the word μυρσίνη to name female genitalia: *myrton*, or "myrtle-berry" meant "clitoris," while *myrtos*, the whole myrtle-bush, meant "vulva."[11] The earliest recorded usage of these terms appears in the anatomist Rufus of Ephesus's treatise on the parts of the body, but they continue well into at least the nineteenth century in English medical dictionaries. The meaning, though not exceedingly well-attested in formal medical documents, was common enough for a captain in Aristophanes's *Lysistrata* to insist that he will "bury [his] sword in the myrtle-bush" (line 631). Later in the same play, a Spartan herald complains that "the women won't let us anywhere near their myrtle-bush" (line 1004).[12] Since Latin acquired the loan word *murtos* for myrtle, it is possible that its anatomical connections came with it. Through this thorny word- and idea-play, the myrtle bushes present themselves as active parts of Venus's femininity and sexuality.

Venus's bushes fail to conceal Adonis's mutilated body, but they successfully reveal his arboreal origins. Both homophonically and etymologically, myrtle points to myrrh, another fragrant flowering bush, although one that tastes decidedly bitter rather than sweet. Both stem from the same

---

10 Pliny the Elder, *The Natural History*, ed. John Bostock and H.T. Riley (Perseus Digital Library), esp. 15.36.

11 See Eva C. Keuls, *The Reign of the Phallus: Sexual Politics in Ancient Athens* (Berkeley: University of California Press, 1985), 30, and Catherine Blackledge, *The Story of V: A Natural History of Female Sexuality* (New Brunswick, NJ: Rutgers University Press, 2004), 227.

12 Aristophanes's Greek uses μυρσίνη, or "myrtle," in conjunction with the word for "shrub" or "stick," in both instances, with clearly salacious intent. Translators working in both English and modern Greek, however, often eschew the innuendo in the first quotation, rendering it more literally along the lines of "I will wrap my sword in a myrtle wreath," connoting the plant's association with victory crowns. The second quotation retains its erotic overtones, but loses its floral associations in favor of another euphemism for female genitalia.

Semitic root (in Arabic, *murr*; in Hebrew, *mor*), but more importantly for this poem, the myrrh tree reaches out to Shakespeare's Ovidian source.[13] The tale immediately preceding the story of Venus and Adonis in the *Metamorphoses* explains how a woman named Myrrha fell in love with her own father and, after deceiving him into an illicit romance, became pregnant with his child. (In some versions of the story, Myrrha's mother boasted of her daughter's beauty, comparing her favorably to Venus, who punished Myrrha with her forbidden desires.) In shame, Myrrha hopes to die but is dissuaded by her nurse; turning instead to the gods, Myrrha prays to be hidden from human sight and so transforms into a myrrh tree. Nine months later, she delivers a beautiful boy named Adonis. Perhaps, then, we can see what Venus cannot: Adonis grows up to shun Venus's advances and reject her argument that sex and reproduction are nature's mandate because his experience has taught him otherwise. Shakespeare conceals the youth's roots, but the myrtle calls out for us to attend to them and incorporate his shameful birth-story into our reading of its next installment.

Venus's bush reveals the disorder, the mess, the chaos inherent in love and sexual desire, but to what end? One answer lies in the myrtle's final revelation. Shakespeare conspicuously conceals the tale's Ovidian narrator rather as the LEGO bushes on my computer pretend to conceal the TARDIS. In the *Metamorphoses*, both Myrrha's and Adonis's stories are narrated by Orpheus, who literally moves his audience of stones and humans-*cum*-trees with his song, his gift animating nature as Venus's presence does in Shakespeare's adaptation. Orpheus sings of evil, fallen women and innocent, beautiful young boys—a milieu into which *Venus and Adonis* comfortably fits; in removing this frame, Shakespeare recasts the story, making Adonis's insistence on the dangers of desire feel misplaced, as evidenced by his particularly grisly end. The obvious homoerotic cast of Adonis's death works even more powerfully in contrast to what Venus offers. Boars are dangerous, the goddess argues, but she really means that *men* are dangerous: she has no problem with Adonis hunting rabbits (though she paints such a tender and tragic portrait of poor Wat that one wonders how anyone could kill a rabbit after hearing it), but the threat of the boar's phallic tusks proves too much for her to bear.

That Adonis dies from a vicious tusk to his lily white flank (line 1055) suggests that Venus rightly argues against the homosocial culture this

---

13 "Myrrh, *n.*, 1," OED.

particular enterprise represents: the masculine hunt, furtively ensconced in the trees, ends with sterile, fatal intercourse, while the feminine hunt takes place on the open meadow and promises fertility and immortality. Adonis, however, insists that he must remain within this group because he is too young to pursue the love of a woman: "Fair queen [...] if any love you owe me, / Measure my strangeness with my unripe years: / Before I know myself, seek not to know me" (lines 524–26). The reflexive phrase "know myself" might easily contain "know others like myself"; only when he has gained this key experience, has known other men, will he look outside his fraternity and consider a heteronormative relationship.

If we consider this argument alongside Venus's rejoinders that reproduction is natural, that the beautiful owe the earth continuance of their beauty, and that children offer a kind of immortality to their parents, we can see Shakespeare building a familiar case. Venus sounds very much like the speaker of the first sonnet group, who argues so eloquently that "from fairest creatures we desire increase" and that a "fair child" can "sum a count and make an old excuse," while Adonis provides the second voice in the conversation. *Venus and Adonis*, *The Rape of Lucrece*, and the sonnets were all dedicated to Henry Wriothesley, the third Earl of Southampton, and while much scholarly speculation has attended to possible connections between Wriothesley and the sonnets, not much has included the narrative poetry. Patrick Murphy, a notable exception, has convincingly argued that Shakespeare intended *Venus and Adonis* as a message to the young man, who had recently backed out of his engagement to Elizabeth Vere and would not marry again for six years, at the age of 25.[14] Murphy's article stops short, however, of promoting a positive reading of Venus's seduction of Adonis, which I believe the poem encourages, despite the consternation that her pursuit causes him. As badly as we might feel for him, plucked from his horse and pinned beneath her gargantuan arms, and as silly as Venus's histrionics might seem, when Adonis rejects her to join his male friends, he meets a brutal and unmistakably homoerotic end.

After Adonis dies, he joins the feminine, floral economy of the poem. First we learn that, as the myrtle echoed Venus's inner turmoil, the plants mirror Adonis's pain: his wound "weeps" with "purple tears," and "no flower was nigh, no grass, herb, leaf, or weed, / But stole his blood and

---

14 "Wriothesley's Resistance: Wardship Practices and Ovidian Narratives in Shakespeare's *Venus and Adonis*," in *Venus and Adonis: Critical Essays*, ed. Philip C. Kolin (New York: Garland, 1997): 323–340.

seem'd with him to bleed" (lines 1056–58). Even Venus responds to this "solemn sympathy," and she begins attempting to vocalize her trauma. During her laments, she envisions all the world bowing before Adonis's beauty, including "some hedge," which hid a lion behind it so the beast would not frighten the youth; like Orpheus, Adonis in Venus's imagination tames the tiger when he sings and coaxes the wolf from the sheep's pasture. The boar only gored him, she reasons, because it did not see his face: "This foul, grim, and urchin-snouted boar, / Whose downward eye still looketh for a grave, / Ne'er saw the beauteous livery that he wore" (lines 1107–09). Finally, the effect of her words of woe is such that Adonis "melted like a vapour from her sight," turning instead into a fragile flower. Plucking it (the goddess gets her quarry at last!), Venus tucks the stem between her breasts in the embrace of both a lover (subject to her constant kissing) and a mother (subject to her constant rocking). He becomes, in the end, yet another of Venus's bushes.

Cordelia's Corpse
Dead as Earth
Sallie Anglin

KING LEAR AND VIDEO GAMES HAVE SOMETHING IN COMMON. IN MOST massively multiplayer online role playing games (MMORPGS) a player's character dies, but it isn't permanent. For a moment after death, a player stares into her computer screen at her own corpse, her removed first-person perspective hovering over it, still attached to but disembodied from the avatar that allows her to experience the virtual space of the game. In this moment, the player knows she is dependent on that object, the body/corpse, that she has been forcibly separated from. The corpse's existence is no longer fully dependent on the player. In this moment, the video game player who is housed in the avatar, in the player character, becomes an audience to her own corpse. She's watching the story of flesh in digital form. The Unreal creates an actual agential demise of the player, at least momentarily.[1]

In video games this is the moment right before a player "respawns." This uncanny moment is a kind of satori, a Buddhist term for "awakening" or seeing, perhaps seeing into one's "essence" or "true nature." But what the player is seeing is not a realization of a divine self, but the realization that there is a fundamental dissociation between the body object, the corpse object, and the object, "I." What the player discovers is that the exchange with the material world is temporary and elusive. Her relationship to that body is not a given, and her human vitality is certainly not

---

1   The Unreal Engine is one of the most used graphics engines in the video game industry. It was developed by Epic Games in 1998, uses the programming language C++, and is utilized for developing the graphics for first person shooters, role playing games, stealth games and online multiplayer games.

required for the body to go on existing. Like the corpse in a game, the corpse on the early modern stage refuses to cooperate with human agency.

The corpse on stage doesn't simply represent an undeniable dissonance between the human body and the dead/inhuman body, it also all at once reifies the material existence of a person, even while it calls into question the agency of that materiality, and the exchanges with the material world a body must negotiate in order to be/stay human. For a human body to be alive, it needs breath, water, a healthy brain, a functioning cardiovascular system and active communication between the brain and the rest of the body. A corpse possesses none of these things. The difference between a corpse and a living body is how it functions, and in early modern England, a corpse's function was not to house a human life, yet a corpse nevertheless possessed vital properties.

In some MMOS (such as EQ, *Team Fortress 2* and *Diablo 2*), multiple avatar corpses remain in the game for a time even after the player is resurrected. The virtual corpse is an extreme example of the corpse-as-object independent from human experience. Its origin is contingent upon the human subject, but its *existence* is not. To see a body that one identifies as one's own is a dissociative experience. To see any human corpse is equally dissociative. As in a video game, tragedy requires a character (the hero?) to die in order for catharsis or transformation to take place. In Shakespeare and his contemporaries, however, characters dying more than once is not wholly uncommon. Although not always, these characters are often women who die at the hands of a man or through the actions of a man, for instance, Desdemona and the Duchess of Malfi.[2]

When King Lear carries Cordelia's corpse onto the stage, he knows she is "gone forever," and yet he continues to look for signs of life, of revival, in her corpse.[3] Lear mistakes Cordelia's corpse for the person of Cordelia. Such a case of mistaken identity seems entirely understandable. A thing should be as it appears. In *Nekrokedeia,* Thomas Greenhill even argues that letting a corpse decay is "disagreeable to the dignity of our nature" because it would reveal us to be other than ourselves.[4] Embalming and burying our dead is a way to preserve the corporeal and

---

2 Although there are plenty of examples of male characters dying multiple times, such as Falstaff's double death and Barabas's commenting about his many deaths, these deaths do not present corpses on the stage.

3 All references to *King Lear* are from William Shakespeare, *King Lear*, in *The Complete Works of Shakespeare*, ed. David Bevington, 7th ed. (Upper Saddle River, NJ: Pearson, 2014).

4 Thomas Greenhill, *Nekrokedeia: or, the art of embalming* (London, 1705), C1r.

boundaried notion of the body and one's identity. What you see is supposed to be what you get. What's more, in one of the source texts, Cordelia is never a corpse.[5] She lives. Shakespeare's Cordelia, however, is dead as earth. The body onstage is a corpse—not merely dead tissue, but an object that challenges the distinctions between existence and non-existence, life and death, and being and becoming.

Cordelia's corpse—and perhaps any human corpse on the early modern stage—represents a peculiar case of difference and deference. While on the one hand, the corpse *belongs* to Cordelia, she does not possess it. It serves as a visual reminder of her non-existence, while at the same time stands *for* her. It exists as Cordelia strictly because of her relationships with the other characters and the audience, but as a corpse, it is alone. Its relational identity is stripped from it. At a funeral viewing, a corpse is never understood as *das Ding an Sich*, a thing-in-itself, in the Kantian or any other sense. It is known by and through the person it signifies. The corpse is also not the Heideggerian thing. A human body imbued with life more closely resembles what Heidegger calls *Das Ding*, "a convocation of human and world."[6] Alternatively, a corpse, while certainly an assemblage of material relations, possesses a unique relationship to the human. A corpse is both human and no longer human. It is *that person* and yet close to nothing because it does not house the human. A corpse refuses to participate. Greenhill describes the emotional justification for burying a corpse:

> By these two fore-going Causes of Burial appears yet a farther Benefit to Mankind, that they may live without that continual Terror of Death, which is occasion'd by seeing such miserable Emblems of Mortality. If you do but consider, when Men at first liv'd dispers'd, the very Abhorrence and Detestation of meeting Dead Bodies, made them to remove such unpleasant Objects out of their sight: Afterwards, when they assembled together and built Cities to dwell in, they used Burial for this Reason says *Lilius Gyraldus…That the Living might not be infested by the most noisom stench of the Dead.*[7]

---

5 Raphael Holinshed, *Holinshed's Chronicle as Used in Shakespeare's Plays* (New York: J.M. Ment and Sons, Ltd., 1927), 227.
6 Ian Bogost, *Alien Phenomenology, or What It's Like to Be a Thing* (Minneapolis: University of Minnesota Press, 2012), 24.
7 Greenhill, *Nekrokedeia*, C2r.

A corpse is an intruder. It refuses human vitality. The properties that make up a corpse are fundamentally transformed from those of a human. It is a stark reminder of death, of the raw materiality of the body, and of any object's ever changing state of being.

In the early modern period, a corpse was more than just dead. It no longer possessed personhood, but it nonetheless carried vital properties unique to itself: both the body of a former person as well as a thing in itself, with uses and values exclusive of its having formerly housed a living identity. According to Philippe Ariès, "the cadaver [was] still the body and already the corpse."[8] The body may have died, but the corpse was thought to possess a distinct sensibility that does not originate from *being alive*. According to Greenhill, we should bury our dead because, "the spiritless Body should be restor'd to the Earth, from whence it was deriv'd."[9] The author's reference to the biblical origin of man reminds his readers that the materiality of the body is transformative: human, corpse, earth or dust. Such transformation stresses the tenuous boundary between the living and the non-living.

The loss of the "soul" was not necessarily an indication of lifelessness; the corpse, while no longer *that person*, had a life of its own, inherently undead. It had no agency, no being to speak of, but still possessed a *vestigium vitae*, residual life. A human corpse's utility was, for the most part, centered around the living and particularly the human. A corpse's perspiration was used to treat hemorrhoids, skulls were used in relief for epileptics, and bones were ground up and ingested. Indeed, many of the remedies created from a corpse's materials implied a sympathy with the human body. Parts of the dead were used to treat the same part of the living.[10] In his book of medicinal recipes, Nicholas Culpepper includes a number of remedies that utilize ingredients taken from a human corpse. He explains, "The fat of a man is exceeding good to anoint such limbs as fall away in Flesh" and that "the skull of a man that was never buried, being beaten to power and given inwardly, the quantity of a drachm at a time, in Bettony water, helps Palsies, and Falling sicknesse."[11] He includes *mummia*, human flesh, as a common ingredient. In his recipe for "A

---

8   Philippe Ariès, *The Hour of Our Death*, trans. Helen Weaver (New York: Vintage Books, 1981), 355.
9   Greenhill, *Nekrokedeia*, B3r.
10 Ariès, *The Hour of Our Death*, 357.
11 Nicholas Culpepper, *A Physical Directory; or a translation of the Dispensatory made by the Colledg of Physitians of London* (London: Peter Cole, 1651), L4v.

powder for such as are bruised by a Fall," he calls for "*terra sigillata a Sanguus Draconis*, Mummy, of each two drachms, Sperma Ceti one dram, Rhubarb half a dram: beat them into powder according to art."[12] In these cases, the corpse is a thing in Heidegger's sense, because it is useful specifically for the human.[13] Yet, its relationship to the human is intricately connected to its existence *as a corpse*, not as a human being. I hesitate to say that its usefulness is connected to its being dead, because the corpse's existence as a dead thing is a primary subject of contention. Such vitalistic properties call into question the corpse as a dead thing. Instead, the corpse is life in another form distinct from that of the once living human.

Cordelia's corpse is appropriated by Lear in order to perpetuate his own identity, and he utilizes it as a remedy for his pain and suffering. He looks for signs of her own rising from the dead: "This feather stirs; she lives! If it be so, / It is a chance which does redeem all sorrows / That ever I have felt" (5.3.265–67). Cordelia's corpse represents the possibility for redemption *if* it possesses life. Lear wants to imbue the corpse with Cordelia. He wants to give it life and to force signification onto that life. The corpse, however, doesn't cooperate. Jane Bennett, summarizing Adorno, explains this phenomenon. She writes, "[a thing] eludes capture by the concept, that there is always a 'nonidentity' between it and any representation."[14] The gap between what the object is and what the living want the object to be is always present. Adorno says, "what we may call the thing itself is not positively or immediately at hand. He who wants to know it must think more, not less."[15] Bennett calls Adorno's concept of nonidentity as "that which is not subject to knowledge, but is instead 'heterogeneous' to all concepts."[16] This appears to be complementary to Bogost's use of speculation. Bogost writes, "That things are is not a matter of debate.…The significance of one thing to another differs depending on the perspectives of both," and that speculative realism "takes existence to be separate from thought."[17] In other words, a thing can have perspective

---

12 Culpepper, *A Physical Directory*, U2v.
13 Bogost, *Alien Phenomenology*, 24.
14 Jane Bennett, *Vibrant Matter: a Political Ecology of Things* (Durham: Duke University Press, 2010), 13.
15 Theodor Adorno, *Negative Dialectics*, trans. E.B. Ashton (New York: Continuum, 1973), 189.
16 Bennett, *Vibrant Matter*, 14.
17 Bogost, *Alien Phenomenology*, 30, 31.

without thinking per se. The perspective of Cordelia's corpse is not the perspective of Cordelia.

In the final scene of *King Lear*, Lear attempts to instill his agency, his desires, and his imagination into the corpse he carries in his arms, but the corpse refuses to be a reflection of the king's interests. The way in which Lear responds to Cordelia's corpse is indicative of the conflict between understanding an object in itself and imbuing it with reflections of selfhood. Lear's imagining of Cordelia's body as living is an attempt to animate the dead. Cordelia *could* breathe in this moment. She is, in fact, a live actor playing a corpse, but this fact does not resolve the tension between Lear's attempts to impose agency upon her and the corpse's rejection of those attempts. Because early modern physiologists and philosophers understood air and breath as fundamentally material and humorally unstable, the moment Cordelia's breath leaves her body, her control over it would be in question.[18] The corpse, however, acts upon Lear and the audience, declaring through inaction that what Lear and the audience might want or might imagine is not indicative of what is. Although it is an object outside of and aside from the human subject, the corpse must remain anthropomorphic. Yet it also rejects any participation in such affects as empathy. Its existence is a reminder of the difficulty of understanding an object without imposing our own perceptions, ethics and selves upon it.

The Countess of Pembroke's 1600 translation of Phillipe Mornay's *A Discourse of Life and Death*, states that when we

> retire we ourselves into ourselves, we finde it there as uncleane as any where. We cannot make the world dye, but by dying in ourselves. We are in the world and the world in us, and to separate us from the world, we must separate from ourselves. Now this separation is called Death.[19]

Mornay describes death as the process of discovering one's ultimate difference, the transformation from a relational identity with "the world" to

---

18 For more on the materiality of breath, air and voice, see Gina Bloom, *Voice in Motion: Staging Gender, Shaping Sound in Early Modern England* (Philadelphia: University of Pennsylvania Press, 2007).

19 Phillipe Mornay, *A Discourse of Life and Death*, trans. Countess of Pembroke (London: William Ponsonby, 1592), D1v.

an existence that is profoundly distinct and lonely. Immediately after this passage, however, he contradicts himself:

> We are, we thinke, come out of the contagious citie, but we are not advised that we have sucked the bad ayre, that we carrie the plague with us, that we so participate with it, that through rockes, through desarts, through mountains, it ever accompanieth us. Having avoided the contagion of other, yet we have it in ourselves. We have withdrawen us out of men: but not withdrawen men out of us.[20]

The body, arguably like any other object, while not necessarily identified via its anthropocentric relationships, nonetheless cannot escape its relational existence to other objects and to its environment. The moment the body becomes a corpse, the object exists as a "universal difference." It is completely alone and yet it is always a part of the assemblage.

When I play a video game, the knowledge that my self and my corpse are distinct is aggressively present. That moment when I die and my perspective changes to hover over my corpse, the button appears: "Return to Spawn Point? Cancel or Okay." I stare at that button for much longer than necessary because that button releases me from my corpse. It forces me to acknowledge that my life is dependent on the body, but that the body is not dependent on my life. And yet, my corpse lies in wait for others to experience, to see, to plunder in some cases. To use.

Lear exploits Cordelia's corpse for his own use. He forces signification and meaning and identity and name upon it. He forces a life upon it. But the corpse is a problem. A corpse represents a kind of *terra incognita*, an object just outside of signification and one that resists its relational identity to other characters. Cordelia's corpse rejects the identity he wants to imbue it with.[21] It refuses to participate; Lear is unable to find hope or life in Cordelia's limp body. For many objects, it's often easy to see them as objects, but audiences and readers want to see the corpse as having been human. The difference is the present. A table *is* a table. A corpse *was* a

---

20 Mornay, *A Discourse of Life and Death*, D1v–D2r.
21 For more on the presentation of the gendered corpse, see Elisabeth Bronfen, *Over Her Dead Body: Death, Femininity and the Aesthetic* (New York: Routledge, 1992). Although this article seeks to argue for a general resistance of the corpse, I do recognize the implications of power and control associated with gender in Lear's attempts to resuscitate Cordelia. Although Cordelia's dead body may be refusing to participate, Lear is still attempting to impress upon the corpse a gendered identity.

person. A corpse, however, is not the person it once was. A corpse is in fact an object, and the person it once was is also an object, but not the same object as *that corpse*. The corpse respawns as an object independent of human vitality. Faced with the paradox of the unliving body, we are forced to see the living as dead and the earth as living. And we are forced to understand the object as a multiplicity.

Thinking with Hives
Keith M. Botelho

IN *THE TUDOR HOUSE AND GARDEN*, PAULA HENDERSON NOTES THAT apiaries, "although at best only architecture in miniature...were vital, if not particularly conspicuous, elements of most gardens."[1] The eight major bee treatises published in England between 1593-1679, as well as many gardening manuals from the same period, devote space to the construction, preservation, and placement of beehives in and around gardens. We see in Thomas Hill's *The Gardener's Labyrinth* a woodcut of a garden, gardeners, and water pump in action, and in the upper right corner we notice two skep beehives (See Figure 1, next page). These skeps, basket hives made in England from coils of wheat or rye straw, have a single entrance at the base with no internal structure provided for the bees—removing the honey often meant the risk of destroying the entire hive.[2] The hives are stationary, fixed objects that are part of a larger network that produced a working garden landscape. Yet they are also lively, embodied, full of activity (as seen with the bees flying about).

As a "way in" to thinking with hives, I want to begin with two seventeenth-century diary entries. In 1625, at the age of seventeen, Elizabeth Isham inherited the responsibilities of managing the family estate at Lamport after her mother passed away, and one of her tasks was caring for the beehives. Isham kept a diary through the late 1640s, and in it she makes numerous references to her beekeeping activities, detailing

---

1   *The Tudor House and Garden: Architecture and Landscape in the Sixteenth and Early Seventeenth Centuries* (New Haven: Yale University Press, 2005): 149.
2   According to Keith S. Delaplane in *First Lessons in Beekeeping* (Hamilton, IL: Dadant Publishing, 2007), hive designs before the Langstroth hive of the mid-nineteenth century "were exercises in fancy designed with little or no understanding of the biology of bees" (29).

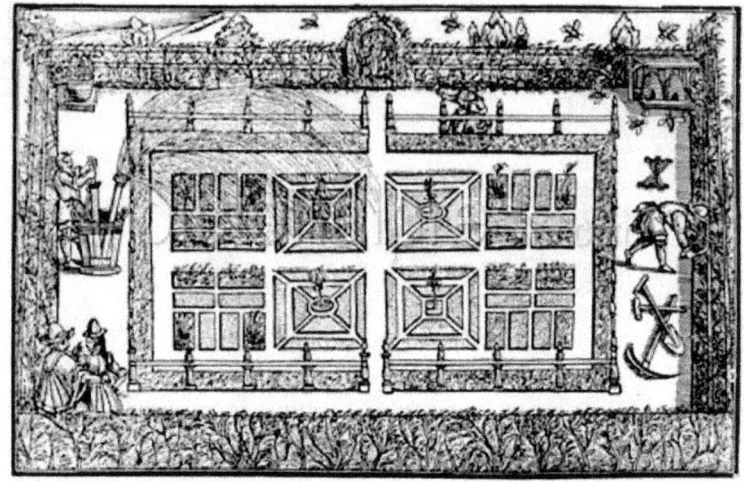

Figure 1. Thomas Hill, *The Gardener's Labyrinth* (London, 1594), CN 20670, The Huntington Library, San Marino, California.

her purchase of bees (presumably from those in her local community), her care in managing swarms, and her selling of both honey and hives, each valued as market commodities. Yet in one striking entry from 1640, she details how she gave hives to two of her female companions. She writes, "Jane dod my Nurse had one hive and Su Allin another to keepe."[3] The following year, Isham writes that she "had a swarm at Sue Allins" while also noting that her Nurse died, although she makes no reference to what became of her hive. And John Evelyn, in a 13 July 1654 diary entry, recounted an evening spent at the home of Dr. John Wilkins. Wilkins, he recalled,

> was the first who shew'd me the Transparent Apiaries, which he had built like Castles & Palaces & so ordered them one upon another, as to take the Hony without destroying the Bees.... he was so aboundantly civill, as finding me pleas'd with them, to present me one of

---

[3] All quotations from Isham's diary can be found on the "Constructing Elizabeth Isham" site at the University of Warwick: http://web.warwick.ac.uk/english/perdita/Isham/.

these Hives, which he had empty, & which I afterwards had in my Garden at Says-Court.⁴

Both Pepys and Charles II would later walk through Evelyn's garden to marvel at these hives, watching the bees conduct their work. Here, Evelyn's hives become sights to see, his garden a destination to observe.

In both Isham's and Evelyn's accounts, the hives become itinerant, unleashed from the garden, traveling things. Isham, in giving hives to two female companions, established a local community of female curators who could manage a hive, women who would order an already female-centered space, what Charles Butler called "A Feminine Monarchie." In fact, John Levett, in his 1634 work *The ordering of Bees*, remarks that it is "good women, who commonly in this Country take most care and regard of this kind of commodity."⁵ Wilkins gives an empty hive to Evelyn with the implication he will fill it with a swarm of bees. Bees and humans are caught, therefore, in a network of profit and pleasure, with the hive as the architecture that allows this exchange to occur.⁶ The gift giver and receiver ensure an object on-the-go will once again become stationary, a stable thing for the coming and going of the bees that will reside within.

But let's give nuance to this term. Hives in nature are found in hollow logs, trees, or crevices high above the ground. Entomologists refer to these as wild bee colonies, not hives.⁷ The *beehive* is the name given to the man-made habitat for bees that is designed so they are subject to humans, who generally oversee their activities. John Worlidge, in his *Apiarium; or a Discourse of Bees* (1676), notes that it is not unusual to find swarms in

---

4   Quoted in Eva Crane, *The World History of Beekeeping and Honey Hunting* (New York and London: Routledge, 1999), 380.

5   John Levett, *The ordering of Bees* (London, 1634), v.

6   This profit / pleasure nexus literalizes the humanist metaphor of a scholar's labor as akin to a bee harvesting nectar. The appeal of Virgil's *Georgics* (particularly Book IV that concerns the honeybee) to Renaissance educational theorists was that the agricultural practices outlined in the text became metaphors for intellectual cultivation, an idea that finds its way into Francis Bacon's *The Advancement of Learning* (1605).

7   See Thomas D. Seeley, *Honeybee Democracy* (Princeton: Princeton University Press, 2010) and Delaplane, *First Lessons in Beekeeping*, 29. Many bee treatises from the period refer to these man-made objects as straw hives or bee houses. See, for instance, Moses Rusden's *A Further Discovery of Bees* (London, 1679), where he writes, "That they set their Bees in the Bee-house to furnish their houses with Colonies as soon in the spring as they can" (75, S4).

trees or hollow places in buildings, but more often you would find swarms "enticed into Hives or other Receptacles prepared for them, which were first made of Rinds or Barks of Trees, in imitation, as may be supposed, of the hollow Trees they naturally placed themselves in. Afterwards by degrees they began to make them of other Materials."[8] A hive is thus a communal *shelter*, temporary and ephemeral (not a *dwelling*, usually marked as lasting), with a logic of activity.[9] *Hive* is etymologically related to *cage* (hollow place, enclosure for animals) and *cell* (small room, concealed hut), yet both are enclosures that without human interference are usually not able to be breached. A hive, whether in nature or manmade, is designed and intended to have an opening, a place for coming and going. Bees cannot be contained, and they work independently of us, and even when humans intervene in the life of the hive, it continues to have a life and complexity of its own.

Yet hives have always been mobile, and by their very nature are always on the move. But bees resist captivity, even as humans have learned to harvest them for profit and pleasure. Bees exhibit what Erica Fudge has called "recalcitrant behavior" in their refusal to be contained, caged, or domesticated.[10] The term *hive*, then, usually represents not only the physical object but also its component parts—Queen and worker bees, drones, honey, wax, cells—in other words, a collective. The bees use manmade hives to reside, but the hive is a temporary shelter, a stopover, a household for rent, a revolving habitation where its tenants will one day be on the move. And although bees are today often raised commercially, a hive's success depends upon humans giving the bees space to return to nature. By resisting containment, bees emerge as a sovereign species, freely leaving and returning not for the sake of humans, but for the sake of their hive.[11] Hives do not take bees out of nature, for it is the natural world to which they will repeatedly return.

---

8   *Apiarium; or a Discourse of Bees* (London, 1676), 3, B2r.
9   For more on these distinctions between shelters and dwellings in nature, see Jeffrey Theis, *Writing the Forest in Early Modern England: A Sylvan Renaissance Pastoral* (Pittsburgh: Duquesne University Press, 2010).
10 Erica Fudge "Renaissance Animal Things," in *Gorgeous Beasts: Animal Bodies in Historical Perspective*, ed. Joan B. Landes, Paula Young Lee, and Paul Youngquist (University Park, PA: The Pennsylvania State University Press, 2012), 44–45.
11 See George Herbert's poem "Providence," where the speaker insists that "Bees work for man." Without human interference, bees generally thrive; in fact, human interference with the natural environment (the use of systemic pesticides or the practice

I want to reorient our looking here, to consider not "the question of the animal" but rather "the question of an object." Bill Brown, in his essay "Thing Theory," notes that

> [W]e begin to confront the thingness of objects when they stop working for us: when the drill breaks, when the car stalls, when the windows get filthy....The story of objects asserting themselves as things, then, is the story of a changed relation to the human subject and thus the story of how the thing really names less an object than a particular subject-object relation.[12]

Bees can leave—in fact, they often do leave their shelter en masse when they swarm—and all humans are left with is an empty hive, an abandoned thing, a man-made object bereft of its livelihood, depriving humans—even temporarily—of its honey and wax.[13] The beehive as empty object is placed in motion only to become stationary in a garden, when it will then, with bees inhabiting, once again become alive, its tenants on the move. Is a hive only a hive if there are bees to make it buzz? In other words, does the object only reach its full potential as a thing—its "hive-ness"—when it is occupied? Is it just straw until its inhabitants move in? When bees swarm and take up elsewhere, does the remaining structure lose its object-ness that made it a hive? The hive invites and challenges us to see it as a thing with agency of its own, imposing its "thing-i-ness" on the mental and physical environs in which it acts. Hives grow and evolve, and they are complex systems that persist over time and adapt to their surroundings. Bees occupy hives but do not build the outer protective part of the hive, as a bird would make a nest. They are rather responsible for constructing the inside, acting as structural engineers that leave their interior architecture behind when they swarm.[14] Each

---

of monoculture, for example) is often pointed to as one of the major factors in the emergence of Colony Collapse Disorder (CCD).

12 Bill Brown, "Thing Theory," *Critical Inquiry* 28 (Autumn 2001): 4.

13 See John Marston's *The Malcontent*, where Maquerelle tells Bianca and Emilia that once youth and beauty are gone, "we are like beehives without honey, out o'-fashion apparel that no man will wear" (2.4.50–53).

14 In fact, it is Virgil who, in Book IV of his *Georgics*, writes that the bees "wall the honeycombs and frame the intricate houses" (4.179). Translation by C. Day Lewis in *The Georgics of Virgil* (New York: Oxford University Press, 1947), 70.

new swarm attests to the marvel of their complexity. The many make the object stable.

Writers of bee treatises often speak of the necessity of trimming or dressing the hive before bees occupy it. To trim or dress hives meant to strengthen, fortify, or make ready. In Edmund Southerne's *A Treatise concerning the right use and ordering of Bees* (1593), he writes that upon purchasing a hive, you must smooth it of any "little superfluous tickling straws" as you begin to dress it for use.[15] He continues, discussing how to ensure that the swarm that you put in to your hive will stay:

> and then, Fennel, Dake, Elm, or Aspen leaves being dipped in fair water with a little honey, besprinkle the Hive, or if you want honey, a little milk, if you have no milk, fair water will serve for a shift, and when you have so done put in your Bees, and they will tarry: but if you have no new Hives ready, then you may take an old Hive and use that as aforesaid.[16]

First, it should be noted that Southerne's receipt describing how to trim a hive, repeated in John Levett's *The ordering of Bees* some forty years later, has the long-term sustainability of the object in mind. Levett himself remarks, through an imagined dialogue between one Petralba and Tortona, that beekeepers often trim or dress the hive with honey or sweet liquor before moving a swarm into it. Yet he notes that while new hives don't need to be trimmed this way ("the Bees will like it well enough without it"), it "may help those that be old, and somewhat unsavory, and cannot hurt any."[17] In both Southerne and Levett, old hives have a robust potentiality, and this process of recycling foregrounds the issue of absence. In other words, old hives are also abandoned hives, hives that have been

---

15 Southerne, *A Treatise concerning the right use and ordering of Bees* (London, 1593), B1v.

16 Southerne, *A Treatise*, B2r. Even more interesting is what Southerne writes next: "But if your Bees be so forward that they will not tarry in any Hive, then take your Hive whether it be old or new, and pull out the sticks, and put therein two handfuls of Barley or Peas, but Mault is the best if you have it, and let a Dog, a Pig or a Sow eat it, turning the Hive with your hands as he eateth, that the froth which he maketh in eating may remain in the Hive, then wipe the Hive again lightly with an old woolen or linen cloth... and so the Bees being put in they will abide without further trouble" (B2r).

17 Levett, *The ordering of Bees* (London, 1634), 20.

subject to a swarm or other natural event. Instead of seeing an abandoned hive as a sign of decline or devastation, as we are apt to do in our own moment in being attuned more than ever to the loss of bees, these writers see opportunity, a shelter that can be occupied multiple times that signals future productivity and activity. Recuperating previously-inhabited hives becomes a regenerative act, and the object of the hive allows for (with some minor trimming or dressing) the opportunity for bees to return and prosper.

To hive bees in an "old" man-made structure is an embodied practice that brings humans and bees together at this object site. In many ways, the hive resembles what Michel Foucault called a heterotopia, a space with multiple or superimposed meanings. Foucault examines the space in which we live inside a "cluster" or "network" of relations, a space that "draws us out of ourselves, in which the erosion of our lives, our time and our history occurs, the space that claws and gnaws at us."[18] The two types of places he describes are utopias and heterotopias. Utopias are sites with no real place that present society in a perfected form or as a place turned upside down. Yet these unreal spaces are opposed to heterotopias, real places that are counter-sites, both mythic and real, outside of all places even though it may be possible to indicate their location in reality. Like the garden of which Foucault writes, so too is the hive a sort of microcosm, "the smallest parcel of the world and then it is the totality of the world."[19] And what did the sight or talk of hives trigger in the early modern imagination? The hive "speaks"—its buzz (the hum made by a hive or a swarm) has agency in its own particular set of behaviors and associations.[20] For instance, the noise of the city was often likened to the hive, as we see in John Earle's *Micro-cosmographie* (1628), where he writes that the noise of Paul's Walk "is like that of Bees, a strange humming or buzze."[21] The hive was layered with extra-literal meanings in the Renaissance, serving as a touchstone from everything from politics ("Again I view'd a Kingdom in a Hive / Where every one did work, and so all thrive") to religion ("the

---

18 Michel Foucault, "Of Other Spaces," *Diacritics* 16:1 (Spring 1986), 23.
19 Foucault, "Of Other Spaces," 26.
20 See Julian Yates, "What are 'Things' Saying in Renaissance Studies?" *Literature Compass* 3/5 (2006): 992–1010. In discussing the exchanges between thing and person, Yates writes of "an overlay of different associations, timings, as literal, referential, metaphorical, richly or minimally semiotized, depending on the text that performs them," 1007.
21 *Micro-cosmographie* (London, 1628), J5r.

Catholick hive of bees").[22] Hives become for early moderns tools through which humans think about their world.[23] Nevertheless, beyond such allegories stands the thing itself, a hive laden with objectal vitality, and it is imperative to remember that the literal lives of bees and their hives matter to early moderns. The hive is not about the individual bee but rather the collective — at a historical moment when the notion of the individual was emerging, bee treatises detail the industry and order of the many. The hive's lively power rests in its ability to move and be moved, both in its absence and in its material presence.

---

22 Anonymous, *A Description of the Four Seasons or Quarters of the Year* (1690); Anonymous, *The Christian sodality* (1652).

23 Catherine Richardson, in *Shakespeare and Material Culture* (Oxford University Press, 2011), notes that material objects were essential to early modern thought processes, "condensing complex concepts and ideas into resonant images in the mind's eye" (9).

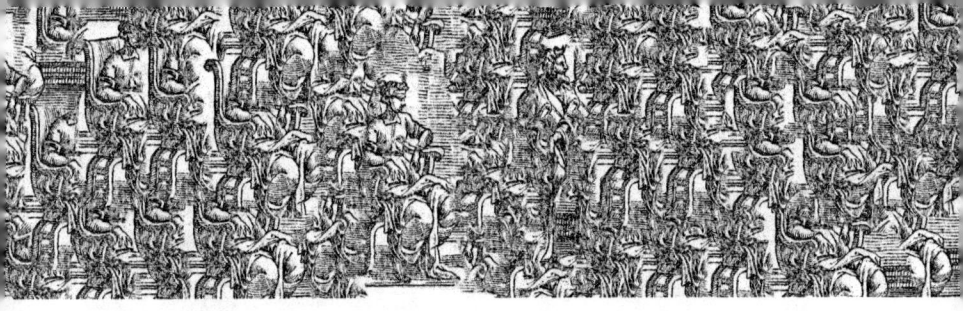

Gloucester's Chair
Object Entanglements on the Early Modern Stage
Patricia A. Cahill

IN GEFFREY WHITNEY'S *A CHOICE OF EMBLEMS* (1586), A WOODCUT entitled "Dolor è medicina" depicts a "Purblinde dame" confronting a devious physician who during his regular visits to her home has been making off with her belongings.[1] (See Figure 1, next page.) As the accompanying short verse details, the woman discovers the theft precisely as the physician requests payment for having restored her sight. Turning the tables on him, she wittily responds to his demand by protesting that she remains impaired: "Bycause my sences either faile, or ells my eies bee blinde./For, where my house before was garnish'd everie nooke:/I, nowe can see no goodes at all, though rounde about I looke." While the woodcut captures this moment in which the duplicitous doctor is stopped in his tracks on the way out the door, Whitney's verse about the woman's failing vision produces a blind spot for his readers. Accordingly, early modern readers, prompted to see a house "un-garnished" of its goods may well have overlooked the one good remaining in place: the gracious, high-backed wooden chair in which the woman sits and surveys her otherwise empty domestic space. This "mistake" could arise not because chairs were so plentiful as to be invisible—in fact, a typical middling-level English household likely contained only one or two chairs, usually made of oak, relying primarily on less costly benches, stools, and chests for seating—but rather because Whitney's verse, with its emphasis on dispossession, invites readers to view the chair as something other than a "goode."[2] Divested of its status as a commodity, the chair exists primarily as the familiar and unobtrusive ally of the bereft woman. It exists, we might say, as her environment.

---

1 Geffrey Whitney, *A choice of emblemes, and other deuises* (Leyden, 1586), 156.
2 Catherine Richardson, *Shakespeare and Material Culture* (Oxford: Oxford University Press, 2011), 101.

Although chairs were not rare on early modern stages, they constitute something of a blind spot for drama scholarship insofar as few critics have sought to address what and how these stage properties acquired meaning.³ Perhaps it is true that once a chair was "set out" or "placed" (to use the terms commonly found in stage directions), it appeared to sit quietly, whether attesting to the social position of its occupants, delineating a domestic interior, or indicating that certain characters are aged, ailing, or wounded.⁴ But why should we assume that stage furniture is merely inert and indexical, that it exists simply to tell audiences how to read space and characters? After all, if even a woodcut hints at intimacies shared by a chair and its occupant, then why should an actual chair not afford the possibility of complex affective encounters? In what follows, I focus on stage chairs that cause unease to their occupants, rather than on an object like Whitney's seemingly comfortable (and perhaps comforting) ally. Put differently, I take as my guide the chairs that appear along with other domestic objects in contemporary Greek architect Katerina Kamprani's "The Uncomfortable Project," which contests the assumption that chairs afford one a place of rest.⁵ Kamprani creates the "lean chair," which reclines in the wrong direction; the "stretching cat chair," whose seat arches upward; and the "half chair," in which the backrest is situated precisely in the middle of the seat. Implicit in the form of these objects, of course, is a narrative about the chair's perversity: its willful movement away from the would-be sitter's desires. Taking aim at the tendency to

Figure 1. "Dolor è medicina," Geffrey Whitney's *A Choice of emblems* (1586).

---

3 But see Richardson, *Shakespeare and Material Culture*, 99–105; Julia Reinhard Lupton, "The Renaissance Res Publica of Furniture," in Jeffrey Jerome Cohen, *Animal, Vegetable, Mineral: Ethics and Objects* (Washington, DC: Oliphaunt Books, 2012), 211–236; and Julia Reinhard Lupton, "Hospitality," in *Early Modern Theatricality*, ed. Henry S. Turner (Oxford: Oxford University Press, 2014), 423–42.
4 "Chair" in Alan C. Dessen and Leslie Thomson, *A Dictionary of Stage Directions in English Drama, 1590–1642* (Cambridge: Cambridge University Press, 1999).
5 Katerina Kamprani, "The Uncomfortable." *kkstudio.gr*. np. nd. Web. 21 May 2014.

regard the world of things as naturally compliant, Kamprani's project, while rooted in our contemporary moment, is instructive for those who think about the objects of the past. Indeed, it may invite us to recognize the chairs of the early modern stage both as objects with which human desires easily become entangled and as objects with their own latent desires, which may be indifferent to our own.[6]

Let's start with an easy chair—namely, the stage property featured in the murder scene of the anonymous true-crime drama, *Arden of Faversham* (1592).[7] In a conversation with a murderer for hire, Alice Arden plans to offer this chair to Mosby, her lowborn lover and co-conspirator in the killing of her husband Thomas, so that Thomas will be forced to sit on a joint-stool and the murderer(s) can sneak up on him from behind. For many readers, this scene turns on the specific symbolism of a chair in the social realm: according to the period's dominant gender norms, the willingness of the master of a household to yield his chair to another is in and of itself blameworthy.[8] But beyond pointing to the failures of a patriarchal figure, this scene also allows audiences to recognize the affective attachments of Thomas's valuable household goods to the persons of this drama. Rather than simply function as an inanimate object in a socially-coded allegory, in other words, Thomas's chair actually seems to animate the play's adulterous lovers and repel its owner. For example, when Alice, having just learned of the chair's signal role in the murder-plot, imagines her future ("I shall no more be closed in Arden's arms, That like the snakes of black Tisiphone / Sting me with their embracings. Mosby's arms / Shall compass me" [XIV, 139–43]), the play's haptic metaphors emphasize the material underpinnings of Alice's desire, conflating the open arms of the chair with those of a husband and lover. Whether soliciting longings or unease, the master's domestic goods often propel the action or otherwise call the shots in *Arden*. Indeed, as the play conflates the agential capacities of the nonhuman with those of the human, it emerges that virtually

---

6   On the indifference of domestic objects see "The Mess" in J. Allan Mitchell, *Becoming Human: The Matter of the Medieval Child* (Minneapolis: University of Minnesota Press, 2014).

7   Citations are to *Arden of Faversham*, ed. Tom Lockwood and Martin White, 2nd ed. (London and New York: Bloomsbury Methuen Drama, 2007).

8   See, for example, Lena Cowen Orlin, *Private Matters, Public Culture* (Cornell: Cornell University Press, 1994), 76 and Frank Whigham, *Seizures of the Will in Early Modern Drama* (Cambridge: Cambridge University Press, 1998), 118.

everyone and everything that Thomas would possess has a hand in the plot to murder him.

While the staging of the murder-plot in *Arden* clearly suggests the extent to which a chair, as much as a master, may make a household, other scenes evoking chair violence foreground a more visceral kind of object ecology: at least five early modern dramas contain lurid scenes of individuals bound against their will to chairs.[9] In George Peele's history play *Edward I* (1593), Alice Arden's Ovidian allusion to the Furies comes to life as a woman is bound to a chair and stung by a deadly serpent she has been forced to nurse at her breast; in Barnabe Barnes's tragedy *The Devil's Charter* (1607), the husband of Lucrezia Borgia unwittingly sits in a chair specially designed to restrain him while she stabs him with his dagger and then unbinds his corpse to make his death appear a suicide; in Thomas Goffe's university play *The Tragedy of Orestes* (1633, but first performed in the 1610s), Clytemestra and Aegystheus are tied to a chair and murdered after having been forced to drink the blood of their murdered infant; in John Ford's revenge tragedy *The Broken Heart* (1633), an unsuspecting brother is trapped in an immobilizing chair and stabbed while mourning his sister's death by the man to whom his sister was once betrothed; and, most famously, in *King Lear* (1610; 1623 but probably composed circa 1605–6), Gloucester is bound to a chair, interrogated as a traitor, and ruthlessly blinded in what is commonly described as one of the most harrowing scenes on the early modern stage. Given how bloody—how utterly corporeal—these chair scenes must have been in performance, it may seem odd to focus on a seemingly quiescent object, a stage property that appears almost incidental to such shocking intensities. But, as I aim to show through the example of *Lear*, the affective power of these scenes has everything to do with the chair as an animate and animating force.

While act 3 of *Lear* is notorious for its performance of Gloucester's blinding, we should not forget the centrality of binding, for the interrogation scene requires both the (presumably offstage) "pinioning" of Gloucester as well as the onstage ordeal of tying him against his will to a chair appropriated from him.[10] Indeed, even before Gloucester comes

---

9 Shakespeare's *King John* also evokes the possibility of the chair-binding and blinding of Arthur, nephew of the king. Less luridly, Francis Beaumont's comedy *The Woman-Hater* shows the misogynist Gondarino tied to a chair and tormented by a group of wronged woman.

10 Unless otherwise noted, citations are to act 3, scene 7 of "The Tragedy of King Lear: A Conflated Text" in *The Norton Shakespeare*, ed. Stephen Greenblatt et al. (New

into view, the scene uncannily foreshadows such entanglements through Cornwall's short speech to Edmund, which twice uses the word "bound" (7, 10). Subsequently, the play moves closer to the staging of this action as Cornwall orders the servants to locate Gloucester and "Pinion him like a thief" (23). Once Gloucester appears on stage, the focus on binding is immediate and, for six lines, unrelenting: Cornwall orders, "Bind fast his corky arms," "Bind him, I say," and "To this chair bind him," while Regan supplements these orders with her own command: "Hard, hard" (29, 32, 34). Signaling debts to Samuel Harsnett's wildly polemical account of young people in Denham who were tied to a so-called "holy chaire" and tortured by priests who feigned exorcism, the scene lingers not only on the broken bonds of hospitality but also on the ligatures joining chair and body.[11] Significantly, such binding—even without the unwatchable blinding—could very well constitute torture: indeed, one of the Denham victims was so firmly anchored to the chair that she suffered severe bruising and, for three years afterward, endured excruciating arm pain (Brownlow, 85).

As *Lear* stages the difficulty and anguish of joining together man and chair, it also ensures that visions of human particularity dissolve, much as Gloucester himself will articulate when he imagines himself as a baited beast "tied to the [presumably wooden] stake" (54).[12] Less obviously, perhaps, when Cornwall suggests that Gloucester's arms be tied together, his use of the word *pinion* evokes what would have been the common practice of preventing flight by cutting off a bird's flight feathers or binding together its wings. As such, the staging of Gloucester's pinioning is much more than a simple insult to Gloucester's social position; it also activates the drama's avian imaginary, which is deeply preoccupied with human vulnerability to death. Through the pinioned Gloucester, in fact, the scene is savagely proleptic. It anticipates both the moment in Act 4 when Edgar, in disguise, will insist that Gloucester is atop a cliff where "crows and choughs...wing the midway air" (4.6.13) and will exclaim that

---

York: W.W. Norton, 1997). My reading is deeply indebted to Vin Nardizzi's incisive commentary on this scene in his unpublished manuscript "'Ripeness is all': Plants, Oedipal Myths, and *King Lear*."

11   F.W. Brownlow, *Shakespeare, Harsnett and the Devils of Denham* (Cranbury, NJ: Associated University Presses, 1993), 234.

12   On the play's staging of human particularity, see Laurie Shannon, *The Accommodated Animal: Cosmopolity in Shakespearean Locales* (Chicago: University of Chicago Press, 2013).

Gloucester's survival of his supposed fall indicates that he too is birdlike, made of "gossamer, feathers, [and] air," (4.6.49) as well as the moment in Act 5 when Lear will hope to find, in the stirring of a feather evidence that the lifeless Cordelia lives (5.3.264).

While the pinioning of Gloucester threatens to evacuate the category of the human, the interrogation scene, somewhat paradoxically, also conjures the human form as it insists upon the chair as a site of disciplinary force. Most notably, the scene of Gloucester's suffering recalls the earlier scene of Kent's confinement within the stocks: in that scene, so the Fool declared, Kent was "tied" like a captive animal and had his legs encased in "wooden nether-stocks" (2.4.7,10). As a site of retributive punishment, Gloucester's chair is also kin to the "trick chairs" of revenge dramas like *The Devil's Charter* and *The Broken Heart*. Just as those plays foreground the manufacture of their "grasping" furniture—Lucretia Borgia, for example, boasts of her superiority to the master craftsman Vulcan while Ford's revenger applauds mechanical ingenuity—so, too, does *Lear* showcase the intentional re-design of an otherwise banal domestic object. As Julia Reinhard Lupton has observed, the play calls attention to the "brutal repurposing" of the chair: "the chair's stately arms and solid back normally support the dignity of the master of the house or his most honored guest; now these very same features afford very different actions as Gloucester's 'corky arms' are tied to the wooden arms of the chair, which is then tilted backward to receive Cornwall's blinding foot."[13] Insisting upon the proximity of chair and torture technology, the scene depicts the chilling fantasy that the most seemingly domestic of objects possesses or, to draw on Graham Harman's lexicon, "withholds," lethal capacities, a fiction realized again in the modern era when an oak recliner associated with the furniture designer Gustav Stickley was deployed for the first electrocutions as capital punishment.[14] Like this cozily domestic electric chair, the chair in *Lear* is positioned on the side of the law. Indeed, for Cornwall who, at the start of the scene, acknowledges that he "may not pass upon [Gloucester's] life / Without the form of justice" (25), the chair is itself the form and, quite literally, the seat of justice.

---

13 "Hospitality," 436.

14 On the chair design and Stickley's connection with the world's first electrocution in 1890, see Mark Essig, *Edison and the Electric Chair: A Story of Light and Death* (New York: Walker, 2003), 230.

And yet to see Gloucester's chair solely as a cruelly indifferent technology of torture may be to overlook how carefully the scene, in staging a domestic object that echoes the form of the body, attends to the object's vulnerability. While Shakespeare's text is curiously silent about where Gloucester's chair ends up, it seems likely that, in performance, the stage property must be jettisoned in some way. Perhaps it would be cast off in the midst of the scene, thereby cryptically revisiting the play's opening in which Lear, in disavowing his kingship, implicitly renounced his (presumably wooden) chair of state. Or perhaps the chair, like Gloucester, would be "thrust out at gates" at the scene's conclusion (96). In any case, as the scene depicts the binding of Gloucester to his chair, the play re-imagines human-object affiliations such that the instrument of torture itself becomes visible as an abject thing, instantiating in its very form the corporeal frailty of its occupant. Rather than merely perform the rigor of the law, the chair thus witnesses to the law's impact: after all, in the very form of a chair, as Alice Rayner has points out, we may see the image of a faltering body, for the "angles [of a chair] follow the skeletal joints of a body halfway to collapse, expecting the bending of the knees and the hinging of the hips."[15] As such, the chair materializes the scene's uncanny temporalities, anticipating by its shape the play's many fainting and falling bodies, including of course that of Gloucester at Dover Cliff.

The chair's vulnerability is made most visible perhaps when Cornwall summons Gloucester's "corky arms" (29), a phrase that is usually read as a signifier of the old man's utter defenselessness in the face of his captors. The unusual adjective, often glossed as "withered," is conventionally traced to Harsnett who insinuated that the exorcising priests were motivated by lust, favoring young victims rather than "old corkie women."[16] But whatever Shakespeare's lexical source, it is hard to overlook the poignancy of the resonance, noted by Lupton, between the wooden arms of the torture chair and the corky arms of its occupant, especially in view of what Vin Nardizzi has taught us to recognize as the presence and potentialities of the playhouse's wooden structures.[17] As is underscored by John Gerard's popular herbal, cork-oak trees, like all trees, were commonly

---

15 Alice Rayner, *Ghosts: Death's Double and the Phenomena of Theatre* (Minneapolis: University of Minnesota Press, 2006), 110.
16 Brownlow, *Shakespeare, Harsnett and the Devils of Denham*, 111.
17 Vin Nardizzi, *Wooden Os: Shakespeare's Theatres and England's Trees* (Toronto: University of Toronto, 2013).

understood via analogy as human bodies ("In all the bodyes of trees as of liuely creatures, there is skinne, senowes, blood, fleshe, vaynes, bones, and marowe: theyr skinne is their barke."), a fact that makes the binding of Gloucester to the chair not unlike a meeting of skin on skin.[18] The affective resonance of Cornwall's reference to corky arms may also have been bound up with early modern understandings of the bark of the cork-oak as an unusually durable and resilient material.[19] Attuned as the play may be to practical knowledge of the cork-oak tree as able to withstand the loss or "pill[ing] off" of its protective skin, this scene in which a corky-armed man endures the plucking of his beard and the putting out of his eyes powerfully substantiates Gloucester's affiliation with the nonhuman.[20]

Without knowing more about the stage properties of the early modern theater, it is impossible to know just how far the reach of Gloucester's corky arms may once have extended. But it is tempting to imagine that these ligneous limbs once found a match in the actors' footwear, for thick cork-soled shoes were then (as the anti-theatricalist Phillip Stubbes lamented) the height of fashion.[21] If so, how painfully tight would be the entanglements of object and human when a cork-soled Cornwall, having instructed his servants to "hold the [wooden] chair," warned the corky-armed Gloucester, "Upon these eyes of thine I'll set my foot" (68–69)? Certainly, as the torture scene constructs this assemblage, it reflects back on an earlier wooden-limbed locales: the scene in which Edgar, having found safety within "the happy hollow of a tree," declares that he will pierce his arms with "wooden pricks," imitating the "numbed and mortified bare arms" of beggars (2.3.2,15–16). By contrast to such insensate human arms, Gloucester's chair seems all-too-sentient.

Through such agonizing interpenetrations of wood and flesh, Gloucester's torture scene challenges human-centered readings of *Lear*, which typically focus on what Caroline Spurgeon once described as "a human body in anguished movement, tugged, wrenched, beaten, pierced, stung, scourged, dislocated, flayed, gashed, scalded, tortured and finally broken

---

18 John Gerard, *The herball or Generall historie of plantes* (London, 1633). As Vin Nardizzi has pointed out to me, Robert Hooke's discovery of plant cells came about while examining cork under the microscope.
19 Gerard, *The herball*, 1348.
20 Charles Estienne, *Maison rustique, or The countrey farme* (London, 1616).
21 Phillip Stubbes, *Phillip Stubbes's Anatomy of the Abuses in England in Shakespeare's Youth*, ed. Frederick J. Furnivall (London: New Shakespeare Society, 1876–9), 57–8.

on the neck."[22] Gloucester's wooden chair surely does not let audiences forget about such "anguished movement." Through its very materiality, however, the chair insists that such anguish entails human affiliation with the nonhuman. In short, even as *Lear* stages the most abject human corporeality, it reminds us of the fragility of the nonhuman, including of the seemingly commanding objects (whether stocks, or stake, or chair) through which its tortures are meted out. Such a reminder is writ large at the play's end when, in response to Lear's collapse, Kent cries out, "He hates him much / That would upon the rack of this tough world / Stretch him out longer" (5.3.313–15). Rather than foreground the human body alone in a brutal world, Kent's plea that Lear be allowed to die undisturbed articulates a more expansive vision, for through the evocation of Lear bound to a rack—that is, of yet another hybrid human / nonhuman wooden assemblage—the play returns once again to Gloucester's chair, a return underscored by the buried pun on "would." Asserting, it seems, that there is no escape from the enmeshment of the object with the human, the play depicts an environment of shared vulnerability in which human and non-human are inexorably bound together. If the emblem of the bereft woman and her chair with which I began quietly hints at the affective possibilities of so-called moveables, Shakespeare's drama turns Whitney's still life into tragedy: that is, it intimates that, even in a world constituted by cruelty and devastating loss, objects are not remote from us, but rather a part of our very being.

---

22 Caroline Spurgeon, *Shakespeare's Imagery and What It Tells Us* (Cambridge: Cambridge University Press 1935), 339.

Much Ado about Planking
Christine Hoffmann

IN 2011, SOMETHING CALLED "PLANKING" BRIEFLY TOOK OVER THE Internet (Figures 1 and 2). Before declining in popularity, this global meme would provoke arrests in Wisconsin, inspire legislation in the Philippines, stir accusations of racism on Twitter, and kill a man in Australia. *Know Your Meme* helpfully defines planking as "lying face down with arms to the sides in unusual public spaces."[1] The site's image gallery includes people planking on desks, chairs, escalators, phone booths, goalposts, even the back of a whale. For me, the photos bring new meaning to Benedick's complaint, in *Much Ado about Nothing*, that he has been "misused" by Beatrice "past the endurance of a block"; he likely means the chopping block—the solid piece of wood "used for various operations," according to the *OED*, such as chopping meat, cutting firewood, or beheading the condemned—an object with a notably high tolerance for use and abuse.[2] Benedick identifies here as a thing, but even more importantly, as a thing among other things—"an oak but with one green leaf on it would have answer'd her. My very visor began to assume life, and scold with her"—each pushed past its limit, compelled into intimate exchange with Beatrice and with each other.[3]

To make an argument about planking is, no doubt, to make much ado about nothing, but out of both the meme and Shakespeare's play emerges an object-oriented ethics. To plank, first of all, is to imitate (the

---

1 "Planking," *Know Your Meme*, last modified June 29, 2013, http://knowyourmeme.com/memes/planking.
2 "Block, *n.*," *OED*.
3 Shakespeare, William, *Much Ado About Nothing*, in *The Riverside Shakespeare*, ed. G.B. Evans, 2nd ed. (Boston: Houghton Mifflin, 1997), 2.1.239–42.

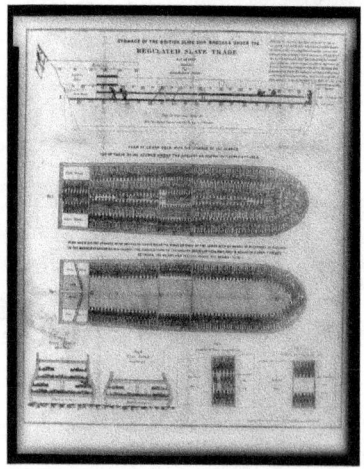

From top to bottom:

Figure 1. Image #134,675 from *Know Your Meme*.

Figure 2. Image #184,865 from *Know Your Meme*.

Figure 3. Image from from "Alexander Hart Planking Spree: Wisconsin Man Convicted Following Prank (PHOTOS)," *The Huffington Post*, December 13, 2011, accessed February 2, 2014, http://www.huffingtonpost.com/2011/12/09/alexander-hart-planking-spree-convict_n_1139162.html.

Figure 4. Image from "Stowage of the British slave ship Brookes under the regulated slave trade act of 1788," *Library of Congress*, accessed 12 February 2015, http://www.loc.gov/pictures/item/98504459/.

posture of) an object; it is also to invite observation as an actor without a code. "We might observe in an object...a way of being, a custom or routine," says Ian Bogost. "But a disposition is quite different from a code," and "the fact of relations shouldn't be sufficient to affirm that the actors involved in those relations act according to an ethics or in violation of one."[4] Granted, many respond to planking as a violation of some kind of behavioral standard, but articulating this violation proves tricky. The blockheads[5] arrested in Wisconsin were found guilty of "disorderly conduct" (believe it or not), although according to the police report the real crime seems to be irreverence:

> I explained to RYAN that the photo of him lying on top of the Memorial Monument was offensive to me, as my friend's name was on it. I asked RYAN if he would go to a cemetery and lay across someone's gravestone to take a picture, and he responded "Of course not". I explained to RYAN that what he did was very similar. At that point, RYAN apologized.[6]

If this officer's logic triumphs under the rubric of good taste, it crumbles under "the rubric of material agency,"[7] because in addition to arrest, injury and the smooth reinforcement of an arresting officer's sense of decorum, planking provokes speculation on a non-normative, object-oriented ethics, the kind Silvia Benso has in mind when she imagines an ethics renouncing its claims "of being a practical guide, or a moral ought, or a science of mores, traditions, behaviors"—or, we might add, a rhetorical trap ("Of course not").[8] Our ethical codes "are always ethics for

---

4 Ian Bogost, *Alien Phenomenology or What It's Like to be a Thing* (Minneapolis: University of Minnesota Press, 2012), 77.
5 The OED also lists figurative definitions for "block": "A person resembling a block or log of wood...in unintelligence: A blockhead" or "in want of feeling: A hardhearted person." The Wisconsin plankers meet these definitions and more.
6 "Wisconsin Man Convicted For 'Planking' Spree," *The Smoking Gun*, December 8, 2011, accessed February 2, 2014, http://www.thesmokinggun.com/documents/stupid/man-convicted-of-planking-765891.
7 Jane Bennett, *Vibrant Matter: The Political Ecology of Things* (Durham: Duke University Press, 2010), 34.
8 Silvia Benso, *The Face of Things: A Different Side of Ethics* (Albany: SUNY Press, 2000), 130.

us," not for objects.⁹ Planking, then, might be one way to recognize how "self-centered" the process of theorizing ethical codes is, because it complicates any confidence we might have that "what a thing tends to do [is] the same as what it considers noble or right."¹⁰

Take the officer, who isn't wrong to assert that RYAN planking on a memorial is "very similar" to RYAN planking on a grave—and thus potentially offensive. He *is* wrong to stop there, however. What RYAN did is also very similar, after all, to what a plank of wood would do. According to some perspectives, what he did is also very similar to disorderly conduct. To certain Twitter users, it is very similar to racism. Rapper Xzibit tweeted in 2011 that planking "was a way to transport slaves on ships during the slave trade, its [sic] not funny."¹¹ (Figure 4). *Gawker*'s Adrian Chen was similarly absolute when, after considering Xzibit's tweet, he concluded that planking is *not* racist because "it's just stupid."¹²

Each of these participants makes justifiable observations, but none reduces planking to a single interpretation. A plank/er becomes what Timothy Morton calls a "strange stranger," a thing impossible to imagine "as an (independent, solid, predictable) object in advance of an encounter" without "domesticat[ing] it (or her, or him) in advance."¹³ Thus ethical arguments about planking are possible, for from an object-oriented perspective, planking on a memorial is less unethical than insisting on one reading of planking on a memorial—the human-centered reading that says planking on a memorial is "very similar" to planking on a gravestone and doesn't quite say, but strongly implies, that it is identical to spitting on someone's grave. When ethics is alternatively defined as "a locative description, not a normative procedure," additional interpretations emerge, as Benso explains: "Ethics opens up a space.... It deals with how much of reality one is able to maintain. What is good is defined in terms of what preserves the maximum of reality from destruction. What is bad

---

9   Bogost, *Alien Phenomenology*, 73.
10 Bogost, *Alien Phenomenology*, 76–77.
11 Xzibit, "#Planking was a way to transport slaves on ships during the slave trade, its not funny. Educate yourselves," *Twitter*, June 6, 2011, 10:22 PM, https://twitter.com/xzibit/status/88795039257468928.
12 Adrian Chen, "Is Planking Racist?" *Gawker*, July 8, 2011, accessed February 2, 2014, http://gizmodo.com/5819185/is-planking-racist.
13 Timothy Morton, "Here Comes Everything: The Promise of Object-Oriented Ontology," *Qui Parle* 19:2 (2011): 166.

is what works against reality."[14] To reduce planking to a single interpretation is thus to work against a reality where there is more to what RYAN did than bad taste, while to preserve RYAN's strange irreducibility is to preserve more of reality, one based not on normative codes but on peculiar, often intrusive, dispositions, and on relations that prove no less intimate for being based on nothing much at all—nothing consistent with any common-sense code of taste, etiquette or morality, that is. Nothing plainly funny or unfunny, orderly or disorderly, human or inhuman.[15]

In Shakespeare's *Much Ado about Nothing* are similar lessons about normative versus object-oriented ethics; so often in the play, making much ado about nothing *is* what preserves the maximum of reality. This is most evident in stage / film versions of Beatrice's and Benedick's eavesdropping scenes in Acts 2 and 3—scenes which portray all characters at their most ethical because most willing to apply "the rubric of material agency" as a "counter to human exceptionalism."[16] The prop humor often utilized in these scenes—Beatrice and Benedick's absurd attempts to camouflage themselves in, behind or as things—also recognizes "the degree to which people, animals, artifacts, technologies, and elemental forces share powers and operate in dissonant conjunction with each other."[17] It is particularly true for Don Pedro and Claudio—so stingily normative for most of the play—that they are at their best in these scenes, because the gentle humiliations they have in mind for Benedick and Beatrice are nothing to the humbling postures into which their own plan forces them, humble because for their designs on Benedick to work, they must adapt to his *redesigns* of the environment. David Tennant's Benedick spits, so Don Pedro and Claudio hold up their palms, checking for rain; the gentlemen flutter their hands after Kenneth Branagh's Benedick turns his involuntary vocalization into a birdcall; Don Pedro directly addresses the bottom of the canoe behind which Sam Waterston's Benedick conceals himself. By imitating (the postures of) objects, these Benedicks encourage their self-important companions to acknowledge that "human design takes place

---

14 Benso, *The Face of Things*, 130–31.
15 Here it is useful to read the "in-" of inhuman "simultaneously as negative prefix and inclusive preposition, surfacing entanglement even at moments of abjection." Planking is an inhuman act in the sense that it invites humans to consider our entanglements with the non-human. See introduction to *Inhuman Nature* ed. Jeffrey Jerome Cohen (Oliphant Books: Washington DC, 2014), i.
16 Bennett, *Vibrant Material*, 34.
17 Bennett, *Vibrant Material*, 34.

This page, top to bottom:

Figure 5. Frame from Joss Whedon's production (2012), starring Clark Gregg, Alexis Denisof, Fran Kranz and Reed Diamond. Note Denisof's Benedick raising his upper body from planking position.

Figure 6. Frame from Josie Rourke's production (2011), starring (from left to right) Tom Bateman, Adam James, Jonathan Coy and David Tennant.

Figure 7. Frame from A.J. Antoon's production (1973), starring Douglas Watson and Sam Waterston.

Figures 8a & 8b. Benedick-as-bird, from Kenneth Branagh's production (1993), which starred himself, Robert Sean Leonard, Denzel Washington and Richard Briers.

Next page, top to bottom:

Figure 9. "See you where Benedick hath hid himself?" Don Pedro's absurd question launches the absurd scene (2.3.40). In Jeremy Herrin's production (2011), Benedick "hides" in a tree. (Image from Manuel Harlan, "Charles Edwards as Benedick...," Cool Connections, accessed February 2, 2014, http://www.coolconnections.ru/en/projects/286/titles/9).

Figure 10. In Rourke (2011), Tennant "hides" behind a towel.

within a gigantic universe of nonhuman design" (see Figures 5–10);[18] plants, bed-sheets, boats and lukewarm cans of beer become integral actors with/around/among whom the human characters must improvise.

As these various objects insinuate themselves into integrality, the scene's object-oriented lesson emerges: these interruptions are inevitable, given the "outrageously full universe of strange and dark designs" we inhabit; "[e]ven our own designs get away from us," writes Morton; "that is what they do."[19] Don Pedro proves as much when he *plans* for Benedick to intrude on his conversation, making interruption a part of his design all along. He may not know it, but planning for intrusion is an ethical move, for it demands (re)actions that preserve the maximum amount of reality. The self-appointed love-gods[20] must be aware of Benedick but *not* aware of him. Haplessly merging with his environment, Benedick becomes for the gentlemen an object lesson, an actor without a code. Made inaccessible at his moments of closest proximity, he becomes the strange stranger—strange *because* of his close proximity, because he/it "emerges from, and is, and constitutes, the environment. The background becomes the foreground."[21]

---

18 Timothy Morton, "Freak Show Ecology: What is the Difference Between a Duck?" *Design Ecologies* 1:2 (2012): 193.

19 Morton, "Freak Show," 193.

20 Shakespeare, *Much Ado*, 2.1.386.

21 Timothy Morton, *The Ecological Thought* (Cambridge: Harvard University Press, 2012), 46.

It is not the first time Benedick has been in this position. "But that my lady Beatrice should know me, and not / Know me!" he muses in act 2,[22] uttering his long complaint about his misuse (partially quoted above) shortly after; in this speech he attacks Beatrice and at the same time credits her with preserving the maximum of reality, for she has positioned Benedick in an environment the parts of which seem entirely in accord with him—man, block, oak and visor, in it together—and yet estranged, for any fellow feeling is the result of *mis*use, these background objects forced unnaturally into the foreground by Beatrice's terrible terminations[23]—more actors without proper, predictable codes. Benedick's complaint thus hints also at the object-oriented lesson of the play: "[f]ar from gradually erasing strangeness, intimacy heightens it."[24] It's the lesson Don Pedro and Claudio fail to carry from one eavesdropping scene to another, only learning it after a visit from Messina's law enforcement, who (like Wisconsin's arresting office), unwittingly remind us how *very similar* strangeness and intimacy always are.

Indeed, after being prepped by Dogberry—a walking reminder that the closer one gets to anything, be it a word or a wrongdoer, the stranger it becomes—Messina's Watch successfully arrest Conrad and Borachio. Their confidence in bidding the villains to "stand"[25] is surprising, given their earlier conversation with Dogberry, that blockhead who withdraws every code of behavior he sets up:

> DOGBERRY
> This is your charge: you shall comprehend all vagrom men; you are to bid any man stand, in the Prince's name.
>
> 2. WATCH
> How if 'a will not stand?
>
> DOGBERRY
> Why then take no note of him, but let him go, and presently call the rest of the watch together, and thank God you are rid of a knave.[26]

---

22 Shakespeare, *Much Ado*, 1.203–204.
23 Shakespeare, *Much Ado*, 2.1.248–49.
24 Morton, *Ecological Thought*, 41.
25 Shakespeare, *Much Ado*, 3.3.165.
26 Shakespeare, *Much Ado*, 3.3.24–30.

Dogberry simply contradicts himself here, but he also suggests that the best way for the Watch to prepare is to prepare for intrusion, for interruption, for the possibility that any men bid to stand might not be "the men you took them for."[27] You might know them, but not know them—like knowing a word, but not knowing it, too. Indeed, Dogberry performs his object-oriented ethics not with prop humor but with mala-prop (humor). Words are the things he trips over and ineptly hides behind, though interestingly enough, Dogberry never stutters; for him, the wrong word *is* the right word, he's sure of it. We might say he misuses words past the endurance of their wrongness. They are at once familiar *and* wrong, and so they intrude into conversation, forcing listeners to adjust their expectations for what the truth must sound like. It is a generous adjustment, a new ethical space where the wrong word can also be the right one, where "tolerable" can mean intolerable, "redemption" can mean damnation, and "a deformed thief" can be a man, Deformed, who "wears a lock" and "goes up and down like a gentleman."[28] Quite literally, the Watch get their men, but not the man they took them for. Strange.

Just as strange, perhaps, is that no character ever bothers to correct Dogberry. Yes, Conrad calls him an ass, and Don Pedro and Claudio mock him in Act 5 as "too cunning to be understood,"[29] but essentially Dogberry is treated as Benedick and Beatrice are treated in their eavesdropping scenes; that is, most characters adjust to his inap*prop*riateness, becoming strangely intimate with it, however briefly:

DON PEDRO
Officers, what offence have these men done?

DOGBERRY
Marry, sir, they have committed false report, moreover, they have spoken untruths, secondarily, they are slanders, sixth and lastly, they have belied a lady, thirdly, they have verified unjust things, and to conclude, they are lying knaves.

---

27 Shakespeare, *Much Ado*, 3.3.47–48.
28 Shakespeare, *Much Ado*, 3.3.36; 4.1.57; 3.3.124, 126–127, 170.
29 Shakespeare, *Much Ado*, 5.1.228.

DON PEDRO
First, I ask thee what they have done, thirdly, I ask thee what's their offense, sixth and lastly, why they are committed, and to conclude, what you lay to their charge.[30]

More mockery from Don Pedro, but as Borachio's bonds should tell him, Dogberry's roundabout way is the better way; his creative (if not fully intentional) violation of normative procedure does far more good than Don Pedro's routine adherence. Borachio asserts as much when he says that "[w]hat your wisdoms could not discover, these shallow fools have brought to light."[31] Indeed, long before this scene, without Dogberry to keep them "vigitant,"[32] Don Pedro and Claudio fall into normative ethics even before gaining proximity to Hero's alleged disloyalty:

CLAUDIO
If I see any thing to-night why I should not marry
her, to-morrow in the congregation, where I should
wed, there will I shame her.

DON PEDRO
And as I woo'd for thee to obtain her, I will join
with thee to disgrace her.[33]

"How if you will not?" one wishes a Watchman would pop his head into the scene to inquire, for Claudio and Don Pedro need to be catechized. They show themselves unprepared for the strangeness of an intimate encounter and the generous ethics such an encounter demands. "The world is real," writes Morton, "but not because you can kick it,"[34] or shame it in a church.

Ultimately, even more than Dogberry and the Watch, it is Beatrice and Benedick, things among things, who prove capable of thriving within a strange environment that *must* remain inaccessible — as the eavesdropping Benedick must remain inaccessible to the gentlemen, as the "right" word must remain inaccessible to Dogberry and the Watch — if they are

---

30 Shakespeare, *Much Ado*, 5.1.213–223.
31 Shakespeare, *Much Ado*, 5.1.232–34.
32 Shakespeare, *Much Ado*, 3.3.94.
33 Shakespeare, *Much Ado*, 3.2.123–27.
34 Morton, "Here Comes Everything," 167.

to have any meaningful designs on / with / for it. "Thou and I are too wise to woo peaceably," Benedick suggests to Beatrice in Act 5;[35] even wiser to say that *nothing* woos peaceably in this play. Relationships are built on error, compulsion or speculation. But if the last act of *Much Ado* teaches us anything, it is that these speculations can be productive, and making much ado about nothing can be an exercise not in tragedy but in constructive humility, the kind that compels us to imagine ethics as locative rather than normative, dealing in metaphors more than certainties. As we can imagine the endurance of a block or plank, the vitality of a visor, we can imagine the "fire in [our] ears" as we choose to be suddenly, "horribly in love";[36] it is through props (humor) that characters learn the moves for a non-normative ethics—horribly strange, but ultimately necessary for progress, for reform, for love.

Whatever props occupy the eavesdropping scenes of *Much Ado*, the best productions will emphasize their proximity, the ways in which objects are integral to and invested in a scene, even if also withdrawn. As Jane Bennett reminds us, "No one really knows what human agency is," so "how can we be so sure that the processes through which nonhumans make their mark are qualitatively different?"[37] Uncertainty and inaccessibility is the point. We can project "violence or ardor" between piston and fuel, says Bogost, but this is "the human metaphorization of a phenomenon, not the ethics of an object. It is not the relationship between piston and fuel that we frame by ethics but *our* relationship to the relationship between piston and fuel."[38] Likewise, the best that Beatrice and Benedick can do by the play's last act is figure out their relationship to their relationship; "here's our own hands against our hearts," Benedick says of the love poems each discover the other has written.[39] They accept the imprecision of *this* relationship and so accept each other, at the same time taking the Friar's advice to "let wonder seem familiar."[40] The preparation for this acceptance, however, occurs throughout the play, through every object lesson, every strangely intimate encounter that inspires in the

---

35 Shakespeare, *Much Ado*, 5.2.72.
36 Shakespeare, *Much Ado*, 3.1.107; 2.3.235.
37 Bennett, *Vibrant Matter*, 34.
38 Bogost, *Alien Phenomenology*, 78.
39 Shakespeare, *Much Ado*, 5.4.91–92.
40 Shakespeare, *Much Ado*, 5.4.70.

actors, equally, negligence and perseverance—encounters that are based on nothing but might mean everything.

BENEDICK
I do love nothing in the world so well as you—is not that strange?

BEATRICE
As strange as the thing I know not.[41]

Here the lovers, in confessing their love, also confess that strangeness is a part of intimacy. It intrudes into all our careful designs. It is invited.

---

41 Shakespeare, *Much Ado*, 4.1.267–269.

Warm Bodies in Plague and Shakespeare's "Womb of Death"
Neal Robert Klomp

> Our own genome probably carries hundreds of thousands of such stowaways. The boundary between [disease] and the 'normal genome' is quite blurred; intrinsic to our own ancestry and nature are not only Adam and Eve, but any number of invisible germs that have crept into our chromosomes.
> —Joshua Lederberg, Nobel Laureate for Medicine[1]

THIS HUMANOID STICK FIGURE IN PROFILE (SEE FIGURE 1, NEXT PAGE) is the image used for Wikipedia's entry "Plague (disease)."[2] The uncanny resemblance to a human highlights the zombie-like objectness of the microbe: it is alive, like a human, but it is also essentially an immobile object; its movements are as imperceptibly microscopic as it is. Further, plague seems to cross the territory between life and death: it returns after years, even centuries, of dormancy—seemingly absent after the eighth century Justinian *y. pestis* outbreak only to remerge with even more virulence in the fourteenth century as the Black Death. Its very nature seems to invite us to think of plague as both alive and dead; incapable of chasing its prey, plague spreads and kills with terrifying efficiency whenever it rises from its own grave-like dormancy. This slightly altered image of

---

1   Joshua Lederberg, "Pandemic as a Natural Evolutionary Phenomenon," in *In Time of Plague: The History and Social Consequences of Lethal Epidemic Disease*, ed. Arien Mack (New York: NYU Press, 1991), 27–8.
2   From the Centers for Disease Control and Prevention, courtesy of Larry Stauffer. "Details - Public Health Image Library (PHIL)," accessed June 11, 2014, http://phil.cdc.gov/phil/details.asp?pid=1918. This is a public domain image. I have rotated it about forty-five degrees, cropped it round, and blurred its edges.

Figure 1 neatly conjoins the plague object with the human, and together they engender an environs populated by the living humans, the still-living soon to be "corpse" of the infected, and the ever growing population of dead objects.

The multibillion-dollar zombie-industry marks a popular exploration into the territory between the living and the masses of corpse-objects that epidemic disease outbreaks, like the plague, produce—this is a territory early modern were all too familiar with. Isaac Marion's *Warm Bodies* contributes to this collective thought experiment by seeming to ask, what dreams may come to the zombie as it shuffles across the un-mortal coil?[3] In the film—a Rom-Com-Zom(bie)-flick, and *Romeo and Juliet* adaptation—the zombie-hero "R" falls for the human "Julie," and their impossible love in the midst of a zombie-disaster "exhume[s] the whole world" by "digging up a corpse" with reciprocated love.[4] But their romance is blocked by feuding "families" that are branches of biological classification: he is the grey, undead (a virus-human hybrid)[5] and she is the still-living and uninfected, thus pure(ified) human free of decay.

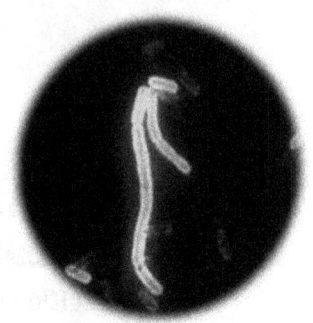

Figure 1. *Yersinia pestis* seen at 200× magnification with a fluorescent label.

The film's purification of life from death is a major revision of *Romeo and Juliet*. In doing away with the undead at the end of the film, *Warm Bodies* offers an important framework for understanding the plague environs of Shakespeare's play in which this purification is denied. It is often overlooked that we learn in act five of *Romeo and Juliet* that the plague was likely in Verona from the play's start, and, in fact, Romeo does not learn that Juliet's death is false because Friar Laurence's messengers are

---

3   Isaac Marion, *Warm Bodies* (New York: Atria Books, 2011).

4   His love grows from the memories within the brains of her boyfriend Perry—punning on the French pronunciation of Paris. *Warm Bodies*, directed by Jonathan Levine (Universal City, CA: Summit Entertainment, 2013), 54:30–54:48.

5   Marion, *Warm Bodies*, 171. This is, essentially, the foundational contemporary popular zombie configuration. The living-dead are infection-human hybrids, and another form of life (or un-life). Max Brooks, *The Zombie Survival Guide: Complete Protection from the Living Dead* (New York: Three Rivers, 2003), 16.

WARM BODIES IN PLAGUE... 49

Figure 2. Todd Lieverman and David Hoberman, *Promotional Poster for "Warm Bodies,"* 2013. (Universal, CA: Summit Entertainment, 2013).

quarantined upon suspicion of being infected with plague.[6] Written in the shadow of the first terrible plague outbreak in Shakespeare's lifetime, the play in some measure explores love in the tragic plague environs. Similarly, *Warm Bodies* explores love in the modern zombie environs; however, Marion's lovers live happily-ever-after, while Shakespeare's lovers of course do not. R's love for Julie and her reciprocation consummates his return to humanity—the opposite trajectory of Shakespeare's lovers, who (re-)consummate their love through death. But, like Romeo and Juliet, R and Julie's love saves their two "families." The film's climactic battle against the dead-too-long, evil "boneys" turns upon the returning-to-life dead's ability to convince the still-living that they are no longer infected; they succeed where those suspected of having the plague in early modern England generally failed to convince the searchers that they were not infected. In a bit of play upon humoral medicine's practice of phlebotomy, it is R's bleeding from a bullet wound that ultimately convinces the human leader (Julie's father) that the undead have come back to life. The question from the poster (Figure 2) has been answered; romance is alive as are the walking corpses.[7]

The living *becoming* the dead would have been a far too familiar sight in early modern England. Indeed, the bodies of traitors were forced into a second life as gruesome public displays of state power—body-objects

---

6 William Shakespeare, *The Tragedy of Romeo and Juliet*, in *The Riverside Shakespeare*, ed. Hershel Baker, et al., 2nd ed. (Boston: Houghton Mifflin, 1997), 5.2.5–16. The plague has been in Verona long enough for the Barefoot Brother to have heard of the outbreak and come to Verona to minister to the sick; and, long enough for searchers and warders to have been organized, probably a few months at least, certainly many weeks.

7 Levine, *Warm Bodies*, 1:25:30–1:27:50.

made to support in death the regime they opposed in life.[8] These heads and other body parts took on a new unlife, that of a silent warning against disobedience. But even the regular course of death and burial meant that the decaying dead remained a presence in the ordinary lives of the living.[9] The division of the living from the dead was hardly absolute. By 1600, the humoral theory of medicine that had been hegemonic for centuries confronted the rival theories of Paracelsus; however, neither of these competing medical theories could offer an effective mediation of the plague. It was both divine and natural—some even thought that it was two different diseases with the same results.[10] For early moderns, as John Donne writes, "There is no health; physicians say that we/At best, enjoy but a neutrality./And can there be worse sickness, than to know/That we are never well, nor can be so?"[11] Illness and health were imagined to exist in an imprecise harmony. The division between the kingdom of health and illness that Susan Sontag describes in *Illness as Metaphor* is absent from Donne's description. Indeed, there was a distinctly non-modern (to use Bruno Latour's language) aspect to early modern notions of illness and health, as well as infection.[12] From the very early days of the Black Death, the disease was understood as at once from within and from without, as plague writers from John Lydgate to Thomas Lodge show.[13] In a sense, the early modern understanding was not entirely inaccurate: all humans are "infected," as Joshua Lederberg describes in this chapter's epigraph:

---

8 Stephen Greenblatt, *Will in the World: How Shakespeare Became Shakespeare* (New York: W.W. Norton & Co., 2004), 173.

9 Stephen Greenblatt, *Hamlet in Purgatory* (Princeton: Princeton University Press, 2001), 18.

10 Margaret Healy, *Fictions of Disease in Early Modern England: Bodies, Plagues and Politics* (New York: Palgrave 2001), 48, 29; Rebecca Carol Noel Totaro, *Suffering in Paradise: The Bubonic Plague in English Literature from More to Milton* (Pittsburgh: Duquesne University Press, 2005), 46.

11 John Donne, "An Anatomy of the World," in *John Donne: The Complete English Poems*, ed. A.J. Smith. (New York: Penguin Classics, 1996), 91–4.

12 Bruno Latour, *We Have Never Been Modern*, trans. Catherine Porter (New York: Harvester Wheatsheaf, 1993).

13 John Lydgate, "Dietary and Doctrine for the Pestilence," in *Lydgate's Minor Poems II*, ed. H.N. MacCracken (Oxford: Early English Text Society, 1933); Thomas Lodge, *A Treatise of the Plague* (London: Edward White and N.L., 1603).

Our own genome probably carries hundreds of thousands of such [disease] stowaways. The boundary between them and the 'normal genome' is quite blurred; intrinsic to our own ancestry and nature are not only Adam and Eve, but any number of invisible germs that have crept into our chromosomes.[14]

Genes are "chemical nomads" building life and evolving on a slower scale of time than we, with our "hurried heartbeat[s]," are easily able to recognize.[15] Over time, the diseases that once plagued us move into our bodies, taking up residence in our very DNA.

Nothing has plagued humans worse than *y. pestis*. War (in particular modern wars like WWI and WWII), famine, the Spanish Flu, and a few other disease outbreaks are the only historical environs that can rival the sheer lethality of a full-blown *yersinia pestis* outbreak, and only thermonuclear annihilation or a zombie apocalypse would clearly surpass it. During a plague outbreak, a staggering number of the living become "corpse-objects." Victims succumb to the disease in a few days, and as the outbreak worsened, their corpses overfilled the burial pits, disrupting the social landscape by both the absence their corpses marked and the rotting presence that must be managed.[16] People who experienced plague outbreaks did not need to imagine mass death (or even "zombies"). They lived in the fictional miasmic plague environ, threatened by an all too real disease-object (as invisible *and* unknown to the early modern world as its effects were visible and well known). The fictional "zombie heralds the termination of human hegemony" in some near future,[17] while the plague was a challenge to human hegemony in the past. Parasitically inhabiting the foregut of the humble flea, this tiny object reigned

---

14 Lederberg, "Pandemic," 27–8.
15 Jeffery Jerome Cohen, "Stories of Stone," *Postmedieval: A Journal of Medieval Cultural Studies* 1.1–2 (2010): 57–8.
16 Robert S Gottfried, *The Black Death: Natural and Human Disaster in Medieval Europe* (New York, The Free Press. 1983), 59; John Saltmarsh, "Plague and Economic Decline in England in the Later Middle Ages," *Cambridge Historical Journal* 7.1 (1941), 25; Daniel Defoe, *A Journal of the Plague Year*, ed. Paula R. Backscheider. (New York: W.W. Norton & Co., 1992), 138; Paul A. Slack, *The Impact of Plague in Tudor and Stuart England* (Boston: Routledge & Kegan Paul, 1985), 17–19, 188.
17 Jeffery Jerome Cohen, "Grey," in *Prismatic Ecology: Ecotheory Beyond Green*, ed. Jeffery Jerome Cohen (Minneapolis: University of Minnesota Press, 2014), 276; Slack, *The Impact of Plague*, 200.

as the ever-potentially-present threat in Europe from 1347 until at least the beginning of the 1700s.

The flea has long been metonymically associated with the disease; Thomas Nashe even mocks those who try to minimize the deadly 1593-plague outbreak by ironically (and in complete ignorance of the truth) claiming that they foolishly imagine it as nothing more than a "flea-byting affair."[18] Beyond such figurative relationships between flea and disease, the infected flea becomes literally joined with the disease as a plague-flea hybrid. Within the flea, the plague forces its dying host into a partnership by blocking the flea's digestive tract—it is the large dark mass in the center of figure 3. The insect tries to satiate its hunger upon the flesh of its mammal host (rat then human). But unable to digest the blood, the flea "backwashes" *y. pestis* into the rat/human, spreading the disease. The plague-flea is slowly starving to death, but the diabolic mechanism of the disease causes the flea to help perpetuate its killer. The insect's fate is sealed after infection; in a sense it is already dead, and exists as a sort of flea-zombie only alive to spread the disease.

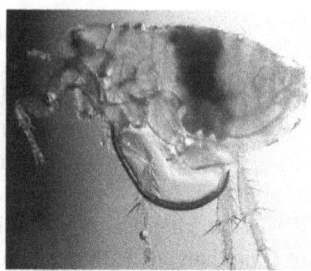

Figure 3. Plague infected male Xenopsylla cheopis 28 days after feeding on an inoculated mouse.

In a world of Donne's "neutrality," everyone was understood literally to carry infectious death within them as the flea-plague does. Everyone was, to some degree, both living and dead; a slight shift in the balance of the humors of one person or a group of people could lead to an epidemic outbreak and mass death.[19] This belief was personified in the dangerous plague victim that Daniel Defoe calls the "walking Destroyer"[20]: a zombie-like figure still alive but also selected for death by the plague. This monstrous potential source of infection might be encountered wandering about the market, perhaps with no visible signs of plague. Unaware that they were infected, they might drop dead in the street or while gathered together in a mass of "dead Corpses...crowded together...[in]

---

18 Quoted in Healy, *Fictions of Disease*, 34.
19 Healy, *Fictions of Disease*, 43.
20 Defoe, *A Journal of the Plague Year*, 139, 159.

Churches."²¹ These walking "Corpses" who, perhaps in the midst of succumbing to disease and in a final act of defiance might have stumbled out into the street, perhaps moaning in pain, reaching out for comfort or someone to infect, further blur the line between the living and the dead in the environs of the plague outbreak.²²

The disease infected its victims, enlisting them in its work—Thomas Dekker even imagined that gravediggers and coffin-makers as part of the plague's host.²³ For Dekker and others²⁴ quarantine was one of the key places where the plague and human joined to create the plague tragedy. He relates the "often"-occurring circumstance of an "amazed husband waking, [who] found the comfort of his bedde lying breathless by his side!"²⁵ Presumably, his wife was infected while she cared for him and died as he recovered with no one to tend to her. The husband wakes to find her and "his children at the same instant gasping for life! and his seruants, mortally wonded at the hart by sickness! the distracted creature, beats at death doors," barred from the outside. He "exclaimes at windows, his cries are sharp inough to pierce heaun, but on earth no eare is opened to receiue them."²⁶ Locked within an infected house, he is a form of undead. John Fletcher's *The Woman's Prize or The Tamer Tamed* shows the difficulty those suspected of being infected confronted when their soundness came into question, as it does for Shakespeare's two monks in *Romeo and Juliet*.²⁷ In the sequel to Shakespeare's *Taming of the Shrew*, Maria (Petruchio's new wife) convinces the searchers that her husband is infected. While the searchers listen to her testimony, his claims of health from behind the locked door are completely ignored — as are Dekker's recovered householder — it is as if because he was locked up, he was already counted among the corpses.

In the act of quarantine, the plague and the human effort to combat the disease blend into one tragedy creating both plagued *and* healthy

---

21 Defoe, *A Journal of the Plague Year*, 67.
22 Defoe, *A Journal of the Plague Year*, 136–7.
23 Thomas Dekker, *The Wonderfull Yeare 1603*, ed. Risa S. Bear (The University of Oregon: Renascence Editions, 2000), 15.
24 Slack, *The Impact of Plague*, 250.
25 Dekker, *The Wonderfull Yeare 1603*, 14.
26 Dekker, *The Wonderfull Yeare 1603*, 14.
27 John Fletcher, *The Woman's Prize; Or, The Tamer Tamed*, ed. George B. Ferguson. (The Hague: Mouton, 1966), 3.4.

victims within an environ in which they were plagued by both disease *and* humanity. Quarantine was the "mortall siege of the plague" that allowed many to die who may have survived with aid and comfort according to Dekker. For him the human effort to combat the plague was too much like the executioner's work: "the drawing windows were hangd, drawne and quartered," a gruesome allusion to the early modern English death sentence.[28] It may have been a time honored measure by desperate people who placed a greater premium on following tradition, but, as Paul Slack notes, quarantine also amounted to a "ritual purification of the social order," along early modern "sort"-lines. It was also a desperate effort to produce modern purification of well from "sick," life from death, and human from disease, and thus to turn into monsters those who existed in the liminal space between infection and death.[29]

Perhaps Mercutio's famous curse calls for the disease already present in Verona to purify as Slack describes, closing off sources of disorder from the social order. "A plague a' [in]"[30] the two houses of Montague and Capulet would have resulted in watchers locking up each family and their servants. The two sites of social unrest in Verona would have faced possible death (divine judgment) and secured quarantine (state control). But the play complicates Mercutio's call to plague intervention: instead of directly unleashing the disease-state plague, the play stills the passionate humors of Romeo and Juliet as well as their fathers through plague-like deaths.

Within the death and undeath of Juliet there are a few noteworthy similarities to another death Dekker describes, the tragic death of "a paire of Louers," whose love is destroyed by the disease.[31] Like Romeo and Juliet, their parents are against their marriage. After persuading them to allow the wedding, the young couple is forced to find a church not "pestered" with "so many coffins" of plague dead.[32] But in speaking the vow "In sicknesse and in health" the bride is revealed as residing in what Susan

---

28 Dekker, *The Wonderfull Yeare 1603*, 14, 18–20; Slack, *The Impact of Plague*, 225.
29 Leeds Barroll, *Politics, Plague, and Shakespeare's Theater: The Stuart Years* (Ithaca: Cornell University Press, 1991), 74; Slack, *The Impact of Plague*, 213; Latour, *We Have Never Been Modern*, 11, 23–5 37, 51.
30 Shakespeare, *Romeo and Juliet*, 3.1.90–2.
31 Dekker, *The Wonderfull Yeare 1603*, 21. Rather than tracing influences here, I am suggesting that there is a common topography of tragedy that *Romeo and Juliet* shares with the plague experience.
32 Dekker, *The Wonderfull Yeare 1603*, 21.

Figure 4. Todd Lieverman and David Hoberman, *Promotional Poster for "Warm Bodies,"* 2013. (Universal, CA: Summit Entertainment, 2013).

Sontag calls the "kingdom of the ill" or in the "night-side of life,"[33] and dies without consummating her marriage. The plague overthrows the household the lovers would have formed before the moment of consumption, transforming their wedding into her funeral. However, unlike either Romeo or Juliet, the surviving lover controls his passions and does not follow his love into the grave.

Crossing over similar territory but in a different direction, Shakespeare's lovers' plague-like death and funeral becomes a sort of wedding: first, the young husband Romeo must see his (un)dead wife. Infected with grief, he strikes down Paris and throws him in the "detestable maw" that becomes a common grave for three. As a dying Romeo looks around, he sees Tybalt nearby: many corpses are buried together in a society of death, as was common in a plague burial pit.[34] Like Dekker's quarantine-critiquing plague story of a husband who awakens to find his wife, his children and all his servants sick or dead, Juliet awakens to find her "household" (Romeo) dead beside her.

Dramaturgically, Romeo's quick (and foolishly passionate) suicide, as the audience knows, has left her with no choice but to prove her love by joining him in death. In *Warm Bodies*, R's exhumation from walking death creates a world without the undead. However, in Shakespeare's play, Juliet's un-death creates a plague-like grave of humanity's making. In killing herself and following Romeo, who has killed himself, she confirms not just her love but also humanity's culpability in the plague's destruction. After all, it is Romeo who killed Paris and Tybalt—even Mercutio's death is a result of Romeo's interference—and Juliet follows him into death. Ultimately, their passion of love opposed by the passion of hatred in their

---

33 Susan Sontag, *Illness as Metaphor* (New York: Vintage, 1978), 3.
34 Shakespeare, *Romeo and Juliet*, 5.3.45–97.

fathers created the circumstances for plague-infected tragedy—even if plague did not kill anyone.

In a cathartic moment, the grief infected fathers make undead "jointure" vows to care for each other's child's tomb, turning the grave into a "womb of death" from which is born their alliance, they exhume their children's love.[35] Within this "jointure" the play marries (as fathers-in-law) the living through the dead, a union of life and death or non-object and object, in a pre-modern plague environs in which the modern distinguishing categories become decidedly indistinct. While the *Warm Bodies'* poster (Figure 4) offers the spoiler that the undead R will warm up and become human, the "star-crossed lovers" in plague-infected Verona were marked for tragic death and cold tomb from the play's beginning. From this plaguey mass-grave—addressed by Romeo as if it were alive, "Thou detestable maw, thou womb of death, / Gorged" and with "rotten jaws"—is born as undead the legacy of the corpses buried there. The grief-infected living accept the loving passion in death, balancing the fathers' hatred with that which was abjected in life.

---

35 Shakespeare, *Romeo and Juliet*, 5.3.296–304, 45; unfortunately, their good intentions come after the Prince hands down punishment, and might merely represent a moment of self-correction to stay the potentially severe sovereign judgment.

The Biology of Rain
Becoming a Distant Master in Early Modern England
Tara E. Pedersen

IN ACT 3 OF SHAKESPEARE'S *RICHARD II*, HENRY BOLINGBROKE REQUESTS the restoration of his family's lands while painting a picture of the ecology of war. Henry claims that if his inheritance is not restored he will "use the advantage of [his] power/And lay the summer's dust with showers of blood/Rain'd from the wounds of slaughter'd Englishmen" (3.3.42–44).[1] In other words, Henry argues that if he is refused the territories that he believes are rightfully his, he will drench the lands with the blood of a people whom he also claims are his own. As he makes this statement, Henry lays out a chain of cause and effect in which he becomes the primary human agent and interpretive consciousness that orders the climate of the surrounding countryside. Objects (be they land, elements, or citizens) exist in order to be possessed and acted upon by him, and ultimately the picture his words paint makes a case for how the listener/viewer is supposed to see the landowner as well as the earth and the English citizen's relationship to it. Henry suggests that the landscape, and the organisms within it, are ordered and sustained at his will.[2]

---

1 All quotations from Shakespeare follow *The Riverside Shakespeare*, 2nd ed. (Boston: Houghton Mifflin, 1997).

2 My argument about Henry's will may be complicated by the claim that he is only a character in a play. I join S.E. Cosgrove in arguing that to see his performance of agency or will as irrelevant because he is only a "character" overlooks the numerous performances that often comprise agency. It may also, by implication, strengthen the notion that only "real human" agents are capable of agency and action. As James Phelan notes: "Silently underlying this discussion of the mimetic component (of the fictional character) are some messy problems. First, all this talk about characters as plausible or possible persons presupposes that we know [with certainty] what a person is" (qtd. in S.E. Cosgrove, "Radical Uncertainty: Judith Butler and a theory of character," in *The Ethical Imaginations: Writing Worlds Papers — The*

It is perhaps unsurprising then that, faced with Henry's rhetorical positioning of himself as a force who determines a series of relations between objects, his rival responds by amplifying and translating Henry's "showers of blood" anew. King Richard looks on Henry's anticipated bloody rain and responds by arguing that, as reigning monarch, he himself is supported by an "omnipotent" force that will also summon "clouds on [his] behalf." Furthermore, the blood rain that Henry spills will not quench the dry "summer's dust." Instead it will:

> ...ill become the flower of England's face,
> Change the complexion of her maid-pale peace
> To scarlet indignation and bedew
> Her pastures' grass with faithful English blood. (3.3.97–100)

Richard draws his listeners' attention to a different interpretation of the form the land will occupy at the end of Henry's threatened attack. In doing so he argues for an alternate understanding of the relationship between actors and objects where interpretive mastery dictates the form and function of the objects that surround the ruler. Henry threatens to turn the blood of English soldiers into rain, but Richard translates and transforms Henry's portrait of the dusty earth into a body—a face—whose complexion will be permanently altered by the dew of citizens' blood. Henry may be able to make it rain, but Richard claims to dictate the effects and meaning of this precipitation.

Although both characters essentially imagine the same incident, they argue from opposing perspectives. Each character claims to shape the substance of the landscape and implicitly places a human actor as the central organizing force in the environment. In the rhetorical volleys of these two characters, we find an example of what Graham Harman identifies as the fight for "cognitive mastery" that an Object-Oriented Literary Criticism attempts to resist. In fact, Object-Oriented theorists might go so far as to claim that there is an "unreal" competition going on between these two characters. As these men fight for possession of objects, they fail to acknowledge the way that blood, rain, and soil also withdraw from the immediate context of their quarrel by always also existing beyond

---

Refereed Proceedings of the 16th Conference of the Australasian Association of Writing Programs, 2011 [http://www.aawp.org.au/publications/the-ethical-imaginations-writing-worlds-papers/]), 2.

the shaping power of the discourse that describes them. Lowell Duckert, describes this succinctly as he claims, "Rain resists our attempts to know its intentions, yet it also resists the separations between climate and culture, life and matter, and subject and object."[3]

Richard and Henry's words, therefore, stand in contrast to the "deeply non-relational conception of the reality of things [at] the heart of object-oriented philosophy."[4] As Richard and Henry fight to translate objects in a given context, they neglect, as Timothy Morton suggests, to consider that these objects "exist prior to the one 'for whom' they are fluid or static."[5] In other words, Henry and Richard assume that the objects around them are within their reach and completely open to their manipulation and mastery. They fail to conceive of objects at a distance.

Graham Harman argues that conceiving of objects at a distance (even from themselves) may serve an ethical purpose, for, as objects are divorced from an individual agent's perception or particular context, "the objects of object-oriented philosophy [become] mortal, ever-changing, built from swarms of subcomponents, and accessible only through oblique allusion." Object-Oriented Ontology offers "not the oft-lamented "naïve realism" of oppressive and benighted patriarchs, but a weird realism in which real individual objects resist all forms of causal or cognitive mastery."[6] OOO refuses to allow objects to become the pawns of masters or kings who rule over them. Instead objects remain always somehow foreign and elsewhere, just beyond reach.

I am intrigued by the liberating possibilities of such a claim. At the same time, I would like to ask if imagining the distant and withdrawn might sometimes lead us back to the familiar and presumably understood.[7] I do this not to reify the human as the primary actor in a world

---

3 Lowell Duckert, "When It Rains," in *Material Ecocriticism*, ed. Serenella Iovino and Serpil Opperman (Bloomington, Indiana University Press, 2014), 116.
4 Graham Harman, "The Well-Wrought Broken Hammer: Object-Oriented Literary Criticism," *New Literary History*, 43:2 (2012), 187.
5 Timothy Morton, "An Object-Oriented Defense of Poetry." *New Literary History*, 43:2 (2012), 208.
6 Harman, "The Well-Wrought Broken Hammer," 188.
7 In this way, my thinking aligns with Nathan Brown's. Brown asks if an object might be productively "constituted by the current context of its relations with other entities and be differentially constituted by relations with new entities and contexts?" See "The Nadir of OOO: From Graham Harman's Tool-Being to Timothy Morton's Realist Magic: Objects, Ontology, Causality," *Parrhesia* 17 (2013), 63).

of subordinate objects but to draw attention to the way that positioning objects as distant may sometimes be an act of interpretive mastery as well, or at least something that looks very much like it. Considering this possibility seems like it would be of vital importance to a movement that concerns itself with the ethical consequences of how we position and conceive of objects. If not mastering sometimes also looks like mastering, then is there more to be said about what this project attempts to achieve and how that, in-and-of-itself, should look?

I would like to begin exploring this question by letting an object lead me. John Tradescant's *Musaeum Tradescantianum*, which catalogs hundreds of items housed in Tradescant's Ark in South Lambeth during the 1600s, describes a location that exhibited a multitude of natural and constructed objects collected from around the globe. These items were put on display for the London viewing audience's entertainment and edification, and I turn to a consideration of this document and the location it depicts precisely because it gives me an opportunity to consider how objects have a long history of being positioned as withdrawn and the ends to which these objects may be put. The items in Trandescant's Ark are often studied as an example of the curious and distant. Tradescant's project then serves as a very apt example of the way that objects may be positioned as withdrawn for a variety of purposes, many of them lucrative.

The Ark, like many other European curiosity cabinets, was a middle-class undertaking that capitalized precisely on an object's ability to resist cognitive mastery. Marjorie Swann puts it particularly well when she points out that: "Not only were objects selected for their anomalousness, but the unusual qualities of individual things were emphasized through their physical juxtaposition with strikingly different items."[8] Furthermore, some scholars of the period have argued that these unusual juxtapositions may be understood as highly theatrical gestures that rely, in part, on the desire to escape rigid systems of organization and ownership. Steven Mullaney, in his work on the relationship between London's theater culture and curiosity cabinets like Tradescant's, highlights the ethical stakes of these locations and argues that both curiosity cabinets and the London stage operate as chaotic sites of disorder that reflect the "suspension of

---

8 Marjorie Swann, *Curiosities and Texts: The Culture of Collecting in Early Modern England* (Philadelphia: University of Pennsylvania Press, 2001), 26. I have written about Tradescant's Ark elsewhere. See *Mermaids and the Production of Knowledge in Early Modern England* (Burlington: Ashgate, 2015).

cultural decorum and discrimination" in early modern society. Although Mullaney is not an ooo scholar, his assessment seems to align spaces like Tradescant's with a desire to resist the strictures of an interpretive practice that can easily account for objects as known, understood, close by, and easily possessed. The collection of items attempts to exist beyond cultural categorization itself. "Ambiguous things" find a place here in an unusual, seemingly arbitrary, assembly that, as Mullaney goes on to explain, "lodges them beyond the bounds of cultural hierarchies and definitions."[9]

Although I find attractive the idea that the seeming disorder present in Tradescant's Ark illustrates a desire to reject the strictures of a rigid system of classification and order, I would also like to propose that this potential disorder might also be marshalled in the service of bolstering other forms of social order. Section VIII of Tradescant's catalog, provides an example of an item I wish to consider further in this regard: "Blood that rained in the Isle of Wight."[10] The blood mentioned in Tradescant's catalog is unusual for two reasons. First, it is indexed next to objects procured, for the most part, from travels abroad. The local blood rests alongside artifacts from North America, charms from Turkey, musical instruments from Portugal and Spain, and even the trunnion from Drake's sailing vessel. Second, the blood is one of the few objects that is connected to an individual, for it is "attested by Sir Jo. Oglander."

We know nothing for certain about how John Oglander specifically "attested" to the blood rain on the Isle of Wight. We do, however, know a fair deal about Oglander's life though the account books that he kept for his estate on the Isle. According to Adam Nicholson, Oglander was an individual whose "entire being was distributed among the structures that framed and supported him."[11] His account books provide a vivid record of daily life, of relationships between land, animals, tools, buildings, purchased luxuries, and humans. Throughout these records Oglander emerges not simply as a landowner who is deeply attached to his

---

9 "Strange Things, Gross Terms, Curious Customs: The Rehearsal of Cultures in the Late Renaissance," *Representations* 3 (1983), 42–43.
10 John Tradescant, *Musaeum Tradescantianum: or, A collection of rarities* (London, 1656), 44, Early English Books Online, http://eebo.chadwyck.com.
11 Adam Nicholson, *Gentry: Six Hundred Years of a Peculiarly English Class* (London: Harper Press, 2011), 119.

property and country, and deeply mystified by the workings of the world, but also as an object himself.

Oglander's tendency to account for himself and his family as objects may seem most notable to a tweny-first-century reader in the moments when, consumed by grief, he dramatically documents the death of family members in his own blood. However, it is apparent throughout the text that Oglander is regularly driven by an impulse to account for himself as he records both the unusual and mundane happenings of a lifetime and meditates on his relationship to his lands and house at Nunwell. In one particularly memorable instance he imagines himself as a vital and familiar participant in the landscape even after his own death. Describing his ghost, he writes:

> I will give thee my owne Carracter. Conceive though sawest an Aged, somewhat Corpulent Man of middle stature, with a white Beard and somewhat big Muchatoes, riding in Blacke or some sad coullored clothes from Westnunwell up to ye West Downe and so over all the Downes to take the Ayre, Morning and Evening, and to see there his ffatting Cattell, on a handsome midlinge blacke stone-horse, his hayre graye and his complexion very Sangwine, and, as Tully sayde, *Nunquam Minus Solus, quam Cum Solus.* [*Never less alone than when alone.*][12]

In this moment, Oglander positions himself as a figure who is simultaneously familiar and withdrawn. On the one hand he conjures a picture of his specter carrying out the daily actions of a landowner who dutifully tends to his property. His descendants may happen upon him some "Morning and Evening" as his shade dons characteristic attire and surveys Nunwell's lands or animals. His presence seems to permeate the land around him. At the same time he depicts himself as mysterious and always out of reach. He is a figure in the distance, a removed presence whose solitude is anything but solitary. By becoming perpetually distant, he also becomes linked with the objects and locations that he surveys and which sustain his being.

This move may, on the one hand, seem unsurprising for a Royalist member of the gentry. After all, as Adam Nicholson notes, "The interfolding of people, land, animals, food, housing, and hospitality was in itself a

---

12 Quoted in Nicholson, *Gentry*, 119. The translation is Nicholson's.

model of the gentry's idea of goodness. It was...civilization attached to a particular place. A form of organizing the land which was also a way of organizing society, an interlocked complexity, which was intended to be both stable and long lived and to lie at the root of the honourable, just and hospitable life."[13] However, faced with the demands of a rapidly changing social order, I would argue that when Oglander depicts his ghost he does more than simply comply with a traditional understanding of the neatly ordered life.

Throughout his accounts, Oglander rarely suggests that he is part of a tidy, ordered system. Interpretive or cognitive mastery seems frequently to elude him. For example, next to a listing of the cattle slaughtered on his estate in 1643, he writes (presumably in reference to the English Civil Wars), "I only knowe this, that I knowe nothing I cannot read eythor my selve, or other men, this world is Changed, and our Antipodes possesseth owr places."[14] As he keeps a record of the mundane workings of an estate, Oglander positions himself as both profoundly connected to and distant from the nation, objects, and land that should be familiar to him. He claims to be incapable of locating himself in context, and we see him hyperbolically invoke, in this passage, a stock example of the withdrawn and foreign as he argues that his familiar land has been exchanged with the Antipodes (also tellingly described as "owr[s]").

I have provided just one illustration of the many instances where Oglander's accounts demonstrate the profound disorientation of a being who is uncertain about how to interpret the objects (including himself) that inhabit the world. However, the question remains: how does thinking about Oglander help me reflect on the blood that Tradescant housed in his curiosity cabinet, and why might it be useful to connect this object to Oglander at all? This seems, after all, to counter the entire purpose of the ooo project.

One answer to this question may be found by returning to the beginning of this chapter's trail of thought. Studying a man did not lead me to this object. Instead, studying a collection of ambiguous objects led me to a man, a man who appears, in a roundabout way, to be asking many questions that are relevant to Object-Oriented Philosophy. I can only speculate, but it seems plausible that Oglander's belief in the idea that familiar objects are beyond his cognitive mastery (and are as distant as the

---

13 Nicholson, *Gentry*, 114.
14 Quoted in Nicholson, *Gentry*, 131.

Antipodes) may help account for how blood rain from the Isle of Wight ended up in Tradescant's collection of rarities. Lowell Duckert notes, that in early modern England, there was an "insatiable appetite for travel writing [that] coexisted with an increasing taste for climatic literature as well."[15] We do not have evidence that Oglander was a voracious reader of either of these genres. However, his reference to distant locations like the Antipodes, perhaps suggests that it is not a stretch to imagine that Oglander recognized the cultural value of placing a piece of his climate and everyday world in the realm of the fantastic, distant, and disordered. Perhaps this object (this blood rain) has drawn a line that points to the specter of a distant master who has always been close by. I would like to suggest that it is valuable to entertain such speculation because in doing so we are challenged to consider the possibility that deeming an object as withdrawn and beyond the grasp of understanding may also be placing it in a kind of context with very real causal effects. Unlike Henry Bolingbroke, Oglander does not claim fully to master the objects around him, but his lack of certainty about objects helps place them in locations that have masters just the same.

---

15 Duckert, "When It Rains," 117.

Shoe Talk and Shoe Silence
Tripthi Pillai

LIKE THE GAIT OF ONE UNFAMILIAR WITH WALKING IN STILETTO HEELS, the two parts of this essay move, at times arhythmically, between explorations of objects in environments. Part one embeds the shoe in human-centric environments as an instrument that's used as much to displace particular autopoietic systems as it is to display others.[1] Part two embeds the human in ontic environs,[2] in the triangulation of semantic disclosure, withdrawal, and density in the shoe-dog-human network in act 2, scene 3, of William Shakespeare's *The Two Gentlemen of Verona*. My purpose is to apply the language and architecture of speculative realism to consider both the gaps in knowledge and the interplay of objects as yet underexplored in historicist critical engagement. The strategic ahistoricism employed by OOO I adopt here enables me to wander and "wonder unburdened" among objects and environments in a manner that is,[3] not unlike the precariousness of some shoes, at once alluring and promiscuous in its embrace of instability.

---

1   I follow the definitions of autopoietic and allopoietic machines laid out by Levi Bryant, who adapts Humberto Maturana and Francisco Varela's terminology developed in "Autopoiesis: The Organization of the Living." Bryant writes of their definitions, "it is sufficient to note that when Maturana and Varela refer to autopoietic machines, they are referring to living objects, while when they refer to allopoietic machines they are referring to non-living objects" (137). See Levi Bryant, *The Democracy of Objects* (Ann Arbor: Open University Press, 2011).

2   Onticology asserts that "there is only one type of being," which is the being of objects. "Humans are not excluded" from onticology, "but are rather objects *among* the various types of objects that exist or populate the world, each with their own specific powers and capacities" (Bryant, *The Democracy of Objects*, 20).

3   Ian Bogost, *Alien Phenomenology, Or What It's Like To Be a Thing* (Minneapolis: University of Minnesota Press, 2012), 133.

I. SHOE TALK

The vocabulary of shoemaking and the language we use to talk about the shoe construct the object as its own other. The established lexicon of shoe parts traces the human body on the object. Let us consider, for instance, some of the parts that comprise a shoe: eyelets, waist, rib, shank, tongue, and breast. While its name does not underscore a link to the human form, the "shoe tree," a device designed to store shoes and retain their shape, health, and appearance, connects the anatomy of the shoe to the anatomy of another familiar living organism within an ecological system.[4] Our insistence in language that shoes are parts of the human body, or at least a body that is capable of life (breathing, reproducing), of absorbing lightness or heaviness, shapes familiar discursive practices in philosophy, art, design, and literature that are applied to our attempts at knowing shoes.

On December 2, 2013, I found a pair of men's shoes sitting atop one of the recycle bins outside my residential complex. The image (opposite page), like many of Vincent van Gogh's paintings of shoes, lends itself to a series of meaning-seeking exercises, remediations that render inextricable the shoes' relationship to the human.[5]

---

4 Wood is a familiar ingredient in the construction of protective shoes. The Swedish clogs and the Japanese *geta* are just two types of wood-based footwear that symptomatize human wearers' desire to use something of the soil—the tree—to avoid soiling our feet. But wood is also the preferred material used by us, both to protect the shoe from a variety of environments and display the object's elevated place in our aesthetics. Thus, Nancy Macdonell notes, in the early twentieth century the American socialite Rita de Acosta Lydig went so far as to have "exotic" shoe trees custom-made "from the wood of violins" to protect and display her shoes (56). See Nancy Macdonell, *The Shoe Book* (New York: Assouline Publishing, 2014).

5 While van Gogh painted multiple images of shoes, most notable among them are *Shoes* (1888) and *A Pair of Shoes* (1886). *Shoes*, now part of the collection at the Metropolitan Museum of Art in New York, is a typical example of van Gogh's preoccupation with the representative potential of shoes. The description, as noted on the Met's website, draws the viewer's attention to the "specific spatial context" within which the shoes are placed. See http://www.metmuseum.org/toah/works-of-art/1992.374. Similarly, *A Pair of Shoes*, which is now part of the collection at the van Gogh Museum in Amsterdam, prompted Martin Heidegger's phenomenological analysis of the painting in "The Origin of the Work of Art." Art historian Meyer Schapiro's claim that Heidegger may have amalgamated multiple van Gogh shoe paintings is crucial. While we may not be able to ascertain which particular pair of shoes or painting caught the philosopher's attention, Schapiro's statement suggests that, for the philosopher, all the shoes in van Gogh's paintings fall under

Whose shoes were these? Why were they abandoned? Given that they were placed on a recycle bin, presumably the person discarding the shoes intended for them to be taken up for use by another. Who might take up these shoes? What might his/her need or desire for the shoes suggest about his/her economic, cultural, aesthetic, and political environment? The shoes disappeared by the morning of December 4, 2013, but my questions persist. Notably, my initial questions about them had less to do with the shoes themselves and more to do with their past and potential human wearer. The questions fed my imagination because their answers promised to reveal something about the shoes' connection to the human. Had I stepped into the shoes and walked around in them for some time, I might have been able to discover something about the previous wearer's height and gait, about whether or not he placed weight or strain on particular parts of his feet and shoes, about the kind of time he spent standing or walking from place to place. The shoes, in other words, might have materialized the wearer as well as parts of his world.

I am not alone in desiring a shoe that tells a human story. Most art historians agree that van Gogh's *Shoes* narrativizes the life and conditions of the human subject, the invisible wearer of the item. That is, the shoes stand not only for the wearer, but also for the wearer's experience (his movements, poverty, plainness, suffering, and humility). For Heidegger, van Gogh's *A Pair of Shoes* reveals the equipmental nature of the object's being by drawing out what he claims is the primary use of the shoe.[6] Although Heidegger declares the painting is just of "a pair of farmer's shoes and nothing more," famously he follows the statement with an elliptical "And yet—" (33). Heidegger anatomizes the shoe's environment, assuming the object in the painting belongs to a female peasant: "[t]he farming woman wears her shoes in the field. Only here are they what they are. *They are all the more genuinely so, the less the farming woman thinks about the shoes,...or is even aware of them*" (33, emphasis added). For Heidegger, the shoes' being hinges on their being forgotten by the peasant woman. At the same time, in those of us that encounter their image, the shoes provoke thought and refuse to be forgotten. Heidegger goes on to frame the shoes in the context of absence and presence, abundance and

---

one interpretive umbrella—they all represent the experience and the labor of the absent wearers.

6 Martin Heidegger, "The Origin of the Work of Art," in *Poetry, Language, Thought*, trans. Albert Hofstadter (New York: Perennial Classics, 2001), 15–86.

scarcity: "From out of the dark opening of the worn insides of the shoes the toilsome tread of the worker stares forth....The shoes vibrate with the silent call of the earth, its quiet gift of ripening grain...and the earth's unexplained self-refusal in the fallow desolation of the wintry field" (33–34). This is the "And yet—" to which Heidegger draws our attention. Had the farmer been present, she may not have been able to tell the story of the earth better than her shoes do. The shoes, then, not only tell the truth about their true identity (their primary use or equipmentality), for Heidegger they also share a greater knowledge about the conflicts inherent in the natural and human environs.

There is no denying Heidegger maintains a representational approach to the farmer's shoes and to the painting. His focus remains the absent subject that is the farmer, whose living conditions or truth he extrapolates from the object that she uses everyday.[7] As I'd attempted to do when I sought answers about the shoes on the recycle bin, Heidegger mobilizes multiple interpretive tools to construct a world or environment within which the shoes operate as a synecdoche of the human network into which their object being is absorbed. As autonomous objects, the shoes in the painting seem to bear no significance for the philosopher.[8] That he

---

7   I'm grateful to Jeffrey Cohen for drawing my attention to *Victims' Shoes*, which is part of the permanent exhibition at the United States Holocaust Memorial Museum. Like Heidegger's observations about human experience codified within/by the shoes in van Gogh's painting, *Victims' Shoes* bears a heavy representational weight insofar as the four thousand shoes in the exhibit stand in not only for the staggering number of humans that died at specific Nazi killing camps in Europe but also for the uncounted victims of the Holocaust whose lives, experiences, and deaths are not linked to the particularities of specific objects. In this sense, *Victims' Shoes* draws attention powerfully to the affective semantics of human absence that is vehiculated by the tactile poetics and survivability of objects. See http://www.ushmm.org/information/exhibitions/permanent/shoes.

8   Heidegger isn't alone here. There is no consensus on the topic of the identity of the shoes' wearer and/or owner. Nor is there agreement on what the shoes represent. Meyer Schapiro's "The Still Life as a Personal Object—A Note on Heidegger and Van Gogh," which focuses on Heidegger's flawed interpretation of van Gogh's painting, remains one of the most influential analyses of *A Pair of Shoes*. Schapiro argues that the shoes depicted in the painting aren't a peasant's but rather the artist's own. As opposed to Heidegger's insistence on situating the shoes in an invisible yet palpable environment of rural agrarian labor, Schapiro positions them as representations of van Gogh's urban wanderings across Europe. Derrida draws attention to the limits of both Heidegger's and Schapiro's interpretations while acknowledging that the objects primarily occupy a representational place, standing

doesn't engage with the shoes' inner life or immanence is symptomatic of a larger, institutionally structured anthropocentricism of which he is a part, one that relies on the potentiality of objects to reflect the human.

Even when work and wanderings do not erupt in the body of the shoe, that is, when the shoe is not clearly demarcated in the world of its function (in its wear and tear), the object represents the wearer's economic position and relationship to labor. Pietro Yantorny, who in the early twentieth century designed and made shoes for wealthy Americans and Europeans, cherished his relations with Rita de Acosta not only because she owned 150 pairs of shoes made by him, each of which cost her approximately $1000, but also because he found she was the only woman he knew who was conscious of "how to place her feet."[9] Indeed, severed from the context of obvious functionality, the shoe is made to represent (take the place of) a variety of human bodily preoccupations and pleasures. It gains life in metaphor, but it is predominantly a human life that the shoe is made to gain.

Certain types of women's shoes have an established history in human sexuality and sex acts, for example.[10] Art, design, and commerce work in

---

for the human. See Jacques Derrida, *The Truth in Painting*, trans. Geoff Bennington and Ian McLeod (Chicago: University of Chicago Press, 1987). Matthew Ruben offers an excellent critique of Heidegger's and Derrida's readings of the painting, as well as a defense of Schapiro's interpretation of the painting, which he contextualizes in the Jewish experience of nomadism during the Nazi regime. See Matthew Ruben, "The Sole of Deconstruction: Preparations for the Truth in Mourning," *Critical Quarterly* 39. 4 (Winter 1997): 25–38. What is clear in all the texts is that, for the authors, the meaning of the shoes contains the meaning of the wearer and the wearer's environment.

9   Macdonnell, *The Shoe Book*, 56.

10 In his discussion of the human practice of collecting certain objects, Jean Baudrillard notes of non-functional objects, which he defines as things that are "no longer specified by (their) function," that their value (to the subject or collector) is "directly linked to (their) regressive character" (92, 107). Baudrillard likens this "regressive character" to perversion, specifically sexual perversion: "If perversion as it concerns objects is most clearly discernible in the crystallized form of fetishism, we are perfectly justified in noting how throughout the system...the possession of objects and the passion for them is...a tempered mode of sexual perversion" (107). See Jean Baudrillard, *The System of Objects*, trans. James Benedict (London: Verso, 1996). Considerably less theoretical in its approaches to objects, *The Shoe Book*, which includes pithy interviews with renowned shoemakers and entertaining anecdotes about collectors of footwear, offers a pop-historical overview of the connections between shoes and sexual desirability and accessibility.

conjunction to map sexual language onto women's shoes. From the strategic positioning of the falling shoe in Fragonard's *The Swing* or Shonibare's *The Swing (After Fragonard)*, to the cover image of the 1953 issue of the "'fetish' erotica magazine" *Bizarre* featuring a "kinky twist on the children's nursery rhyme 'The Old Woman Who Lived in a Shoe,'"[11] to the sculpted images of unwearable shoes in Louboutin and Lynch's *Fetish* pieces, the *useless*ness of the shoe is made to bear sexual meaning in the context of femininity. Alienated from the context of practical functionality, the shoe not only becomes sexy, as metaphor it becomes a visible element that displays a system of sexual organs and organization.

But the shoe is also made to bear resemblance to other parts and organizations of the human body. In an interview held in 2011, shoe designer Christian Louboutin discusses the traits of the particular shoe varietal that is the pump, a woman's shoe, and refers to it as a human face: "When I am designing shoes, the most important thing is the bone structure. A shoe, a pump, is basically a face with no makeup.... A pump is...a whole silhouette; it's a heel, it's a front, and it's an arch. So it really is like a bone structure of a face."[12] The shoe, then, holds a unique place within the autopoietic environments in which we locate it. If our relations to the shoe are the limited means by which we understand the thing, the language that we mobilize to speak about a shoe—its parts, its types—manages to transform it into something other than a shoe and, in its idealized form, even into ourselves.

Useful or useless, shoes are bound to our interpretations of the human body and subjectivity: as ironic or sincere commentary on or representation of the affects of human-ness (of sexuality and class, for example). Constructed to extend, represent, or reflect on our autopoietic relations, the shoe entices us with its mysterious ability at once to display and displace us. Yet, without consistent interface with the human, it loses its relevance to the environment within which we construct subjectivity. The slipper in Fragonard or Shonibare and the stiletto in Lynch / Louboutin serve as examples of the confined affective relations within which we understand the shoe. But the triangulation of shoe, human, and environment remains a closed network precisely because determined by human

---

11 Julia Pine, "In Bizarre Fashion: The Double-Voiced Discourse of John Willie's Fetish Fantasia," *Journal of the History of Sexuality* 22.1 (2013), 1, 4–5.
12 The interview with Louboutin is available at http://www.youtube.com/watch?v=-wpLa6f5fxE.

directives. The shoe's other, undisclosed, relations—for instance, the stiletto heel's with the earthworm—contribute to its density.[13] Indeed, never is the shoe "just a shoe," as Heidegger and Louboutin, among others, discover. But especially as a thing that recedes from human-centered histories and other systems of knowledge, the shoe is not "just a shoe." Heidegger's "And yet—" haunts *us*, just as the shoe's ontic being closes itself off from being accessed completely.

II. SHOE SILENCE

In *The Democracy of Objects* Levi Bryant studies "the self-othering of objects in terms of the relationship between the perpetually and necessarily withdrawn virtual proper being of objects and the local manifestations of objects that take place through the internal dynamics of substance and the exo-relations they enter into with other objects."[14] Appropriating Alfred North Whitehead's language, Bryant states that objects "must have a structure for the 'how' of prehensions to take place at all and that this endo-structure constitutes the substantiality of objects."[15] It is the "endo-structure" of the object, in other words, that comprises its "virtual

---

13 In a section of *Vibrant Matter* Jane Bennett tells a story about worms. Taking both Charles Darwin's and Bruno Latour's observations on the agency of worms as her starting point for theorizing ontological heterogeneity, Bennett argues that we need to "consult nonhumans more closely, or to listen and respond more carefully to their outbreaks, objections, testimonies, and propositions" (108). See Jane Bennett, *Vibrant Matter: A Political Ecology of Things* (Durham: Duke University Press, 2010). I bring up the example of the relations of the earthworm and stiletto heel to suggest there is no certainty we will be able fully and successfully to "listen and respond" to the calls and languages of allopoietic beings. Yet it is important that we pay attention to them more variedly than we are trained to do, which is anthropocentrically.

14 Bryant, *The Democracy of Objects*, 136.

15 Bryant, *The Democracy of Objects*, 137. According to Whitehead, "[E]very prehension consists of three factors: (a) the 'subject' which is prehending, namely, the actual entity in which the prehension is a concrete element; (b) the 'datum' which is prehended; (c) the 'subjective form' which is how *that subject prehends the datum*" (qtd. in Bryant, *The Democracy of Objects*, 135). For Bryant, both the prehending entity and the material prehended are objects or substances.

proper being."¹⁶ The problem, as noted by most practitioners of OOO, is that things lock out other things, including individuals, groups, and systems, thus making their structure difficult, even impossible, to discern. Bryant refers to this locking out process or phenomenon as "*operational closure*" and suggests that the shifting nature of things is marked by their selective exposure (self-exposure) to other objects and environments.¹⁷ But even as they lock and unlock themselves, objects "perturb or irritate one another,"¹⁸ producing information in the process. Bryant is careful to note that it is the irritated or perturbed system that constructs information and, following Niklas Luhmann, he asserts that the information produced is something that cannot be exchanged among systems to result in a transparent and complete knowledge of objects. Moreover, the information produced is tentative and constituted, and there is no guarantee that the "receiver" or the system attempting to make sense of its irritation decodes "the information received as identical to the information transmitted."¹⁹

I'll turn to Launce's monologue in *The Two Gentlemen of Verona* to explore the various intersections of perturbations and irritations, of knowledge produced and withheld by systems and things. Launce enters the scene with his dog Crab and states:

> Nay, 'twill be this hour ere I have done weeping. All the kind of the Launces have this very fault. I have received my proportion, like the prodigious son, and am going with Sir Proteus to the imperial's court. I think Crab, my dog, be the sourest-natured dog that lives. My mother weeping, my father wailing, my sister crying, our maid howling, our cat wringing her hands, and all our house in a great perplexity, yet did not this cruel-hearted cur shed one tear. He is a

---

16 Bryant, *The Democracy of Objects*, 140.
17 Bryant, *The Democracy of Objects*, 140. Critics of OOO focus on concepts like operational closure to argue that, not only does onticology remain rooted in an anthropocentric engagement with things, it also romanticizes the identity of objects by presenting them as a mostly voluntary phenomenon that is independent of its relationship to the human. For example, see Andrew Cole, "The Call of Things: A Critique of Object-Oriented Ontologies," *The Minnesota Review* 80 (2013): 106–18. The scope of this essay does not permit me to elaborate on or respond to the criticism, which Bryant addresses in the penultimate chapter of *The Democracy of Objects*.
18 Bryant, *The Democracy of Objects*, 153.
19 Bryant, *The Democracy of Objects*, 153.

stone, a very pibble stone, and has no more pity in him than a dog. A Jew would have wept to have seen our parting. Why, my grandam, having no eyes, look you, wept herself blind at my parting. Nay, I'll show you the manner of it. This shoe is my father. No, this left shoe is my father. No, no, this left shoe is my mother. Nay, that cannot be so neither. Yes, it is so, it is so—it hath the worser sole. This shoe with the hole in it is my mother, and this is my father. A vengeance on't! There 'tis. Now, sir, this staff is my sister, for look you, she is as white as a lily and as small as a wand. This hat is Nan, our maid. I am the dog. No, the dog is himself, and I am the dog—O, the dog is me, and I am myself. Ay, so, so. Now come I to my father: "Father, your blessing." Now should not the shoe speak a word for weeping. Now should I kiss my father—well, he weeps on. Now come I to my mother. O, that she could speak now like a wood woman! Well, I kiss her—why, there 'tis: here's my mother's breath up and down. Now come I to my sister: mark the moan she makes. Now the dog all this while sheds not a tear nor speaks a word, but see how I lay the dust with my tears.[20]

Launce makes no attempt to conceal he is irritated by Crab, the dog that refuses to share in the Launce household's environment of "great perplexity." The perplexity, which has been brought about by the event of Launce's imminent departure from Verona, results in unified action among most autopoeitic beings that inhabit the household. They shed tears and make sounds that express their sorrow. But while these things, human and nonhuman, produce information that is consistent with the clown's understanding of his environment, Crab's semantic withdrawal from the otherwise unified household response to the impending event of Launce's departure perplexes his master. More precisely, Launce is struck by "wonder" at Crab's withdrawal from his environment. "Wonder," Bogost states, "describes the particular attitude of allure that can exist between an object and the very concept of objects." It is also an event that detaches us "from ordinary logics, of which human logics are but one example." Wonder destabilizes and unhinges us from familiar systems of interpretation; it

---

20 William Shakespeare, *The Two Gentlemen of Verona*, ed. Mary Beth Rose, in *The Complete Pelican Shakespeare*, ed. Stephen Orgel and A.R. Braunmuller (Middlesex: Penguin, 2002), 2.3.1–31.

compels us to "suspend all trust in (our) own logics...and to become subsumed entirely in the uniqueness of an object's native logics."[21]

Wonder is not unlike what Deleuze and Guattari call "unnatural participation."[22] (It is no surprise that the philosophers' influence on present and anticipated directions of vibrant materialism is profound.)[23] They explain the phenomenon of unnatural participation using (somewhat uncannily) an example of human-shoe-dog triangulation of beings. Such participations among autopoietic and allopoietic beings, they claim, are the result of "a composition of speeds and affects involving entirely different individuals, a symbiosis."[24] They turn to Vladimir Slepian's short story *Fils de Chien* to map the success (the deterritorializing line of flight) but also the limit (the reterritotialization) of participations among human, dog, and shoe:

> Being expresses (speeds and affects) in a single meaning in a language that is no longer that of words, in a matter that is no longer that of forms, in an affectability that is no longer that of subjects. Unnatural participation....Vladimir Slepian formulates the "problem" in a thoroughly curious text:...I'll have to become a dog—but how? *This will not involve imitating a dog, nor an analogy of relations*. I must succeed in endowing parts of my body with relations of speed and slowness that will make it become dog, in an *original assemblage proceeding neither by resemblance nor by analogy*. For I cannot become dog without the dog itself becoming something else. Slepian gets the idea of using shoes to solve this problem, the *artifice* of the shoes. If I wear shoes on my hands, then their elements will enter into a new relation, resulting in the affect or becoming

---

21 Bogost, *Alien Phenomenology*, 124.
22 Gilles Deleuze and Félix Guattari, *A Thousand Plateaus*, trans. Brian Massumi (Minneapolis: University of Minnesota Press, 1987), 258.
23 Jane Bennett makes this point in "Systems and Things," where, citing Deleuze and Guattari's example, she invites practitioners of ooo to consider such a direction in the future as might "make both objects and relations the periodic focus of theoretical attention, even if it is impossible to articulate fully the 'vague' or 'vagabond' essence of any system or any things, and even if it impossible to give equal attention to both at once" (227). See Jane Bennett, "Systems and Objects: A Response to Graham Harman and Timothy Morton," *New Literary History* 43, no. 2 (Spring 2012): 225–33.
24 Deleuze and Guattari, *A Thousand Plateaus*, 258.

I seek. But how will I be able to tie the shoe on my second hand, once the first is already occupied? With my mouth. Which in turn receives an investment in the assemblage, becoming a dog muzzle, insofar as a dog muzzle is now used to tie shoes. *At each stage of the problem, what needs to be done is not to compare two organs but to place elements or materials in a relation that uproots the organ from its specificity, making it become 'with' the other organ.* But this becoming, which has already taken in feet, hands, and mouth, will nevertheless fail. It founders on the tail....The tail remains an organ of the man on the one hand and an appendage of the dog on the other; their relations do not enter into composition in the new assemblage.[25]

Launce's experience of wonder fails in a manner similar to that of the character in Slepian's story who, in the end, fails to become dog. If anything, Launce jolts himself all too quickly out of his suspended state of wonder. To do so, he relies on interpretation and representation, two autopoietic tools (of language) essential to his re-establishment of familiar relations with and control over the surrounding environment. I'll elaborate on his use of each of these. First, his dog's refusal to shed a tear or speak a word becomes, for him, a sign of the animal's cruelty: Crab becomes a "cruel-hearted cur." What's more, Crab's cruelty and silence liken him to "a stone" in his master's mind, that is, to an object whose semantic withdrawal and silence Launce accepts readily. Next, he turns to a reproduction of his household's environment in hopes of representing Crab's withdrawal. He seeks with his reproduction to get to the bottom of the dog's motivation, to make his being accessible and thus manageable.

Launce unleashes a series of interpretive systems to discover the knowledge that Crab withholds. He attempts to interpret Crab's silence as a language that might be learned and understood. Launce's clinging to language as the familiar key with which to unlock knowledge is an anthropocentric fallacy against which Harman and Bryant, following Bruno Latour,[26] might warn us. "*Objects themselves* are already more

---

25 Deleuze and Guattari, *A Thousand Plateaus*, 258–59; emphasis added.
26 In *Pandora's Hope*, Latour expounds on his theory of the multiplicity of and in language: "I am attempting to redistribute the capacity of speech between humans and nonhumans....Of course this means an altogether different situation for language. Instead of being the privilege of a human mind surrounded by mute things, articulation becomes a very common property of propositions, in which many kinds of

than present-at-hand," Harman notes, even though we mostly overlook their secret being until they perturb us "in cases of malfunction."²⁷ This is Launce's experience: it is because Crab malfunctions as loyal pet and vocal participant in the household grief that his master is perturbed by the animal and wishes through use of language to unravel his secrets. It is also the event of malfunction that prompts in Launce a series of concatenations. Since the differences among allopoietic and autopoietic beings are, as Adam Miller notes, "messy, muddy, blurry, constructed, and mobile," all their "connections must always be forged by way of concatenation, a method that preserves the errant singularity of each object even as it finds ways to provisionally string some aspects of them into directional networks."²⁸

Let us consider the various concatenations in the scene from *The Two Gentlemen of Verona*. In a basic sense, we only encounter the one Launce (Launce the serving man) in the play. But in another sense Launce introduces us to the assemblage of links that comprises the Launce household. While the others in the household, even the cat, who wrings her hands, primate-like, to mobilize her sorrow, display attributes that Launce is able to interpret readily as expressions of sadness, the dog displaces himself from the family system by refusing to participate in a performance of semantic unity. Unable to grapple with Crab's withdrawal, Launce seeks out the dog's intention: *why* is Crab silent and unwilling to behave like the rest of the Launce household? For answers Launce leans on familiar interpretive schemas of what he takes to be natural participation. He begins unpacking the hitherto unbearable load of Crab's silence by contrasting it to the utterances and actions of the Launce household. Except for the dog, "[a]ll" the Launces share the condition of tearfulness (2.3.1), he finds. (As I've noted earlier, where words fail them, most members of the family rely on the language of tears to convey their sadness at Launce's departure from his home.) He itemizes each one's actions in the context of the information he receives from them and which he assumes is "identical to

---

entities can participate." See Bruno Latour, *Pandora's Hope: Essays on the Reality of Science Studies* (Cambridge: Harvard University Press, 1999), 141–42.
27 Graham Harman, *Tool-Being: Heidegger and the Metaphysics of Objects* (Chicago: Open Court, 2002), 18.
28 Adam Miller, *Speculative Grace: Bruno Latour and Object-Oriented Theology* (New York: Fordham University Press, 2013), 18, 25.

the information transmitted" by them.²⁹ Their tears are identical, Launce maintains, because they are of one mind.

Theirs is not the "unnatural participation" lauded by Deleuze and Guattari, insofar as it is not a "symbiosis" that involves "entirely different individuals."³⁰ It instead is a unity based on similarity among members of a household. Launce craves such harmonious activity particularly because it is accompanied by assurance that his family's response is both transparent to him and consistent with his expectations of the functions of a single network: "[m]y mother weeping, my father wailing, my sister crying, our maid howling, our cat wringing her hands, and *all* our house in *a* great perplexity" (2.3.4–6, emphasis added). While each being listed by Launce makes a unique sound and/or movement that might be wonderfull, these singularities and differences are collapsed because they seem to signify one and the same recognizable thing: sorrow. The difference isn't what he chooses to focus on, but rather he assures himself of the uniformity of his interpretation of the various sounds and actions of his family. If "wonder is a void," Launce quickly transforms it into "a tunnel that leads somewhere more viable."³¹ Launce accesses the "somewhere" suggested by Crab's silence and gives it a meaning that, though undesirable, seems to him logical. Thus, Crab no longer is impenetrable but becomes translatable as a being whose silence represents cruelty, a trait that Launce associates with autopoietic being. Crab still remains outside the family structure, but now he is outside for reasons that make sense to the human.

Of course it isn't only the dog that prevents Launce's smooth cooptation of wonder into the logical flow of knowledge. As he proceeds from interpretation to representation, he encounters other irritations. The shoes he uses to represent his parents are significant in this context. Launce's recreation of the scene of Crab's withdrawal from the household stumbles when he encounters the endo-structure of his shoes. "This shoe is my father," he first claims in his adaptation, only to be confronted by a rivaling possibility: "No, this *left* shoe is my father" (2.3.10, emphasis added). The left and right shoe each contains unbridgeable differences that cannot be overcome without concatenation. Nor can their differences be eliminated. So, after going back and forth—"[n]o, no, this left shoe is my mother. Nay, that cannot be so neither"—Launce concludes that his left

---

29 Bryant, *The Democracy of Objects*, 153.
30 Deleuze and Guattari, *A Thousand Plateaus*, 258.
31 Timothy Morton, *The Ecological Thought* (Cambridge: Harvard University Press, 2010), 126.

shoe is his mother, for it *resembles* her: it has a "hole in it" and "hath the worser sole" (2.3.11–12). The hole in the shoe becomes a metaphor for his mother's female sexual organization, which in turn vehiculates a familiar Judeo-Christian misogyny about the inferior condition of her soul. In Launce's adaptation, the left shoe's sole becomes a soul and its stench becomes his mother's foul breath, even as its hole remains a hole.

Other beings are also concatenated in Launce's reproduction of his family farewell scene. Most of these don't cause him trouble, for they do not seem to resist his adaptive logic. For example, the staff is transformed effortlessly into his sister, for it is "as white as a lily and as small as a wand" (2.3.14–15); and the hat stands for the maid Nan without need of explanation or justification. Unlike the character in Slepian's story, who tries in his project to create "an original assemblage" that avoids both "resemblance" and "analogy," Launce limits representation to comparative practices rooted in simile and metaphor, in a word, in likeness.

But the slippage among likeness, unlikeness, and becoming is inevitable when Launce once again finds himself unable to navigate Crab's semantic opacity. Having managed tentatively to fold the dog into his autopoietic logics that aim at knowledge, Launce falters in prolonging his understanding of Crab. His adaptive narrative comes to a standstill as he struggles and fails to find a properly unique representative to stand in for Crab: "I am the dog. No, the dog is himself, and I am the dog—O the dog is me, and I am myself" (15–16). Hastily, Launce concludes this section of his reproduction with words not unlike Heidegger's "And yet—": "Ay, so, so." Crab's being and silence remain mysterious, hinting at the complications that arise when objects are simultaneously interactive and closed. "Ay, so, so," Launce states resignedly, and returns to the more comforting parallels and analogies he drew earlier among other autopoietic and allopoietic beings.

Familiarly, therefore, the right shoe-father "weeps on," the left shoe-mother's breath stinks, and the stick-sister moans. The dog-self stands apart from all the other couplings; for even as the self (the "I" in the speech) "lay[s] the dust with (his) tears," the dog "sheds not a tear nor speaks a word" (2.3.29–31). That is, the concatenated dog-self continues "to press in," as Eileen Joy might state, and its paradoxical, "sensual and metaphysical thingness" demands attention,[32] Launce's and ours. Or, to adopt Timothy Morton's words, the scene leaves us "in a bind," in that

---

32 Eileen Joy, "You Are Here: A Manifesto," in *Animal, Vegetable, Mineral: Ethics and Objects*, ed. Jeffrey Jerome Cohen (New York: Punctum Books, 2012), 156.

neither can we "in good faith *cancel* the difference between humans and nonhumans," nor keep the links "*intact*."[33] Despite ourselves, we participate in connections that preserve the errant singularities of both the autopoietic and allopoietic machines that comprise the environment of which we are a variable part and about which we attempt to tell stories. Through these connections "life…names a restless activeness, a destructive-creative force-presence that does not coincide fully with any specific body," but "tears the fabric of the actual without ever coming fully 'out' in a person, place, or thing."[34] Between the disclosures and withdrawals of absent and present objects there peeps a multivalence of being that never does come "fully 'out'" at once. But uncontained by modes of autopoietic citizenship and human fantasy, it trembles nomadically at the fringes of knowledge and language, inviting us to step out.

---

33 Morton, *The Ecological Thought*, 76; emphasis added.
34 Bennett, *Vibrant Matter*, 54.

Performing Meat
Karen Raber

> Who can be made to believe that our cultures are carnivorous because animal proteins are irreplaceable?
> —Jacques Derrida[1]

JOHN WECKER'S SECRETS OF NATURE OFFERS A RECIPE FOR ROASTING A goose alive. Advising the application of a ring of fire to some "lively Creature," the recipe includes pots of water to slake the dying goose's thirst, while it "fl[ies] here and there" within the fire-ring.[2] The cook should baste the goose's head and heart so that "her inward parts" will roast before she dies: "when you see her giddy with running, and begin to stumble, her heart wants moisture: she is Rosted, take her up, and set her upon the Table to your Guests, and as you cut her up she will cry continually, that she will be almost all eaten before she be dead."[3] Recipes like this one have attracted only a limited range of scholarly analysis: Wecker's recipe appears, for instance, in the introduction to Patricia Fumerton and Simon Hunt's collection *Renaissance Culture and the Everyday*, where it serves as a reminder of the casual cruelty of Renaissance practices that estrange everyday early modern culture for a generation of historicist critics.[4] Culi-

---

1 Jacques Derrida, "Eating Well, or the Calculation of the Subject: An Interview with Jacques Derrida," in *Who Comes After the Subject*, ed. Eduardo Cadava, Peter Connor, and Jean-Luc Nancy (New York: Routledge, 1991), 112.
2 John Wecker, *Eighteen Books of the Secrets of Nature*, trans. R. Read (London, 1660).
3 The recipe appears on p. 148. Wecker's is not precisely a cookbook, but rather a grab-bag of "secrets" in various fields, accompanied by recipes both for foods and for medicines.
4 *Renaissance Culture and the Everyday* (Philadelphia: University of Pennsylvania Press, 1999), 2.

nary historians might situate the recipe as an example of the new interest in food's aesthetic complexity during the Renaissance. To animal lovers and vegetarians, the recipe would speak for itself, highlighting the intolerable suffering of living creatures rendered as mere meat for the table: animal studies scholars like Simon Estok and Erica Fudge have discussed early modern resistance to, and rare embrace of, vegetarianism based on the dehumanizing influence of meat-eating exemplified by cases of animal torture like that in Wecker's recipe.[5]

While welcome and a clear inspiration to this project, the various agendas of such recent work have tended to ignore or erase the nuanced process by which meat acquires cultural dominance as a main part of meals, and the consequent cultural negotiations of its inherent complexity as a performer at the table. In this essay, I use the work of new materialists who offer a way to talk about the metaphors mobilized by and through meats, about meat's role as actant, and about what Jane Bennett calls its "vagabond" quality, and its vitality-in-death.[6] In what follows, I take up the question of what is at stake in the appearance of two groups of performing meats included in early modern feast and banquets: zombie or undead meats, in the vein of Wecker's goose; and the related creation of early modern "transgenic" or "masquerading" meats, those created by engastration (the stuffing of one meat with another) and those otherwise transmogrified by culinary art. What these performing meats have in common is the multidimensionality of their required acts at table. They do not simply entertain, although certainly that is part of their purpose. Rather their performances illuminate early modern ideas and desires about the significance of turning living animals into a dietary mainstay. Early modern banquets created performed and performing meats that violated species and other categories; and that while this theater of meat announced and celebrated human exceptionalism and human control over nature by testifying to the creative and transformative power of the human cook (and host), it also revealed the limits of that power by

---

5   See Erica Fudge's essay, "Saying Nothing but Concerning the Same: On Dominion, Purity, and Meat in Early Modern England," in *Renaissance Beasts: Of Animals, Humans and Other Wonderful Creatures*, ed. Erica Fudge (Urbana: University of Illinois Press, 2004), p. 70–86; and Simon Estok's "Theory from the Fringes: Animals, Ecocriticism, Shakespeare," *Mosaic* 40:1 (March 2007): 61–78.
6   By "vagabond," Bennett means "a propensity for continuous variation" (Jane Bennett, *Vibrant Matter: A Political Ecology of Things* [Durham: Duke University Press, 2010], 50).

conceding or granting to animal flesh a type of agency in the process of making it act out a part in a meal. Ultimately, what meat performed was all the distortions, complications and ideological dimensions of its production *as meat*.

I. ZOMBIE MEAT

Wecker's goose is no lonely outlier. Fumerton's account mentions other examples of such kitchen barbarity as a pig whipped to death, or a capon "pulled" and gutted while alive as evidence that the goose's fate is a common one in early modern cookery. A recipe in *The Vivendier* (ca. 1450) offers a comic take on the goose's lyric performance, describing the preparation of a chicken that looks dead, but isn't: plucked and painted with "roast meat" color, and massaged into sleep, when the chicken is about to be carved, "it will wake up and make off down the table upsetting jugs, goblets and whatnot."[7] What happens to the naked chicken after it amuses the guests is not reported.

Like many elaborate banquet dishes, Wecker's goose and the *Vivendier's* chicken accomplish a number of things at once. They confuse the distinction between living and dead, between animal and meat; they also collapse the meal's function as sustenance with its function as entertainment. The latter is not surprising since the basic job of a banquet or feast for guests was precisely to affirm or create social ties through a ritualized communal event. Banquet courses were often interspersed with theatrical, musical or other diversions also nicely calculated to demonstrate the host's status, authority, good taste, education and virtue. What the goose and chicken recipes do, then, is ensure that the host will be remembered for providing a miraculous performance by the entree itself. But in early modern Europe, changing habits with regard to meat-eating required the animal at the center of this performance to take on complex roles that cannot be explained only through the social.

In our own historical moment meat rules the table, unquestioned monarch of the meal, surrounded by fawning courtiers (vegetables and other side dishes), often enthroned and crowned (resting on beds of starches,

---

7 *The Vivendier, A Fifteenth Century French Cookery Manuscript*, trans. Terence Scully (Devon, England: Prospect Books, 1997), 81.

or doused with sauces). Recent adventures in pink slime and petri dish meats have brought home how hard it is to decenter "real" meat from this sovereign position: petri dish meat in particular offends through its very status as simulacrum.[8] But it hasn't always been this way. Only at a fairly late date in its etymology, at the same moment Wecker's goose and the *Vivendier*'s comical chicken appear, did the term "meat" begin to signify specifically the flesh of a dead animal meant for human consumption in a meal. Prior to the fifteenth century, meat or *mete* was almost uniformly used as a generic term for all food. The alternative to the current association of "meat" with cooked animal is the more obsolete use of the word "flesh," but flesh referred as often to human beings as to animal bodies, and so did not restrictively designate a component of a meal.[9] The etymologies of "meat" and "flesh" thus suggest that something was happening culturally that required the role of dead animals at the table in the period we are looking at to be recoded, to be divided off from other categories of food and bodies.

There are a number of practical reasons why such a transition might have occurred: on the one hand, the huge medieval appetite for meat was displaced during a subsequent period of agricultural change that saw food animals reduced in number, thus associating meat consumption with class and wealth.[10] A growing role for the culinary arts in ever broader

---

8 In August 2013 Mark Post, a vascular biologist, offered his lab-grown meat in a publicity stunt for which it was cooked as a hamburger by a famous chef and tasted by two food critics (see, for instance, http://www.theguardian.com/science/2013/aug/05/first-hamburger-lab-grown-meat-press-conference or http://www.the-scientist.com/?articles.view/articleNo/36889/title/Lab-Grown-Burger-Taste-Test/ for online articles covering the event). Public reaction ran the gamut, but one constant was the momentary wince at the mere thought of consuming meat that did not have its origins in an authentic cow.

9 The OED gives initial instances from 1325 and 1475 for this more narrow usage; the *Middle English Dictionary* (http://quod.lib.umich.edu/cgi/m/mec/med-idx?type=id&id=MED27542) confirms that through the Middle Ages, meat meant "Food, nourishment, sustenance; also, digested food, chyle"—anything that could be eaten, from vegetables to sweets—rather than animal flesh. Noëllie Vialles notes that the same shift happens to the French *viande*, in *Animal to Edible*, trans. J.A. Underwood (Cambridge University Press, 1994), 4 .Meanwhile, "flesh" functions as a reference to the human body (as in "all flesh is weak") in the Middle Ages and Renaissance, as well as to communion bread, in addition to the muscle and other tissues of a living mammal (thus exclusive of fish or fowl).

10 See Ken Albala, *The Banquet: Dining in the Great Courts of Late Renaissance Europe* (Chicago: University of Illinois Press, 2007); and Roy Strong, *Feast: A History of*

segments of society throughout the sixteenth and seventeenth centuries also focused the attention of many on feats of cookery applied to meat; meanwhile, widening popular concern for the medical role of meat in dietary regimes encouraged people to think carefully about distinctions among meats, and between meat and other foods. Whatever the economic, medical or other material-historical reasons for meat's changing role, it was transformed into a cultural focal point through its various representations as an object, one engaged in complex interactions with human bodies, with other meats, with other "players" at the banquet table. But that new status for meat only makes more potent the problem of establishing what it is that "makes meat." Is the living animal always already incipient meat? At what point in its metamorphosis is its meaty nature fully achieved: when slaughtered, when divided by the butcher, when cooked, when eaten? As it's being cooked and eaten, meat acts on human senses and imagination: odor, texture, taste all simultaneously generate responses in body and brain, most not fully under the conscious control of an individual. During digestion, flesh melts into flesh, becomes categorically indivisible with its "host," yet can generate discomfort, illness in the short term, or obesity and debility in the long term. "In the eating encounter," remarks Bennett, "all bodies are shown to be but temporary congealments of a materiality that is a process of becoming, is hustle and flow punctuated by sedimentation and substance."[11] The simplistic observation "you are what you eat" thus hides a rich and complex set of processes and intra-actions that shape the process of becoming meat.[12]

Grand Eating (New York: Harcourt Inc., 2002); in his introduction to early modern food in *Food: A Culinary History from Antiquity to the Present*, ed. Jean-Louis Flandrin and Massimo Montanari, trans. Albert Sonnenfeld (New York: Columbia University Press, 1999), Jean-Louis Flandrin points out that archaeological evidence suggests that "diet ceased to be determined by the hazards of production and began to be shaped instead by consumer preference" (405).

11 Bennett, *Vibrant Matter*, 49.

12 The term "intra-action" belongs to Karen Barad, as does a version of the concept of "performativity." I intend both terms to resonate throughout this essay. Barad argues for the body's, and all matter's, agential realism (an account of human and non-human ontology that takes seriously the idea of matter's agency, so that rather than "words" and "things" the world consists of relationalities that are material in nature). Her neologism, "intra-action," insists that there are no pre-existing entities before relation, that only through intra-action do the boundaries of phenomena come to exist. See "Posthumanist Performativity: Toward an Understanding of How Matter Comes to Matter," *Signs* 28:3 (2003): 801–831.

Wecker presumably describes an act of cookery that happens in a kitchen well away from the guests who will partake of the dish, yet he does so in excruciating detail, constructing a scene that resembles nothing so much as a miniature drama. Surrounded by kitchen staff, including the cook, who must bank the fires that roast her, the goose has an audience to her immediate suffering, mirrored in the reading audience of the cookbook once the recipe is printed. She is active, flying around looking for escape, periodically basted with water to encourage her further struggles. A death scene more lingering and pathetic could hardly found on the early modern stage, suggesting that what matters in this recipe is not only the eventual dish that results, but the imaginative pleasure (whatever that consists of) in vicariously witnessing this transition from "lively" animation to zombie-like living death. Wecker's goose had, of course, already been the target of another kind of human-engendered imaginative transformation on a global scale. Domesticated millenia before, the goose is a touchstone for the entire concept and process of human improvement of, and control over nature. Before arriving at the dinner table, a goose is already a mutant, its physiology and behavior meddled with by human breeding, and so it functions as a mirror of human power over nature.[13] The goose's performance includes the trace of her compliance in domestication, and again in her agonizing death, her gentle expiring cry the piquant sauce to her double surrender.

At the same time, however, the "cut" that *should* mark the goose's flesh as object, as dead and therefore edible meat, instead disrupts any neat distinction.[14] The diner carves into an animal that announces by voice and gesture that it is still animate, still conscious, still a participant in the drama of the table. The bloody theatrics usually assumed to end in the kitchen arrive at the table, and instead of passive audience or consumers, guests themselves become actors on stage, butchers, but also creators of category, settling a whole series of existential dilemmas. But as co-performers, diners simultaneously reopen exactly those dilemmas, cooking their own goose even as they dispatch this dying one.

---

13 Albala observes that the predominance of domesticated over wild meats grew exponentially in the late sixteenth and early seventeenth centuries, and that the preference for meats generated from human control over nature; Albala, *The Banquet*, 33.

14 Barad, "Posthumanist Performativity," 815, contrasts the Cartesian "cut," which relies on inherent differences between subject and object, to an "agential cut," that creates a "local resolution *within* the phenomemon of the inherent ontological indeterminacy."

II. MAKE YOUR OWN (DEAD) ANIMAL

Everywhere in the early modern kitchen, an observer could find examples of transmutation, things being turned into other things, often involving various forms of meat. "Turn your meat," writes Lady Elinor Fettiplace in one recipe, "to pure blood."[15] Wendy Wall notes that cookbooks "underscore the importance of flesh mutating into flesh...everywhere hearkening toward dinner's vitality and the precariousness of embodiment."[16] Food was used to create almost anything, from small objects to entire environments: Strong describes fake gardens made of sugar, vessels and instruments, statues and sculptures, even entire buildings made of food.[17] The feast was a "game of deceit," with edible trenchers, cups and so on—but also featuring meats layered or fused within, around and on top of other meats, meats disguised as other creatures or as their own living selves.[18]

Meat's "vagabond" nature in the early modern culture may be generated in part through its preparation. Whether because of sinewy animals, human dental debility, or a sheer love of complexity, nearly every period recipe requires meat to be stewed, seethed, or minced, and then mixed, stuffed or sauced with other ingredients; many meat dishes end with the resulting "paste" reconstituted through baking or incorporation into puddings, hashes, or other blended dishes. What this means is that early modern meat dishes obscure their origins: one could not necessarily perceive in the resulting food the shape or other physical attributes of the living animal. The sheer act of butchering already transformed food into something vastly different from its first incarnation, while every culinary intervention was by definition a process of transformation. At the simplest level, by creating re-formed and re-dressed dishes cooks were thus merely restoring visual cues to the animal's identity, and a less ambiguous connection between the transformed meat and its prior condition as a live animal. *Epulario or the Italian Banquet*, for instance, includes a recipe for how "to dresse a Peacocke with all his feathers" that produces

---

15 *Elinor Fettiplace's Receipt Book*, ed. Hilary Spurling (London: Faber and Faber Ltd, 1986), 334.
16 Wendy Wall, *Staging Domesticity: Household Work and English Identity in Early Modern Drama* (Cambrdige, 2002), 338.
17 Strong, *Feast*, 188–97.
18 Wall, *Staging Domesticity*, 335.

a dish that "seems to be alive."¹⁹ The cook removes the bird's feathers and skin, cooks its meat, then restuffs it with its own flesh, and re-feathers it. While this is the most frequent process cited in recipes, it turns out that the dis-integration of meat through cooking opened the door to much more inventive results. Rendering meat edible also provided an opportunity to quite literally make meats "cross-dress," like one of Shakespeare's boy actors done up in women's garb. Early modern meat thus becomes the material of experiments with nature, transforming and translating what *was* into what *might be*. If "dressing" (meaning to form, order, arrange, straighten, or manage) referred to meat's preparation either for cooking or for serving, then we might say that meats were also "re-dressed" in other attire for their appearance at the dinner or banquet table, re-clothed and amended in the process.

Consider the turducken—a turkey stuffed with a duck, which is in turn stuffed with a chicken—a dish now primarily served at Thanksgiving feasts in the United States. Although its name is new (dating, according to the OED, only from the 1980s), its origins lie in the period we are discussing, in the fascination with engastration that informs many early recipe books and banquet tables. Perhaps the grandeur of the turkey has led us to overlook the smaller animals inside, but from the perspective of the chicken in a turducken the outer layers are a form of cloaking device, concealing its "nature" until the moment when the turkey is carved and reveals itself to be not a singular dead animal, but one inhabited by other creatures. It is, thus, a variation on the many surprise theatrical food-based revelations included in famous banquets like the *Vivendier*'s dormant chicken, or the familiar four-and-twenty blackbirds in a pie.

The turducken is really quite a tame critter: the most extreme example of animal experimentation comes in attempts to create entirely new creatures from dead flesh. For his banquet in honor of the French King, Francis I, at the Field of the Cloth of Gold in 1520, Henry VIII's cooks whipped up a "cockentryce," by sewing together the head of a pig and the rear end of a chicken (Figure 1). While it might look like a bizarre violation of nature, it was not so rare a dish, having already graced the table of John Stafford, Bishop of Bath in 1425, and probably many more banquets besides.²⁰ If Wecker's goose and the *Viviendier*'s chicken are proto-zombies, then perhaps these "redressed" meats count as early experiments

---

19   *Epulario, or the Italian Banquet* (London, 1598), Sig. C1r.
20   Harleian MS. 279 (ca. 1430), p. 62, lists a "cockyntryche" among the banquet dishes.

Figure 1. Cockentryce prepared at Henry VIII Kitchens at Hampton Court Palace. Photo © Richard Fitch, used with permission.

in transgenesis—the manipulation of animal DNA to produce new species, to recode dead flesh and give it a new "nature."

What do engastric, cross-dressed, or amended meats in early modern cookery tell us, either about meat, or about what it represents? While the engastration of meats can be assimilated to other forms of transformation at the banquet table (like *Schauessen* or *trionfi*, confections in all sorts of shapes and forms made out of a variety of materials), making meat into a simulacrum of itself or of other meats suggests that "meat" functions as figurative and symbolic *matter*—it is in itself metaphor, or perhaps an example of what Ian Bogost calls "metaphorphosis" in the sense that "meat" as a descriptor of dead flesh detaches from any "natural" or confirmed "thing" in the world and instead becomes a thing in itself.[21] Each of these masquerading dishes is an ontologically confused and confusing thing, its existence made possible precisely because of the mobile (in every sense of this word) thing-ness of a thing (dead flesh) that was once a living creature-object (the animal). The boundary-crossings of these masquerading meats can be assimilated to the same narrative as our performing

---

21 See Ian Bogost, *Alien Phenomenology or What It's Like to be a Thing* (Minneapolis: University of Minnesota Press, 2012), 66. Bogost coins the term to address how metaphor can function not merely representationally, but as a "means to apprehend reality."

meats above. However, I think the process of creating redressed meats carries a particular cost: by provoking cooks and diners to reconsider meat's apparently inert, passive status and the reliability of meat's self-identity, such dishes raise questions about the dangerous potential in making an animal into meat, and so also about dangers for the body that ingests it.

Early modern dietaries and medical texts posited a humoral human body, porous and vulnerable to external influences, constantly struggling to achieve equilibrium. Geography, class status, gender, and other factors could influence an individual's basic humoral complexion, while everything from air to food could disturb the precarious balance of that body's internal machinery.[22] Whole categories of meats were understood to define the bodies that ate them: pork, for instance, was a lower-class dish, suitable for crude palates and crude bodies, while tender fowl were for more refined diets. Food was never simply fuel: it was physic for a range of ailments, with effects on everything from individual morality to national identity. "All acts of ingestion and excretion," Michael Schoenfeldt argues, were "very literal acts of self-fashioning."[23] If one can't tell the identity of the meat that one ingests, however, then obviously any prescription regarding appropriate consumption of the stuff is rendered ineffectual. Moreover, if meats can be recoded, not merely as different meats (as in the case of layered and blended meats) but as completely new creatures (as in the case of the cockentryce), then the entire edifice that rests on dietary discernment falls apart. Instead of policing social, political, national and other boundaries, meat violates the whole notion of decipherable categories. Again, Bennett's use of the term "vagabond" describes meat's inherent variability, its itinerant nature, resistant to the kind of fixity required by dietary regimes of the period. In an accident of history and language, we might recall here that early modern stage performers, actors in the public theater, were regarded as vagabonds and "masterless men" by authorities. Like human performers, banquet meats promised a theater of order and discrimination, but in their mobility often delivered the opposite.

If transgenic meats expose meat's susceptibility to transformation, and redressed or masquerading meats suggest the difficulty diners might

---

22 See Ken Albala's *Eating Right in the Renaissance* (Berkeley: University of California Press, 2002); and Joan Fitzpatrick, *Food in Shakespeare: Early Modern Dietaries and the Plays* (Burlington, VT: Ashgate Press, 2007).

23 Michael Schoenfeldt, "Fables of the Belly in Early Modern England," in *The Body In Parts: Fantasies of Corporeality in Early Modern Europe*, ed. Carla Mazzio and David Hillman (New York: Routledge, 1997), 243.

have in even recognizing the meat being served to them, then not only does meat *not* enable the policing of social, moral, political and other categories as it is supposed to, but it might lead to the complete collapse of all categories, full stop. Meat's mobility generates anxiety—it is always in the process of becoming something else, animal becoming flesh, flesh becoming "meat," meat being cooked, cooked meats being consumed, consumed meats becoming (human) flesh again, and so on. At each stage, what meat is or isn't is uncertain; in the last stages when animal flesh is transmuted into human flesh, meat enacts a mingling of bodies that confronts the diner with the porousness of her body, and its essential material instability. Matter is never itself, it is always becoming other. Engastric concoctions like the turducken and cross-species confabulations like the cockentryce deliberately try to reproduce this indistinction as a circumscribed byproduct of human intervention in the making of meat in order to confront and defang the anxieties aroused by the act of eating a dead animal. It might be useful here to reconsider the practice of redressing meats as the animals that the flesh originally belonged to. A peacock dressed up in its feathers is dead meat masquerading as living animal—or, in another formulation, an animal masquerading "as itself," just in a more culinarily compliant form. Such redressing attempts to introduce stability and a different kind of vitality to the dead, confused, and confusing object being presented to diners. But what does it mean to say the bird is dressed as "itself"? What "self" does the bird—dead, dismembered, mixed with other ingredients, reassembled, shaped, and re-feathered—have? The act of culinary re-dressing imports a fantasy of self-identity, of a prior subjectivity invested in the living animal that can stabilize its meaty self and so its meaty actions; but what is really created is matter with potential lingering agency. Dangerous stuff, in other words.

Early modern meat had to be made, first by cultivation of living animals as domesticated breeds suitable for consumption, then by flaying and dismembering carcasses, then by transforming flesh into culinary objects. What makes meat, however, is also its performance of itself (of *a* "self") *as meat*. But at the banquet table, "performance," in its more common sense of theatrical action, bleeds—literally—into "performativity," the construction of matter *as matter*, a construction that entangles human with non-human, and suggests that the former only arises in its intra-actions with the latter. In its tales of zombie geese and chickens, its transgenic and cross-dressed pheasants, turkeys, and ducks, early modern culinary practices stage the perilous cultural drama of becoming (human-animal) meat.

Eye and Book
Species and Spectacle
Pauline Reid

MY THINGS, THE EYE AND THE BOOK, UNEASILY TRANSGRESS THE BOUNDARY between objects and media. Following Bruno Latour's call to investigate the ways objects "block, render possible," or "forbid" rather than merely structure our experiences, this essay explores how visual perception complicated early modern encounters with the book as object.[1] I situate the relation between eye and book within a historically specific early modern material and intellectual environment. Material things shape, to cite Graham Harman, how we perceive perception. Even so, our cultural models of perception necessarily color how we approach these things. A focus on objects' environs implies an ecological, networked reading of objects and, I would argue, a historical one. Historical phenomenology can link objects with their temporal as well as spatial environs. Rather than following Husserl and Heidegger's model of a transcendent human consciousness that intentionally "brackets" off the object from its environs, I here adopt phenomenology as a method for discovering co-habitations and disturbances between body and object. Traditional phenomenology often removes perception from a historical and spatial index in order to determine first principles. Instead, as I will explore with the eye, the body manifested as part of a network of objects that continuously patterned and altered perception in early modern thought. This characterization of the human body and its parts as objects as well as perceptual media draws in part from Rosalyn Diprose's claim that phenomenology acts as an "interworld" between the human body and the external object,[2] as well as

---

1   Bruno Latour, *Reassembling the Social: An Introduction to Actor-Network-Theory* (Oxford: Oxford University Press, 2007), 72.
2   Rosalyn Diprose, *Corporeal Generosity: On Giving with Nietzsche, Merleau-Ponty, and Levinas* (Albany: State University of New York Press, 2002), 102.

from Sarah Ahmed's claim that objects and spaces "impress" themselves on the body to the point where they become a "second skin."[3] Perception is here not transcendent, but physically situated; the percipient-object relationship is not static, but mutually dynamic.

In early modern thought and practice, objects were seen to relate to one another and to us in ways radically different from our current moment. Hence, we can not only employ the new materialisms and object-oriented ontologies of scholars such as Jane Bennett, Ian Bogost, Levi R. Bryant, Jeffrey Cohen, Graham Harman, Eileen Joy, Bruno Latour, Timothy Morton, and Julian Yates for novel readings of early modern texts, we can also use early modern discussions of objects and networks to interrogate our own phenomenological assumptions.[4] Object-oriented ontology has been used as an antidote to an entrenched historicism. For instance, Julian Yates criticizes the historicist tendency to use the thing as a "theatrical metaphor" for the human past[5] and posits a greater attention to how "the way in which the use or performance of a 'thing' changes both the 'thing' and the user."[6] Several of our panel discussions at the SAA, too, seemed to

---

3   Sara Ahmed, *Queer Phenomenology: Orientations, Objects, Others* (Durham and London: Duke University Press, 2006), 54. Ahmed criticizes Husserl and Heidegger for using the object as a mere case study for their phenomenological theories: as a field, phenomenology often purports to turn towards objects, but in fact uses them as allegories for human consciousness (25–26). Further, she argues, the practice of "bracketing" an object from its surroundings assumes a "fantasy that 'what we put aside' can be transcended in the first place" (33).

4   Jane Bennett, *Vibrant Matter: A Political Ecology of Things* (Durham and London: Duke University Press, 2010); Ian Bogost, *Alien Phenomenology: Or What It's Like to be a Thing* (Minneapolis: University of Minnesota Press, 2012); Levi Bryant, *The Democracy of Objects* (Ann Arbor: Open Humanities Press, 2011); Jeffrey Jerome Cohen, ed., *Prismatic Ecology: Ecotheory Beyond Green* (Minneapolis: Univesrity of Minnesota Press, 2014) and *Animal, Vegetable, Mineral: Ethics and Objects* (Washington, DC: Punctum Books / Oliphaunt Books, 2012); Graham Harman, *Guerilla Metaphysics: Phenomenology and the Carpentry of Things* (Open Court: Chicago and La Salle, IL, 2005); Eileen Joy, "You Are Here: A Manifesto," in *Animal, Vegetable, Mineral*, 153–172; Timothy Morton, *The Ecological Thought* (Cambridge: Harvard University Press, 2012) and "Here Comes Everything: The Promise of Object-Oriented Ontology," *Qui Parle* 19.2 (2011): 163–190; Julian Yates, *Error, Misuse, Failure: Object Lessons from the English Renaissance* (Minneapolis: University of Minnesota Press, 2003) and "What Are Things Saying in Renaissance Studies?" *Literature Compass* 3.5 (2006): 992–1010.

5   Yates, "What are Things Saying," 992.

6   Yates, "What are Things Saying," 998.

cycle back to the issue of historicism: can, for instance, OOO instead offer us novelty, a fresh reading of Shakespeare and other literary texts? Can and should OOO become, to borrow respondent Julia Lupton's wonderful abbreviation, an alternative to HHH (historicism, humanism, hermeneutics)? HHH tends to use objects for explanation (for human culture) and OOO tends to use them for estrangement (from a hermeneutics of the human). Yet in practice, as Lupton describes, the effect of OOO has been as much to open up alternative histories as to act as an alternative to historical interpretation. A historicized engagement with early modern perceptions of things and an environs-based approach to objects might serve as co-informants rather than rivals. Strictly ontological object theories, removed from a spatial/temporal ecology, could otherwise risk placing objects—as well as history—on a flat surface, where object relations are theorized as more or less the same through time and we project our own intellectual models onto an environment of the past that could otherwise be productively alien to us. OOE can offer us an *altered*, or transformed, history. The ways in which we structure object relations will transform the questions we ask of history, just as historical models of perception have already shaped our own.

Indeed, Harman's description of a "glue that binds the material of perception,"[7] a "network" or "global ether" that connects phenomenal objects,[8] recalls the concept, popular in classical and early modern thought, of visual species that objects emanate. These species form a wider field of perceptual matter; they mediate between object and perceiver. Plato, Aristotle, and Democritus believed that objects gave off "images, copies, or representations" of themselves, "replicas of their shape and colour" that passed "through the air into the eye."[9] Classical, medieval, and early modern philosophers used visual terms to describe these object replicas. Democritus called them *eidola*; Aristotle, Roger Bacon, and Theophrastus, *imagines*; Leonardo da Vinci, *simulacra*; and Kepler, *picturae* and *illustrations*.[10] The term *species* could imply reflections, phantoms, or illusions in the sixteenth and seventeenth centuries (*OED*, senses

---

7   Harman, *Guerilla Metaphysics*, 3.
8   Harman, *Guerilla Metaphysics*, 4.
9   Alistair C. Crombie, *Science, Optics, and Music in Medieval and Early Modern Thought* (London: Hambledon Press, 1990), 177.
10 Crombie, *Science, Optics, and Music*, 177.

3a, 3c, 4).[11] Species trouble the concept of a thing in itself, fully present or "bracketed" from human perception, as well as what Chris Jenks calls the positivist "doctrine of immaculate perception."[12] In a pre-Cartesian worldview, objects, their replicas, and the viewer instead each mediate and, at times, alter one another. For instance, Kellie Robertson discusses how rocks and their species were used as exempla in medieval culture. Rocks symbolized the relationship between material form and immaterial impression in visual perception: "the species (or inner rock) was thought to be generated by the rock, thus linking the rock to the viewer."[13] The rock and its observer co-produce their relation to one another. Both visual *species* and Harman's global network mediate between object and its perception in their phenomenal models.

In Shakespeare's historical moment, common metaphors of perceptual media included visual imprints rather than Harman's global network—phenomenal theories of perception may parallel transformations in media technology. In his *Anatomy of Melancholy*, Robert Burton declares that we "perceive the Species of Sensible things present, or absent, and retaine them as waxe doth the print of a Seale."[14] In this wax metaphor, our perception of a thing is a copy or impression on the mind of the thing's own emanated copy or species. Perception is doubly mediated by object replicas and cognitive impressions. Burton's metaphor of perception as an imprint was common to Aristotelian and Platonic thought: the growth of print media encouraged its wide use in early modern discourse. Physicians Ambrose Paré and Levinus Lemnius also describe perception in terms specific to print.[15] Paré links the ability to retain sense impressions with an imprint on the brain matter itself: "Those who have a dry braine, are also slow to learne; for you shall not easily imprint any

---

11   For a wider historical discussion of visual uncertainty in the early modern imagination, see Stuart Clarke's *Vanities of the Eye: Vision in Early Modern European Culture* (Oxford: Oxford University Press, 2007).

12   Chris Jenks, "The Centrality of the Eye in Western Culture," in *Visual Culture*, ed. Chris Jenks (New York: Routledge, 2002), 5.

13   Kellie Robertson, "Exemplary Rocks," in *Animal, Vegetable, Mineral*, 97.

14   Robert Burton, *The Anatomy of Melancholy*, 2nd ed. (Oxford: 1621), 150, *Early English Books Online* (EEBO), http://quod.lib.umich.edu/e/eebo/A17310.

15   Bruce R. Smith also employs these examples to further his analysis of physical memory in acoustics in *The Acoustic World of Early Modern England: Attending the O-Factor* (Chicago: University of Chicago Press, 1999); I instead emphasize their connection to the graphical elements of the book as object of visual perception.

thing in dry bodyes."[16] Lemnius similarly contrasts slippery, overly liquid brains with overly hard brains, which "will not easely suffer the poynte of anye engravinge Toole to enter and pearce into it."[17] Engraving was a common print illustration method. Again, early modern metaphors of perception drew from material culture, even as these materials would be experienced vis-à-vis these perceptual models.

The eye itself was described as a glass or spectacle, a metaphor drawn from optics. This analogy emphasizes the human eye's dual role as medium and thing: a glass can mediate, reflect, or distort what is seen. As Queen Margaret describes her journey to England in *2 Henry VI*, she loses view of England's shore: "And bid mine eyes be packing with my heart, / And call'd them blind and dusky spectacles, / For losing ken of Albion's wished coast" (3.2.111–113).[18] Her eyes, as "spectacles," are objects of sight, now dusky or clouded over, reflective mirrors or windows now made obstructive (*OED*, "spectacle" *obs.*, sense 5a). Conceptions of the book also drew from an English tradition of mirror imagery in late medieval and early modern book titles that included the terms *Mirror, Speculum,* or *Glass*.[19] As Ian Bogost notes, the mirror or speculum in medieval and early modern culture was a technologically "imprecise device," "a funhouse mirror made of hammered metal, whose distortions show us a perversion of a unit's sensibilities."[20] The material metaphors of books and eyes as glasses in early modern culture, then, do not imply a straightforward model of visual perception: instead, looking and reading can be disorienting and transformative acts. In his *Microcosmographia* (1615), Helkiah Crooke employs glassy metaphors for the eye's anatomy, including two inner membranes that he calls the "glassy" and the "cristalline" humors. Crooke's visceral portrayal of the "cristalline" membrane links

---

16 Ambroise Paré, *The workes of that famous chirurgion Ambrose Parey*, 2nd ed. (London: 1634), 166, sig. P3.v, EEBO, http://quod.lib.umich.edu/e/eebo/A08911.
17 Levinus Lemnius, *The touchstone of complexions generallye appliable, expedient and profitable for all such, as be desirous & carefull of their bodylye health...*, 2nd ed. (London: 1576), 120.v, EEBO, http://quod.lib.umich.edu/e/eebo/A05313.
18 William Shakespeare, *2 Henry IV*, in *The Riverside Shakespeare*, ed. G. Blakemore Evans et al. (Boston: Houghton Mifflin, 1997). All Shakespeare references are to this edition.
19 See Herbert Grabes, *The Mutable Glass: Mirror-imagery in Titles and Texts of the Middle Ages and the English Renaissance* (Cambridge: Cambridge University Press, 1973), 25–35.
20 Bogost, *Alien Phenomenology*, 31.

the eye-as-spectacle metaphor to the process of looking at a book. Crooke tells readers to take the "cristalline" membrane of a disembodied eyeball and spread it across a page to magnify letters:

> if you take out the cristalline humour compassed with his Membrane and lay it upon a written paper, the letters under it will appeare much greater then indeed they are, from whence haply came the invention of Spectacles, and indeed this humour is a very spectacle to the Opticke nerve[21]

Reception and magnification of images here takes place through a process of refraction across the eye's multiple membranes in an indirect, multiplied, and even visually uncertain process—the eye becomes a hall of mirrors. Visual mutability is indeed crucial for cognitive perception: "naturally," Crooke argues, "the images of visible things are no longer retained in the Cristalline then is necessary for their perception, but give way to others."[22] Past images must disappear for new visual impressions to take place. Once the image has passed through the crystalline membrane, "the alteration" or perceived image "vanisheth," "so there is way made for a new alteration."[23]

Crooke's description of the image as it passes through the crystal membrane as an "alteration" characterizes visual perception as ephemeral and mutable. The term "alteration" could also suggest a "disease or disorder" in Crooke's time (OED, sense 2b): the process of perceiving images in a healthy eye also suggests disability, even blindness. Crooke describes alteration as necessary to perception; however, the boundary between the sensation and cognition of an object, and the object and its perceptual trace, remains ambiguous and complex. As phenomenologist Maurice Merleau-Ponty would much later claim, "the visual field is that strange zone in which contradictory notions jostle each other"[24]: "one never manages to determine the instant when a stimulus once seen is seen

---

21 Helkiah Crooke, *Microkosmographia a description of the body of man*, 2nd ed. (London, 1615), 571, EEBO, http://quod.lib.umich.edu/e/eebo/A19628.
22 Crooke, *Microkosmographia*, 571.
23 Crooke, *Microkosmographia*, 571.
24 Maurice Merleau-Ponty, *Phenomenology of Perception*, trans. Colin Smith (London: Routledge, 1981), 6.

no longer."²⁵ Crooke's continuously altered eye recalls Harman's proposition that things infinitely withdraw.²⁶ Ahmed characterizes sensation as an encounter between bodies and things,²⁷ but one which can both transform the orientation of our bodies in space, to the point of disorientation.²⁸ Where does the object end and the eye begin, in this interactive, yet refracted, even disorienting, environment of sensation?

For Crooke and his contemporaries, appearance and disappearance, vision and blindness, a form or object and its trace, jostle together in our perception of objects and images. The term "alteration" could even imply magnification and doubling, a sense that most often appears in early modern music and again troubles the divide between a thing and its mediating image or copy (see OED, sense 1b).²⁹ We may recall Shakespeare's opposition of a permanent "fixed mark" and a love that is "not love," "which alters when it alteration finds," in sonnet 116, or Polixenes's confrontation of Camillo in the *Winter's Tale*:

> Your chang'd complexions are to me a mirror
> Which shows me mine chang'd too; for I must be
> A party in this alteration, finding
> Myself thus alter'd with 't. (1.2.380–84)

In Crooke's (and Shakespeare's) configuration of the eye as a glass which can alter the perceptual field, the human body and brain themselves behave as networked objects, assemblies of parts that always already mediate our encounters of objects.³⁰ In early modern visual perception,

---

25 Merleau-Ponty, *Phenomenology of Perception*, 4.
26 Graham Harman, *Tool-Being: Heidegger and the Metaphysics of Objects* (Chicago: Open Court, 2002), 126–27.
27 Ahmed, *Queer Phenomenology*, 54.
28 Ahmed, *Queer Phenomenology*, 4.
29 John Dowland describes an alteration as a "doubling of a lesser Note in respect of a greater," "the doubling of the proper value" of a note, or a repetition of "one," "self-same Note" by two voices in *Andreas Ornithoparcus his Micrologus, or Introduction: containing the art of singing Digested into foure books*, 2nd ed. (London, 1609), sig. R.r, EEBO, http://quod.lib.umich.edu/e/eebo/A08534.
30 The early modern perception of the human body as an assemblage has been long established by scholars such as Carla Mazzio and Gail Kern Paster. In *The Melancholy Assemblage: Affect and Epistemology in the English Renaissance* (New York:

external objects are continuously interwoven and networked through our own multifarious membranes.

Visual perception conceived as a paradoxical "alteration," a transformation, doubling, or disease, informs Shakespeare's narrative of false blindness in *2 Henry VI*. Gloucester interrogates the pilgrim Simpcox, who claims that his blindness was cured at the shrine of St. Alban's. Gloucester questions Simpcox about the colors of his outfit, which Simpcox names. Gloucester responds: "Sight may distinguish of colors; but suddenly / To nominate them all, it is impossible" (2.1.126–27). Why does Gloucester believe that a previously blind Simpcox could distinguish or see colors, but not name them? Simpcox's potential act of "nominating" colors implies an act of perception that is different than viewing them. Gloucester's interrogation of Simpcox's vision interrogates the entire uncertain enterprise of visual perception. In *Theaetetus*, Plato argues that colors are created through the meeting of the eyes with the object's own motion: "what we call a colour is neither the thing which does the meeting, nor the thing which is met, but something generated in between, which is peculiar to the individual perceiver."[31] Simpcox's (falsely) disabled sight calls into question how any of us can see, perceive, and name objects.[32]

This scene adapts the richly visual source material of John Foxe's *Acts and Monuments*. After Foxe describes Simpcox's false miracle, he figures Gloucester as an icon of virtue: "whether it was that the nature of true vertue commonly is suche, that as the flame ever beareth his smoke, and the body his shadow: so the brightnes of vertue never blaseth, but has some disdayne or envy wayting upon it."[33] These references to smoke and flames, light and dark, brightness and blaze, resemble the fire imagery

---

Fordham University Press, 2013), Drew Daniel more explicitly links early modern notions of the body with actor-network-theory (ANT).

31 Plato, *Theaetetus*, trans. Robin H. Waterfield (London: Penguin, 1987), 34.

32 For a more directly political analysis of Simpcox's false visual disability, see David M. Turner's "Disability Humor and Meanings of Impairment in Early Modern England," in *Recovering Disability in Early Modern England*, ed. Allison P. Hobgood and David Houston Wood (Columbus: Ohio State University Press, 2013). Turner convincingly argues that this scene "renders all vision and sightedness unfamiliar" (109). Lindsey Row-Heyveld situates disability in early modern English culture as a potentially troubled form of performance in "The Lying'st Knave in Christendom: The Development of Disability in the False Miracle of St. Alban's," *Disability Studies Quarterly* 29.4 (2009).

33 John Foxe, *Actes and Monuments of Matters Most Speciall and Memorable, Happenying in the Church with an Universall History of the Same, Wherein is Set Forth*

of Foxe's woodcuts—Protestant martyrs burning at the stake—and the light/dark contrast of these woodcuts' chiaroscuro technique. In both Platonic and Aristotelian thought, "the proper object of vision" was color.[34] Color was thought to be created through the "interaction" between the perceiver and medium, or "fire particles streaming off the coloured object"[35]: the mutual encounters of perceiving eye, medium, and object form colors and images.

Directly after his interrogation of Simpcox's vision, Margaret interrogates Gloucester's guardianship of Henry. Margaret threatens, "Gloucester, see here the tainture of thy nest, / And look thyself be faultless, thou wert best" (2.1.184–85). "Tainture" can imply a stain or degradation (OED, sense 2). Another, earlier meaning of tainture is "colouring" (OED, sense 1). Margaret commands Gloucester to examine himself for flaws and to, himself, gaze upon the colors of his own "nest." Margaret portrays Gloucester himself as blind and lacking in the perception necessary to discern images. The OED locates the first use of the term "tainture" in William Caxton's English translation of the *Aeneid*, *Eneydos* (1490). Caxton employs the term in a digression on the Phoenician alphabet and its capability to retain historiographical memory with its "letters cronykes [chronicles] and historyes," things that would otherwise "have be forgoten it and put in oublyaunce."[36] Caxton claims that the Phoenicians would

> note wyth rede colour or ynke firste the sayd lettres of which our bokes ben gretely decorated soucured & made fayr. We wryte the grete and firste capytall lettres of our volumes bookes and chapytres wyth the taynture of reed coloure[37]

Here, Caxton claims a heritage of book ornamentation (the red colors of capital letters in a book) from the Phoenicians, who both developed the alphabet, and, in his account, allowed ancient history to be later

---

At Large the Whole Race and Course of the Church..., 2nd ed. (London 1583), sig. ppiiii.r, EEBO, http://quod.lib.umich.edu/e/eebo/A67922.

34 Crombie, *Science, Optics, and Music*, 178.

35 Crombie, *Science, Optics, and Music*, 178.

36 Virgil, *Here fynyssheth the boke yf [sic] Eneydos, compyled by Vyrgyle, which hathe be translated oute of latyne in to frenshe, and oute of frenshe reduced in to Englysshe by me wyll[ia]m Caxton...*, 2nd ed. (Westminster: William Caxton, 1490), sig. Biiiir, EEBO, http://quod.lib.umich.edu/e/eebo/A14476.

37 Caxton, in Virgil, *Eneydos*, sig. Biiiir.

remembered. In Caxton's account, remembrance relies on the arrangement and coloring of letters in books. Here, the color (image) and the nomination (letter, language) combine to form historical memory. The visual and material elements of the book-object—in Caxton's text, the book's red, taintured letters—act as a cognitive, mnemonic aid. The language of Gloucester's own "taintures" emphasizes both his iconicity, located in the specific material object of the book, and a material decay, degradation, or stain. Again, magnification and blindness, a seen object and its vanishing point or trace, and a material reminder and its decay occupy the same textual and phenomenological field. Foxe's shadows and flames, Gloucester's nominated colors in 2 *Henry VI*, and Caxton's taintured letters refer to the uneasiness of visual perception, an uneasiness conveyed by metaphors that combine visual materials with phenomenal uncertainty: imprint, copy, color, glass, species, spectacle, idol, phantom, flame.

The Book/Body in
The Duchess of Malfi
Emily Rendek

FOR HELEN SMITH, IN "EMBODYING EARLY MODERN WOMEN'S READING," "the text enacts a physiological change" on the reader.¹ In this essay, I should like to revise this statement to suggest that this "change" is actually an *exchange* between text and body. The marginalia left behind by early modern readers are visible traces of their bodily imprints upon the text and suggest that by their reading, the text becomes an extension of the reader's body. Such exchanges need not be limited only to such visible marks. Recent scholarship has begun to study the often slightly less visible marks left behind by book users; Katherine Rudy's work employs the use of a densitometer to examine these marks, which include oils from fingerprints, food stains, tears, and even blood stains that help to create a better idea of what parts of a text a reader read and how often that text was read.² It is not just that "[t]he process of accessing the text was a corporeal one…impressing key content on the reader's memory," but that the

---

1 Smith gives the example of Sir John Spencer recounting in *Discourse of Diverse Petitions* (1641) his speaking with a young woman who had left her father and was no longer talking to him. Spencer uses a book as a means of persuasion to affect the young woman: "'then I took a Bible and bad her read the first commandment, and then she fell a reading and into a passion of weeping, and afterward spake with her father.'" Smith points out that the act of reading has physically affected the woman—causing a bodily change. Elsewhere, Smith also makes a connection between the appetite and reading, arguing, "the empty stomach creates cognitive space." Helen Smith, "Embodying Early Modern Women's Reading," *Huntington Library Quarterly* 73.3 (Sept. 2010): 418, 425.
2 Katherine Rudy, "Dirty Books: Quantifying Patterns of Use in Medieval Manuscripts Using a Densitometer," *Journal of Historians of Netherlandish Arts* 2 (2010): accessed 10 July 2014, doi:10.5092 / jhna.2010.2.1.

text itself also becomes embodied, taking on features of its reader.[3] Text and reader exchange properties. To say only that "[r]eaders' bodies were molded and altered by the texts they read" is to ignore the other side of the equation.[4] The reader is not only imprinted by the text but imprints the text itself (both literally and figuratively). The relationship between book and reader proves symbiotic, an example of facultative mutualism (where two entities are interdependent but not completely dependent upon each other), something, as I shall show, is illustrated perfectly in the figures of the Cardinal and his Bible in John Webster's *The Duchess of Malfi*. The Cardinal's overpowering, poisonous character—he would be "able to possess the greatest devil, and make him worse"[5]—is both altered by his (mis)reading of the Bible and other religious texts (see 5.5.1–10), as well as being able to infect the book itself, allowing it to literally become poisonous, thereby killing Julia. In the play, the use of the book as murder weapon demonstrates how the boundary between book and body (of the reader) become blurred as both the permeability of the page and of the body is emphasized throughout the play.[6]

Here, it's useful to consider the way the many meanings the term "body" describe or comprehend these blurred boundaries. From "the physical form of a person, animal, or plant" to "the main portion of a document or other text," as well as "more widely: a material thing, an object; something that has physical existence and extension in space," the OED lists approximately a dozen definitions that are applicable to the interpretation of "body" in *The Duchess of Malfi*.[7] This permeability of both page and body serves in direct contrast to the repeated prison imagery set throughout the play. An example of the use of prison imagery can be found at

---

[3] Smith, "Embodying," 426.

[4] Smith, "Embodying," 431.

[5] All citations from *The Duchess of Malfi* come from the 1998 New Mermaids edition. John Webster, *The Duchess of Malfi*, ed. Elziabeth M. Brennan (London: A&C Black: 1998), 1.1.46–47.

[6] For further discussion of the body and embodied texts see Gail Weiss, "The Body as Narrative Horizon," in *Thinking the Limits of the Body*, ed. Jeffrey Jerome Cohen and Gail Weiss (Albany: SUNY Press, 2003), 23–35. And for additional discussion of posthuman hybrid relationships see Jeffrey Jerome Cohen's essay, "The Inhuman Circuit," in *Thinking the Limits of the Body*, ed. Jeffrey Jerome Cohen and Gail Weiss (Albany: SUNY Press, 2003), 167–86.

[7] "Body, n.," OED. See also Caroline Bynum, "Why All the Fuss about the Body? A Medievalist's Perspective," *Critical Inquiry* 22.1 (Autumn 1995): 1–33.

3.2.137–139, as the Duchess asks Ferdinand, "Why should only I, / Of all the other princes of the world / Be cas'd up, like a holy relic?" This quotation also serves as an example of the Duchess being conceived of as an object. The desire to "cas[e] up" demonstrates an attempt to prevent and stop up the leakiness of bodies and texts, but these attempts ultimately fail. Early modern skin, as described by Helkiah Crooke in *Mikrokosmographia* (1615), "serue[s] either for receyuing in or letting out, or *both* as neede shall require."[8] Bosola also speaks to the porousness of skin in act 4, noting that flesh is "fantastical puff-paste: our bodies are weaker than those paper prisons boys use to keep flies in: more contemptible; since ours is to preserve earth-worms: didst thou ever see a lark in a cage? such is the soul in the body."[9] Here, and elsewhere in the play, the body represents the capability of being both / and. The body can both take in and let out, be "weaker than those paper prisons" and serve as a more sturdy (bird) cage to entrap the soul — though just as with a bird cage there must be a door for the bird to get in / out, so too does death enable the soul's escape from the body. This both / and imagery occurs numerous times during the play and is also key to understanding the relationship between book and reader.[10]

---

8   Helkiah Crooke, *Mikrokosmographia* (1615), 71; emphasis added. For Crooke, reading also relies upon more than just sight: "a man cannot see to read vpon a booke that is layd vpon his eye; because there wantenth the meane the obiect and the instrument of sense" (72). Reading is a multi-sensory experience with both text and reader affecting the other. See also Joshua Calhoun's account of the palimpsested nature of paper, Calhoun, "The Word Made Flax: Cheap Bibles, Textual Corruption, and the Poetics of Paper," *PMLA* 126.2 (March 2011): 327–44.

9   Webster, *Duchess*, 4.2.125–128.

10 The hybrid nature of the book and body—where each is neither fully what it is supposed to be, fully text or fully human—is reflected in the animal / human imagery employed throughout the play. This quality of being "not quite" x or y is perhaps explained by Bruno Latour's insistence that the world is full of "quasi-objects" and "quasi-subjects." Bruno Latour, *We Have Never Been Modern*, trans. Catherine Porter (Cambridge: Harvard University Press, 1993). Additionally, animals are often depicted as better off than humans (for example, see 1.1.58–61). (Cf. Donne's "Confined Love.") Humans are also called by animal names; Ferdinand calls the Duchess's children "cubs" (4.1.33) and then "young wolves" (4.2.253). Perhaps most significantly Ferdinand is said to have "A very pestilent disease...lycanthropia" (5.2.4–5). Afflicted with the wolf-madness Ferdinand is representative of the (in)human relationship fostered between book and body. When the doctor announces that Ferdinand is afflicted with lycanthropia a direct connection

The Cardinal should be thought of not so much as a "man of the cloth" but as a "man of the book." His own moral corruption has affected his book. I find it particularly interesting that the Cardinal does not deliver poison through what might be considered the more traditional routes (in food, drink, or even poison on a blade).[11] In fact, I have yet to find another case of a book used as a murder weapon in a Renaissance drama. While the Cardinal's use of the book is ostensibly related to the nature of his profession, and therefore tied to his identity, it also marks the intimate relationship between reader and book. The reader (of the play)[12] is not aware of when the Cardinal has poisoned his book; instead, it appears that he simply speaks his desires into being:

> Yond's my ling'ring consumption:
> I am weary of her; and by any means
> Would be quite of—[13]

Julia's appearance interrupts the Cardinal's lines, and less than 50 lines later, Julia kisses the poisoned Bible; it is almost as if the blurred boundaries between reader and book here are such that the Cardinal's corruption, a corruption that Bosola describes in act 1,[14] seeps instantaneously over to his book.

After Julia has kissed the Bible, the Cardinal tells Julia

> Now you shall never utter it, thy curiosity
> Hath undone thee; thou'rt poison'd with that book.

---

is made to books when Pescara, not knowing what the term means, says, "I need a dictionary to't" (5.2.6).

11 For examples of each see Marlowe's *The Jew of Malta*, Shakespeare's *Hamlet*, and Middleton's *The Second Maiden's Tragedy*. There is also the additional common trope of a poisoned skull seen in such plays as Middleton's *Revengers Tragedy* and Massinger's *Duke of Milan*.

12 I use the word "reader" rather than "audience" because of the title page's insistence that this text is both "As it was Presented priuatly, at the Black-Friers; and publiquely at the Globe, By the Kings Maiesties Seruants" *and* "The perfect and exact Coppy, with diuerse things Printed, that the length of the Play would not beare in the Presentment."

13 Webster, *Duchess*, 5.2.225–27.

14 "Some fellows, they say, are possessed with the devil, / But this great fellow were able to possess the greatest / Devil, and make him worse" (1.1.45–7).

Because I knew thou couldst not keep my counsel,
I have bound thee to't by death.[15]

The Cardinal secures Julia's silence through the use of a corrupted text. The imagery the Cardinal uses also suggests that through his counsel his spoken words have become engraved upon Julia's body, binding her as a text to his book. However, much like ink from an annotation that bleeds through cheap paper, the Cardinal discovers that his words have seeped through and also imprinted upon Bosola, who has overheard his secret. More explicit cases of the body being written upon occur elsewhere in the play when the heart is described as a text to be read. As Ferdinand tells the Duchess to kiss a dead man's hand, he also commands her to "bury the print of it in your heart."[16] Here the hand is seen as a text that should be imprinted upon the texts already implicitly present in the heart, thereby creating layers of text.

As Julia kisses the book, the action can be likened to that of a wax seal being applied to a letter, preventing Julia from being able to "utter" anything. This connection might not seem as far-fetched as it initially appears when one considers that wax imagery is in fact abundant throughout the play—most often associated with the Duchess—and therefore ever-present in the reader's mind.[17] Aside from being malleable, and therefore easily molded and imprinted upon, wax imagery also recalls the use of wax tablets for writing, thereby making the human both an active and passive agent (both imprinting and being imprinted upon), as well as tying the human body to the text.[18] As was mentioned in the previous paragraph, the Cardinal's secret is not kept—Bosola overhears. So while Julia is effectively silenced in her death, she has, however, imprinted upon Bosola, further emphasizing the both/and, hybrid nature that exists between text and reader. Julia and Bosola embrace at 5.2.161–62 as Bosola

---

15 Webster, *Duchess*, 5.2.272–76.
16 4.1.46. Other examples of the heart as a text occur at 3.2.145–46 and 4.1.16–17. Additionally, in 1.2.379–80, the Duchess tells Antonio, "Being now my steward, here upon your lips / I sign your *Quietus est*."
17 For examples of wax imagery see act 4 scene 1, especially lines 62–63, and 110–11. See also Lynn Maxwell, "Wax Magic and *The Duchess of Malfi*," *Journal of Early Modern Cultural Studies* 14.3 (Summer 2014): 31–54.
18 For more on wax tablets see Peter Stallybrass, Roger Chartier, J. Franklin Mowery, and Heather Wolfe, "Hamlet's Tables and the Technologies of Writing in Renaissance England," *Shakespeare Quarterly* 55 (2004): 379–419.

tells Julia, "Come, come, I'll disarm you / And arm you thus." The idea that human touch has the potential to engrave upon another—imparting information and enacting change—is first seen when Bosola touches the dying Duchess. It is only after Bosola notes "She's [the Duchess's] warm"[19]—implying touch—that his motives switch from concern about repayment for his deeds to that of avenging the Duchess's death. Bosola asks "where were / These penitent fountains while she was living? / Oh, they were frozen up."[20] This can be viewed as the inverse of Julia's lips being sealed—if the Duchess is often thought of as a wax figure, then here, the interaction between Bosola and the Duchess melts her wax figure—enabling Bosola to enter into the textual body of the Duchess.

The death of Julia by book also figures as a manifestation of the relationship we see between books and readers throughout the play. Act 3 contains several instances of this relationship as detrimental, sometimes even dangerous.[21] Count Malateste's dependence upon books as his only source of knowledge leads to him being described as only *seeming* like a soldier:

> DELIO: He hath read all the late service,
> As the City chronicle relates it,
> And keeps painters going, only to express
> Battles in model.
> SILVIO: Then he'll fight by the book.
> DELIO: By the almanac, I think.[22]

Delio's clarification that Malateste will fight by the almanac rather than the book is an important one. Almanacs were second in popularity only to the Bible in terms of books that early modern people would have

---

19 Webster, *Duchess*, 4.2.337.
20 Webster, *Duchess*, 4.2.358–360.
21 Shortly after the reader learns of Malateste's dependence upon books, Delio describes Bosola as a "fantastical scholar" (3.3.40) who "hath studied himself half blear-ey'd" (3.3.43–44). Bosola only demonstrates the possibility of the proper relationship between reader and text when he is imprinted upon by the Duchess (4.2). In act 5, the Cardinal also implicitly connects bad fortune with books: "the Prince set up late *at's book*" and was "altr'd much in face / And language" after seeing a figure (5.2.93, 96–97) (emphasis added).
22 Webster, *Duchess*, 3.3.17–21.

owned;²³ they also were normally sold alongside writing utensils. These writing tools, as well as the "blanks," or inserted pages, that were included in almanacs, implicitly encouraged writing on the owner's part. Malateste's explicit connection to almanacs rather than books generally puts him in the position of reader *as* text—he becomes "A marginal note in the muster book."²⁴

The "thingliness" generated by the act of reading—transforming objects into quasi-humans and humans into quasi-objects—is also represented by the large number of transformations the reader witnesses throughout the play. As Martha Lifson notes, "dramatic metamorphosis has been prepared for throughout the play, as things keep forming, deforming, reforming in rapid succession…the Cardinal turns soldier, the steward turns husband, a wife turns whore, a baby grows instantaneously, i.e., in stage time to a boy, [and] the Duchess turns grey overnight."²⁵ The act of reading creates a fluidity between book and reader—one where the topsy-turvy nature of the play helps to emphasize that book and reader can't be separated. I would also argue that it is the Cardinal's moral corruption and therefore corrupt relationship with his book that affects and brings about these bodily changes in the other characters.²⁶

In a play that is heavily aware of its theatricality, the playtext is also aware of its nature as a material text. The play is the first published English play to contain a cast list,²⁷ but most importantly it also contains marked *sententiae* throughout the play through the use of quotation marks or italics.²⁸ My point in listing all these details is to emphasize the material nature of the printed book, which also serves to demonstrate how the page tries to exert authority over the reader. The play includes 16 marked *sententiae*, with the highest number of sayings spoken by Bosola (a total of 4 instances, amounting to 25%). Even though "Q1 was published

---

23 Esutace F. Bosanquet, "English Seventeenth Century Almanacks," *The Library* 10.4 (1930): 371.
24 Webster, *Duchess*, 3.3.10-11.
25 Martha Ronk Lifson, "Embodied Morality in 'The Duchess of Malfi,'" *Pacific Coast Philology* 23.1-2 (Nov. 1988): 54.
26 The idea of a ripple-like effect—one person's actions spreading out and affecting everyone else's—is brought up in the opening lines of the play as Antonio likens "a Prince's court" to that of "a common fountain." See 1.1.11-15.
27 Elizabeth M. Brennan, ed., *The Duchess of Malfi* (London: A&C Black, 1998), 2.
28 Brennan, ed., *Duchess*, xl.

with the reader rather than the actor in mind,"²⁹ the playtext attempts to restrict the act of reading for its audience with its pre-marked phrases (perhaps in the same misguided fashion as the Cardinal's attempts to keep his secret by killing Julia). This does not account for the reader's effect on the text. At the end of the play Delio speaks of the misguided nature of the Cardinal, Bosola, and Ferdinand:

> These wretched eminent things
> Leave no more fame behind 'em, than should one
> Fall in frost, and leave his print in snow,
> As soon as the sun shines, it ever melts
> Both form and matter.³⁰

This suggests that the characters' corrupted nature negatively affected the text's ability to influence the reader. The page again attempts to exert its authority over the reader as the last two lines of the play (spoken by Delio) are also marked as sententiae.³¹

And yet, as is fitting with a play that highlights the both/and of the body, there is also a hopeful quality to the ending of the play, one that I prefer over the negative outlook that argues for the futility of the characters' actions in a chaotic world.³² Delio's final words again remind the reader of the use of wax tablets for writing and the ease with which content can be erased—like one who "leave[s] his print in snow,/As soon as the sun shines, it ever melts,/Both form and matter." The text, with its final two lines marked as sententiae, looks to the reader for recuperation—it does not place its hope in the world of the play. The characters the reader has been confronted with are just that—characters. Over and over again the reader is given a description by one character of another, coupled with repeated moments that highlight the play's metatheatricality. The potential for starting over lies with the reader. Here then, the play's many connections between reading and poisonous behavior merely serve

---

29 Ibid., xl.
30 Webster, *Duchess*, 5.5.112–116.
31 "Integrity of life is fame's best friend, / Which nobly, beyond death, shall crown the end" (5.5.119–20).
32 For further discussion of the different interpretations of the final passages of the play see Elizabeth M. Brennan, ed., *The Duchess of Malfi* (London: A&C Black, 1998), 136–37.

as a warning—they are not condemnations of the hybrid relationship between book and reader.

The knowledge that this is a corrupt world is something that the reader is confronted with from the beginning as Antonio states that

> a Prince's court
> Is like a common fountain, whence should flow
> Pure silver-drops in general. But if't chance
> Some curs'd example poison't near the head,
> *Death and diseases through the whole land spread.*[33]

These lines also appropriately contain the play's first marked sententiae. Several lines later Bosola, describes the Cardinal by saying, "Some fellows, they say, are possessed with the devil, but this great fellow were able to posses the greatest devil, and make him worse."[34] Antonio then describes Ferdinand as having "a most perverse and turbulent nature."[35] From the start, the reader understands that this is a corrupt world. But the bookending of the play with sententiae emphasizes not only the material object of the book, but also the importance of the reader in relation to the playtext. The reader is called on to commonplace selections from the text—to interact with and make the (new) text the reader's own. It is in this action—of commonplacing—that the relationship between book and reader can begin again.

---

33 Webster, *Duchess*, 1.1.11–15.
34 Webster, *Duchess*, 1.1.45–47.
35 Webster, *Duchess*, 1.2.91.

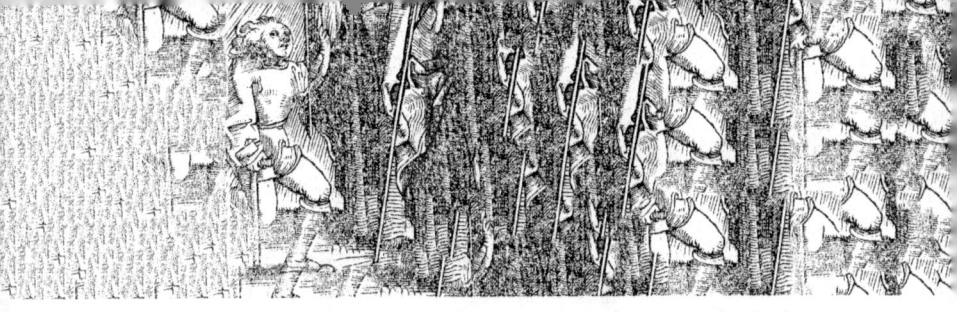

Crutches and Cripistemology in *The Fair Maid of the Exchange*

Lindsey Row-Heyveld

THE CRIPPLE, THE CENTRAL CHARACTER OF THE ANONYMOUS 1607 CITY comedy *The Fair Maid of the Exchange*, describes the onset of his disability as "the visitation of my legges, and my expence in timber."[1] His statement frames this experience in both enlivened and economic terms. "Visitation," defined as affliction with illness or trouble, was usually accompanied by the subject performing that action, for instance, "the visitation of the Lord" or "the visitation of death."[2] In this case, however, his phrase suggests that the legs themselves enacted the visitation. "Expence in timber" describes his adoption of crutches as an investment in the high-stakes early modern timber market.[3] The Cripple's merging of agential objects and commercial objects exemplifies a union that occurs throughout the play. In exploring the liveliness of things in the commercial environment of the play, I suggest that this text carefully attends to their vitality, while the play's characters are primarily attentive only to their financial power. The exception is the Cripple, who seems occasionally capable of seeing both their value and vitality. Considering how and why he possesses such a capability illuminates the ethical limits and

---

My thanks to Allison Hobgood of Willamette University and especially to Andy Hageman, my colleague at Luther College, for their invaluable help thinking through these issues and this text.

1 Anonymous, *The Fair Maid of the Exchange*, ed. Peter H. Davidson (Oxford: Malone Society Reprints, 1962), 677. All subsequent quotations from this text appear parenthetically by line number.
2 "Visitation, *n*., 6–8," OED.
3 For more on the roles of wood in early modern theater, see Vin Nardizzi's *Wooden Os: Shakespeare's Theaters and England's Trees* (Toronto: University of Toronto Press, 2013).

potential of object-oriented theory, specifically as it relates to prosthesis and disability.

The crutches stand (or lean?) at the center of the plot of *The Fair Maid of the Exchange*. With the assistance of his crutches, the Cripple maintains a successful business as a drawer of textile designs, running a shop in London's Royal Exchange.[4] Wielding one of his crutches as a weapon, he stops the attempted rape of two of the Exchange's shopgirls, and his courageous actions win him the devotion of one of them, Phillis Flower. However, the attackers return, steal his crutches out from underneath him, and the Cripple finds himself in need of rescuing alongside the women. Luckily a passing young gentleman, Frank Golding, saves all three of them and falls in love with Phillis in the process. The Cripple is clearly uncomfortable with the debt of gratitude he feels he owes Frank for saving his life, and the majority of the plot focuses on his efforts to restore equilibrium to their relationship. With Frank in love with Phillis, Phillis in love with the Cripple, and the Cripple indebted to Frank, the Cripple devises an ingenious (albeit improbable) solution to everyone's problems: he lends Frank his crutches and helps him win Phillis's affections while disguised as the Cripple himself.

The Cripple's crutches become especially active—even agential—in the scenes where Frank pretends to be the Cripple. The crutches enact the imitation of the Cripple more than Frank does. *Fair Maid* contains a range of evidence attesting to Frank's generally shoddy performance skills. He is usually a rather half-hearted actor (particularly in his disguise as a porter named "Trusty John" earlier in the play) whose success depends on his careful supervision by the Cripple and/or the general gullibility of his audiences. While the Cripple proves a talented stage-manager elsewhere in the play, when it comes to Frank's crucial performance as the Cripple himself, he remains surprisingly hands-off. Given all these factors, Frank's impersonation shouldn't work, but instead it is a resounding success.

And this success rests entirely on the crutches.

In the many references made to these crutches before Frank's performance, characters speak of them directly ("Snatch away his crutches,"

---

4   The only shops in the Royal Exchange were located on the building's second floor, the "Pawn"; the play confirms this (1265). This means that the Cripple's shop and the play itself are set in a uniquely inaccessible location for someone with a mobility impairment.

119); the Cripple swears by them ("By this crutch but I will," 726); other characters even synecdochically call the Cripple "crutch" ("Come crutch, thou shalt with us," 719.) But after Frank's performance as the Cripple, the crutches are not named again in the play. The absence of their name corresponds to their increase in agency; at this point in the play, attention turns from the crutches themselves to what the crutches *do* and specifically what they *make*: a new body for Frank. Anyone who has experience with crutches will tell you that, for all that people control crutches, crutches also manipulate people. They dig into your armpits, hunch your shoulders, curve your upper body forward, and reorder your gait. Early modern crutches, which employed the traditional T-shape model, had no built-in handholds like the Y-shape model in use today, and so twisted the arms of their users around their central shaft. Crutches are demanding, and their ability to evoke a response from a human body—even to create a new human body out of an old one—demonstrates their vitality. This is evidenced in the text. No costume change seems to mark the beginning of the performance (although it seems reasonable to assume one occurs). Instead the crutches are the primary component of Frank's disguise.[5] Even so, the crutches are rarely named directly; instead, once animate, they are defined by their activity/creation. Over and over, Frank's disguise is described as a "shape": "Assume this shape of mine," (1966); "Now to employ the virtue of my shape" (2043); "Give me leave / To come and court hir in my borrowed shape" (2394).[6] Although Frank may "assume" the shape, it would be impossible for him to fully make it without the force of the crutches reforming his body into a new configuration. The "shape" that they create becomes the focus of these scenes, and they remain active throughout the rest of the play. Not only do they form Frank's body, they shape the Cripple, too; they assault would-be rapists;

---

5 The crutches' ability to signal the Cripple's whole identity hints at how entirely they have become a projection of the Cripple's body. Elaine Scarry details the phenomenon of projected materialization of the human body and how that materialized objectification extends the powers of sentience, concluding that, "It is not objects but human beings who require champions." *The Body in Pain: The Making and Unmaking of the World* (New York: Oxford University Press), 305.

6 "Shape" could refer to costume or stage dress exclusively, but it was more frequently used during the early modern period to describe material form, specifically the form and contours of the body. See "Shape, *n.*, 1," OED. The play itself conflates the two meanings of the word earlier when a gentleman attempts to proposition a shop girl by asking to "weare / This shape of thine, although I buy it deere" (1236).

they straighten and measure cloth; they create accessibility in the inaccessible world of early modern London.

For me, the crutches also call out to a constellation of similarly vital objects that populate the play. Handkerchiefs send detailed messages; a cache of letters confers social capital and defers unwanted suitors; a counterfeit diamond punishes a villain; and all these examples are in addition to items continuously in action as a result of the play's setting in a proto-shopping mall.[7] But while the play itself seems to acknowledge the power of objects, the play's characters seem only aware of their financial value. Both the Cripple and Frank imagine the crutches in terms of economic worth: as discussed before, the Cripple does so by describing them as "my expence in timber" (677). Frank offers to improve on that investment when he hyperbolically promises to "make thee chrutches of pure silver" in order to repay the Cripple for his scheming (1537), an offer that underscores his exclusively financial focus since solid silver crutches would be economically valuable but worthless as mobility aids. If other characters in the play see objects as active at all, they regard that animation as a product of commerce and not something intrinsic to the objects.

Certainly these objects have commercial power and are animated by forces of the market. In many ways this play offers a model of nascent commodity fetishism, with the lively crutches, handkerchiefs, letters, and diamonds serving as early modern counterparts to Marx's dancing table, the ordinary object transformed into an animated thing that "stands on its head, and evolves out of its wooden brain grotesque ideas" as a result of "step[ping] forth as a commodity" into the enlivening marketplace.[8] In fact, Juana Green and Jean Howard have both commented on the play's obsessive attention to human relationships (and humans themselves) transformed into objects by market exchange.[9] The characters and the

---

7   For a sense of the range of objects that may have been included in stage properties for *Fair Maid*, see Kay Staniland's assessment of the inventory of real haberdasher in London's Royal Exchange in 1572, "Thomas Deane's Shop in the Royal Exchange," in *The Royal Exchange*, ed. Ann Saunders (London: London Topographical Society, 1997), 59–67. For more on the uses and value of textiles, especially handkerchiefs, in this play, see Juana Green, "The Sempster's Wares: Merchandising and Marrying in *The Fair Maid of the Exchange*," *Renaissance Quarterly* 53 (2000): 1084–118.

8   Karl Marx, *Capital, Vol. 1*, in *The Marx-Engels Reader*, ed. Robert C. Tucker, 2nd ed. (New York: Norton, 1978), 320.

9   Juana Green and Jean Howard, *Theater of a City: The Places of London Comedy, 1598–1642* (Philadelphia: University of Pennsylvania Press, 2009).

critics are not wrong: such readings are important, even necessary, to understanding this play. But what if commodity fetishism isn't the only thing animating these objects?[10] Can they be seen as more than just dancing tables? Uniquely for a character in *Fair Maid*, the Cripple can, sometimes, extend his consciousness to see the vitality of objects while also remaining attentive to their commodity power. His first lines, for instance, are directed to his crutches: "Now you supporters of decrepite youth /... Be strong to beare that huge deformitie, / And be my hands nimble to direct them, / As your desires to waft me hence to London" (85-89). While clearly guided by his hands, he sees that the crutches also have "desires" of their own. This ability to imagine his way into the lives of things shows up elsewhere in the play, too: the Cripple reads an embroidered handkerchief, not just for the message its design was intended to send, but for its ability to send new messages of its own. He keeps a collection of papers because he understands their potential for reshaping intellectual identity. The Cripple seems especially attuned to the ways in which objects withdraw, receding from presence into an incomprehensible reality and distancing themselves from humans and all other things.[11] As I have mentioned, the crutches disappear from the text but they also withdraw from the Cripple. Frank never returns them at the end of the play; it seems that their intense usefulness causes them to fade out of presence. The Cripple's cache of papers is disseminated, also disappearing into use, as are the textiles to which he dedicates so much of his time. Even the other characters withdraw from him; in fact, the whole gambit with Phillis rests on his anticipation of her rejection. The Cripple seems to understand that the more one knows a thing, the less one can access it. When a customer asks him about a textile she has commissioned, the Cripple responds by saying, "I have beene mindefull of your work" (663-64). It seems that he has "beene mindefull" of objects in many ways. All of this is not to say that the Cripple isn't also deeply invested in his commercial work, nor do I think his attention to thing-power nullifies the commodity fetishism that he facilitates

---

10 This question seems especially important because of the way the constant valuation of objects in the play actually creates a devaluation of their vital potential, parallel to Jane Bennett's assessment of the way in which American materialism is actually antimateriality. Bennett, *Vibrant Matter: A Political Ecology of Things* (Durham: Duke University Press, 2010), 5.

11 Graham Harman, *Tool-Being: Heidegger and the Metaphysics of Objects* (Chicago: Open Court, 2002), 126-27.

and exhibits. Instead, his epistemological privilege allows him to see how tightly sutured are the commercial and the vital, evidenced especially by the inseparability of "visitation of my legges" and "my expence in timber."

What makes the Cripple capable of such insight? The text does not offer a direct explanation for his ability to engage with objects this way, but I would like to suggest one possibility: his legs. The Cripple is unique among other crutch-users in early modern drama in that he retains his legs. The majority of other early modern characters with mobility impairments, including Stump in the anonymous *A Larum for London* (1602) and Rafe in Thomas Dekker's *The Shoemaker's Holiday* (1600), are amputees. With stage amputees, focus is placed on the dexterousness of their abbreviated bodies, showcasing how they can still fight battles, perform productive labor, woo women, etc. However, characters in *Fair Maid* seem weirdly fixated on the absent presence of the Cripple's legs, regularly commenting on their non-functionality and drawing particular attention to the way they operate as an assemblage with his crutches. This is especially evident in the instances where characters describe the Cripple as "four-legged" (97, 819). Identifying his crutches as legs themselves attests to their vitality, since it grants them an agency equal to the Cripple's body, but calling him "four-legged" also highlights way the Cripple's legs are equated with the crutches, granting his body a pointedly material quality.[12] Like Heidegger's broken tool, his legs reveal themselves as things through their disability, drawing attention to themselves as objects.[13] Disability theorists also frequently describe this material conspicuousness, noting the way in which physical functionality equals invisibility/inattention equals social capital and privilege. Yet Rosemarie Garland-Thomson has also identified the way in which this lack of "material anonymity" for people with disabilities creates a unique awareness of the material world and the way in which its normalized functionality (its Heideggerian *Zuhandenheit*) are revealed — and specifically, revealed to be provisional and temporary. She says, "When we fit harmoniously and properly into the world, we forget the truth of contingency because the world sustains us.... So whereas the benefit of fitting is material and visual anonymity, the cost of fitting is

---

12 It also suggests an animalistic component to the Cripple's leg-crutch assemblage, further reinforced by the slurs "cur" and "dog" frequently leveled at him by the braggart Bowdler.

13 Martin Heidegger, *Being and Time*, trans. Joan Stambaugh (Albany: State University of New York Press, 1996), 67–71.

perhaps complacency about social justice and a desensitizing to material experience."[14] The misfitting of the Cripple's legs within the world of early modern London certainly makes him more obviously an object than his nondisabled counterparts, but foregrounding that object-ness may account for his attentiveness to material experience and to the experience of material as well. Merri Lisa Johnson and Robert McRuer term this misfit knowledge "cripistemology," a type of "thinking from the critical, social, and personal position of disability" that also "explore[s] disability at the places where bodily edges and categorical distinctions blur or dissolve (where the disabled body as literal referent is, if not dematerialized, then differently materialized.)"[15] The Cripple's awareness of agential objects emerging from his embodied experience of disability provides an early modern example of cripistemology.[16]

But attending to the Cripple's cripistemlogy means seeing the limits of focusing on his conspicuous materiality as well as the potential of that focus. As Steven L. Kurzman so effectively argues, when discussing the vitality of objects, especially prostheses, wholeness or brokenness often tends to be constituted in visible and objective terms. The broken tool (or tool-being) is identified as broken because an outside observer notices it to be broken, but the broken tool-being may not perceive of itself that way.[17] Frequently relying on (and therefore affirming) a naturalized and stereotypical notion of wholeness, especially corporeal wholeness, prevents the extension of human imagination into the lives of objects, and

---

14 Garland-Thomson, "Misfits: A Feminist, Materialist Disability Concept," *Hypatia* 26.3 (Summer 2011): 597.

15 Johnson and McRuer, "Cripistemologies: Introduction," *Journal of Literary & Cultural Disability Studies* 8.2 (July 2014): 134.

16 McRuer's work on queerness and disability also suggests that the Cripple may be attentive to desires beyond those of his crutches. As in McRuer's theorization of queer/crip intersections, the Cripple is both barred from sexual desire in that he cannot or does not engage in a romantic relationship with Phillis but remains the object of perverse—in this case voracious—sexual desire, as he reports that he is "hourly solicited" by women in his shop (888). For more on the crip/queer sex and sex objects, see McRuer, *Crip Theory: Cultural Signs of Queerness and Disability* (New York: New York University Press, 2006); for more on the Cripple's complicated sexual positioning and the erotics of early modern disability, see Lindsey Row-Heyveld, "Disability and Masculine Commerce in *The Fair Maid of the Exchange*," *Allegorica* 29 (2013): 88–105.

17 Kurzman, "Presence and Prosthesis: A Response to Nelson and Wright," *Cultural Anthropology* 16.3 (2001): 380–81.

yet when the "broken tool" is a person, paradoxically, the reliance on naturalized wholeness tends to privilege the agency of the prosthetic over that of the human using prosthetic technology. Vivian Sobchack similarly pushes back against the theorized prosthetic with her material prosthesis. She states that her desired relationship with her prosthetic left leg is one of "transparency," wherein it is not regarded as an object but seamlessly incorporated "not 'into' or 'on' but 'as' the subject."[18] However, Sobchack specifies that this "desired transparency, however, involves my incorporation of the prosthetic—not the prosthetic's incorporation of me (although, seen by others to whom a prosthetic is strange, I may well seem its extension rather than the other way around.)"[19] Sobchack and Kurzman both circumscribe the limits of matter's vitality even as they defend the vital matter of their own materiality. In discussing their cripistemoplogical stances, both are careful not to overvalue personal anecdote or privilege autobiographical over discursive experience, but seek to reground discussions of prosthesis in "a more embodied 'sense-ability.'"[20] I suggest that we should do the same with the Cripple and with other disabled characters. While his awareness of his own body as a thing may open the Cripple's understanding to other lively objects, it may also reveal to him the intertia of those objects. If we are to consider his attentiveness to his uniquely animated crutches, we must also consider what it is for his material self to maneuver on those crutches through the irregular streets of early modern London, to haul them up the stairs to the Pawn of the Royal Exchange, to negotiate his kiosk-sized shop packed with textiles and customers while balancing on them. How does he feel—materially—about the way they shape him: exhilarated, exhausted, indifferent, frustrated, thrilled? When he uses his crutches as a weapon, does he feel the impact ringing through his fingers? When they're stolen away from him, does it hurt when he falls?

Theorizing the prosthetic, and considering the vitality of objects more generally, has the potential to reveal the Cripple's crutches at the expense

---

18 Sobchack, "A Leg to Stand On: Prosthetics, Metaphor, and Materiality," in *The Prosthetic Impulse: From a Posthuman Present to a Biocultural Future*, ed. Marquard Smith and Joanne Morra (Cambridge: MIT Press, 2006), 22.

19 Sobchack, "Beating the Meat/Surviving the Text, or How to Get Out of this Century Alive," *Body and Society* 1.3-4 (1995): 210.

20 Sobchack, "A Leg to Stand On," 18–19. The tension between identarian knowledge and other more theoretical modes of knowing is also central to McRuer and Johnson, "Introduction" and its accompanying roundtable.

of obscuring the Cripple. However, extending that same material attention to the Cripple himself, orienting ourselves to his object-ness, also has the potential to create the "sense-ability" Sobchack calls for, to meet the ethical demands of disability studies, and, possibly, to demonstrate the political consequences object-oriented ontology is often accused of eliding. Focusing primarily on the agency of the crutches can limit understandings of the Cripple's material reality, but paying attention to the Cripple's full cripistemology not only reveals his material and epistemological experience, but also that of the crutches as well, since his unique "bodymind" (to borrow a term from Babette Rothschild via Margaret Price) is the very thing that makes the vitality of the crutches visible.[21] At the end of *The Fair Maid of the Exchange*, the Cripple recedes from the text. In spite of the central role he occupies throughout the play, other characters carry out all the action of the final moments and he remains strangely silent. It is possible that his extreme functionality as an object in the environment of the play allows him to disappear into the communal assemblage he has crafted in these final moments. It is possible that he is just worn out by all the unacknowledged work he has done and, since his one-time friend Frank will not return his crutches, he has nowhere to go and nothing else to say. Or it is possible that he stands/leans there thrumming with silent satisfaction at what he has made. The Cripple and his crutches both fade in the final scene; however attending to their cripistemology revives them.

---

21 Robert McRuer and Merri Lisa Johnson, "Proliferating Cripistemologies: A Virtual Roundtable," *Journal of Literary & Cultural Disability Studies* 8.2 (July 2014): 153.

Imagining Early Modern Wish-Lists and Their Environs
Debapriya Sarkar

WHAT WAS AN EARLY MODERN WISH-LIST? WAS IT AN OBJECT OF INQUIRY, an instrument of the imagination, or one of cognition? Why did these catalogues (incomplete in form, and projective by nature) fascinate early modern writers? I begin with these questions to explore the status of the wish-list as a "thing" that enabled thinkers to curate new ways of interacting with their environs, both real and imagined.[1] Wish-lists became instruments through which writers attempted to make intelligible a world that was fundamentally in flux, one in which new geographies were being discovered through travels and a new cosmology was displacing both earth and man from the center of the universe. In this environment of uncertainty, the wish-list propelled naturalists and travelers to search for non-existent objects and propose new epistemological systems.

These lists took multiple forms, from the *desiderata* of speculative knowledge and epistemic systems, to the *optativa* of operative knowledge and specific objects, to query lists (which directed investigation and provided methodical instruction for travelers).[2] In her contribution to a recent *Isis* volume on list-making, Vera Keller differentiates empirical lists, *optativa*, and projected lists based on their stated aims and the temporalities conjured by each. The *desiderata* (which demanded long-term collaborative projects) were the most ambitious of such lists, since they

---

1   I draw on the definitions of "thing" as developed, among others, by Bill Brown, "Thing Theory," *Critical Inquiry* 28.1 (2001): 1–22; Ken Adler, "Thick Things," *Isis* 98 (2007): 80–83; Bruno Latour, "Can We Get Our Materialism Back, Please?" *Isis* 98 (2007): 138–42.

2   Vera Keller, "The 'New World of Sciences': The Temporality of the Research Agenda and the Unending Ambitions of Science," *Isis* 103.4 (2012): 727–34.

"surpassed the abilities and lifetimes of individuals."³ Guido Pancirolli's *Two Books of Things Lost and Things Found* (1599, 1602), an extremely popular work that set the research agenda for many early modern philosophers, offers one example of how *desiderata* could project futures by appealing to pasts. As Keller describes elsewhere, Pancirolli's work influenced writers as diverse as Francis Bacon and John Donne.⁴ While Keller distinguishes among different wish-lists, Justin Stagl's combination of various kinds of epistemic catalogs under a broader category of *interrogatoria* implies that the boundaries were more fluid than the terminology might suggest.⁵ Even the differences Keller marks in Bacon's writing between "*desiderata* as missing pieces of learning" and "*optativa* as wished-for-things" become unstable when we explore how individual things in the list constitute Bacon's *Instauratio Magna*.⁶ Wish-lists, most broadly, propelled readers to undertake new projects and expand the scope of the conceivable.

Historians of science have demonstrated how the wish-list enables us to examine research proposals that linked the past to the future. But as Bacon's "Catalogue of Particular Histories by Titles" (which concludes the *New Organon* and the *Preparative toward Natural and Experimental History* [1620]) intimates, it also facilitates interactions between fact and imagination.⁷ In the "Catalogue," readers encounter a concrete list: 130 experiments and observations to be performed, limited to categories of generations, pretergenerations, and arts. The entries range from histories of the cosmos, planets, and astronomical bodies to histories of gems, stones, and non-human beings, to studies of human bodies and motions, medicines, mechanical arts, and mathematics. Yet this list immediately invites projections into the actual world and into the future, converting what we might think is a query list of discoverable objects or particular

---

3   Keller, "'New World of Sciences,'" 729.
4   Vera Keller, "Accounting for Invention: Guido Pancirolli's Lost and Found Things and the Development of *Desiderata*," *Journal of the History of Ideas* 73.2 (2012), 228, n.21.
5   Justin Stagl, *A History of Curiosity: The Theory of Travel, 1500–1800* (Chur: Harwood Academic Publishers, 1995).
6   Keller, "Accounting for Invention," 237. The *Instauratio Magna* is Bacon's unfinished six-part project that aimed to restore learning and reorganize the sciences.
7   The *New Organon* is the second part of the *Instauratio Magna*. The *Preparative* was supposed to be the third part.

"optatives" into ambitious *desiderata* that demand the production of entire knowledge-systems.

The projective nature of Bacon's catalogue also invites us to consider whether any list could express, or even generate, wishes. James Delbourgo and Staffan Müller-Wille gesture to the plausibility of such a claim, when they characterize the list as an "attempt to give finite expression to potentially limitless series of things."[8] Exploring literary lists, Robert E. Belknap too marks the "generative capacity" of lists: "because it can be considered shapeless it has the capacity to spark endless connections and inclusions in a multiplicity of forms."[9] Umberto Eco, focusing on European art, argues that the list enacts a "poetics of the 'etcetera,'" an infinite "enumeration" that "may never stop."[10] And Ian Bogost develops the concept of "Latour litanies": lacking a distinct logic, the numerous lists that Bruno Latour presents in his work "functio[n] primarily as provocations."[11] To demonstrate the scope of these lists as well as the "diversity of things" they capture, Bogost creates a "Latour Litanizer," a tool that randomly generates litanies by drawing on entries from Wikipedia.[12]

What Eco terms "etcetera," Bogost calls "provocations," and Belknap characterizes as "expandability,"[13] I argue, captures the condition of Baconian lists. They "conclude" the *New Organon*, but the ideas contained in them expand to other works including the catalogue of experiments in *Sylva Sylvarum* and the list (the "Magnalia Naturae") punctuating the *New Atlantis*. The "Catalogue" generates a model of the natural world by recording particulars through natural history and induction: it extends into nature as Baconian method invites naturalists to fulfill the author's desire for complete knowledge. But at its most expansive, the Baconian list *suggests* an "etcetera" which can range from nature to the no-place that is utopia. Despite Bacon's continual attempts to limit the role of the

---

8   James Delbourgo and Staffan Müller-Wille, "Introduction to Focus: 'Listmania,'" *Isis* 103.4 (2012), 710.
9   Robert E. Belknap, *The List: The Uses and Pleasures of Cataloguing* (New Haven: Yale University Press, 2004), 1–2.
10 Umberto Eco, *The Infinity of Lists*, trans. Alastair McEwan (New York: Rizzoli, 2009), 15.
11 Ian Bogost, *Alien Phenomenology, or, What It's Like to Be a Thing* (Minneapolis: University of Minnesota Press, 2012), 38.
12 Ian Bogost, "Latour Litanizer," *Ian Bogost*, accessed February 19, 2015, http://bogost.com/writing/blog/latour_litanizer/.
13 Belknap, *The List*, 31.

imagination in natural inquiry, his lists become instruments of speculation about a world that might be fully knowable.

As the "Catalogue" prescribes the collection of natural history (which begins with the aid of "factors and merchants [who] go everywhere in search of [the materials on which the intellect has to work]" [xx]),[14] it captures tensions between this condensed form and the expansive desires for knowledge contained within it. The list includes 130 diverse entries, including "History of the Heavenly Bodies; or Astronomical History," "History of Air as a whole, or in the Configuration of the World," "History of Flame and of things Ignited," "History of Fossils; as Vitriol, Sulphur, etc.," "History of the Generation of Man," "History of Life and Death," "History of Basket-making," "History of Gardening," and categories under "*Pure Mathematics*" (285–91). The work promises that a collective of laborers can record facts; the list immediately suggests a query list of objects to be found in the world if one methodically follows instructions of inquiry. But items in the catalogue are already beyond the capacities of Bacon's proposed collaborators, the "factors and merchants." What does it mean to provide a history of "Life and Death," or an "observation" of mathematics (288, 291)? Are these discoverable in the same way as a gem, or a new star? These entries demonstrate how a list enumerates what exceeds its grasp, while other items, such as the two examples of mathematical observations—"Power of Numbers" and "Power of Figures"—offer only an inadequate "catalogue" of the complex signification of mathematics in this period. The list registers a realm of possibility even as it exposes a desire for what does not, and perhaps may not, exist.

Hovering between the empirical and the thinkable, Bacon's list-making participates in a rich culture of collecting and cataloguing. Different catalogues (including inventories, recipe or receipt books, and *Wunderkammern*) mediated between objects and environments through logics of incompletion. Recipes were instruments of household remedy and practical knowledge, and they listed ingredients alongside prescribed instructions. Popular books of recipes such as the *Secrets of Alexis of Piedmont* contained lists of strange objects (including "wild boar's teeth, skin of a dog, 'dung of a blacke Asse, if you can get it; if not, let it be of a white

---

14 Francis Bacon, *The New Organon and Related Writings*, ed. Fulton H. Anderson (New Jersey: Prentice Hall, 1960).

Asse'").[15] Yet until these objects were combined with stated instructions, the recipe did not fulfill its role as "a prescription for an experiment, a 'trying out.'"[16] As William Eamon argues, a "recipe's 'completion' is the trial itself."[17] But lists could suggest absences without prescribing activity; incomplete catalogues would invoke different kinds of environments, from the mundane to the extraordinary. At one end of this spectrum lies a catalogue like the inventory, which listed personal items of the deceased. Although such inventories of "objects to answer debts" are usually read as objective catalogues of early modern households, these were treacherous documents. As Lena Cowen Orlin demonstrates, inventories were partial and misleading, and they did not provide accurate pictures of domestic or public spaces.[18] At the other end lies the "peculiarly Renaissance phenomena" of the *Wunderkammer*—collections of marvels proliferating among the wealthy at the turn of the seventeenth century—which promised glimpses of strange locations and cultures.[19] The singular contents of the *Wunderkammer* paradoxically became "'everyday' emblems of cultural formations that are at one and the same time different from that of England."[20]

These imperfect catalogues are united by an emphasis on the accessibility of objects: an ingredient required in a recipe, a household item to address a debt, a wonder to represent a culture. The wish-list, however, catalogs absent, potential, and non-existent entities. Its contents might exist, but their presence *in* the list rehearses absence. Wish-lists, we could argue, document *potential* rather than *actual* modes of being.[21] And it is this logic of potentiality that places Bacon's catalogue not only alongside

---

15 Quoted in William Eamon, *Science and the Secrets of Nature: Books of Secrets in Medieval and Early Modern Culture* (Princeton: Princeton University Press, 1994), 144.
16 Eamon, *Science and the Secrets of Nature*, 131.
17 Eamon, *Science and the Secrets of Nature*, 131.
18 Lena Cowen Orlin, "Things with Little Social Life (Henslowe's Theatrical Properties and Elizabethan Household Fittings)," in *Staged Properties in Early Modern English Drama*, eds. Jonathan Gil Harris and Natasha Korda (Cambridge: Cambridge University Press, 2002), 102.
19 Jonathan Gil Harris, "The New New Historicism's Wunderkammer of Objects," *European Journal of English Studies* 4.2 (2000): 115.
20 Harris, "The New New Historicism's Wunderkammer of Objects," 116.
21 I draw on Giorgio Agamben, "On Potentiality," in *Potentialities: Collected Essays in Philosophy*, ed. Daniel Heller-Roazen (Stanford: Stanford University Press, 1999),

lists produced by naturalists, but also beside those created by poets and dramatists. As Sir Philip Sidney famously claims in *The Defence of Poetry*, *poesie* dealt with the "may be and should be" rather than the "bare was" of history.[22] Documenting objects and systems that "may be and should be," wish-lists seem to enact a crucial aim of *poesie*: they imagine ontological crossings from the "brazen" world of nature to unverifiable "golden" worlds.[23] While the wish-lists of *poesie* deviate in structure from the *desiderata* of natural philosophy, they echo similar desires to expand the limits of the thinkable. In the rest of the essay, I follow the invitations implicit in several literary wish-lists to ask what kinds of "golden" worlds they conjure and comment on.

Responding to Polixenes's claims in *The Winter's Tale* that there "is an art/Which does mend nature" (4.4.95–96), Perdita defends nature over art, offering him flowers appropriate to the season and his age ("Here's flowers for you:/Hot lavender, mints, savory, marjoram,/The marigold,...These are flowers/Of middle summer, and I think they are given/To men of middle age" (4.4.103–108).[24] Next, she launches into a wish-list for Florizel:

> my fair'st friend,
> I would I had some flowers o'th' spring that might
> Become your time of day; [*to* MOPSA *and* DORCAS] and yours,
>   and yours,
> That wear upon your virgin branches yet
> Your maidenheads growing: O Proserpina,
> For the flowers now, that frighted thou letst fall
> From Dis's wagon! — daffodils,
> That come before the swallow dares, and take
> The winds of March with beauty; violets, dim,
> But sweeter than the lids of Juno's eyes
> Or Cytherea's breath; pale primroses,

177–84. Agamben argues that actuality is not the teleological fulfillment or destruction of potentiality, but the full realization and exhaustion of impotentiality.

22 Sir Philip Sidney, *A Defence of Poetry*, ed. Jan Van Dorsten (Oxford: Oxford University Press, 1966), 23.
23 Sidney, *A Defence of Poetry*, 24.
24 William Shakespeare, *The Winter's Tale*, in *The Norton Shakespeare*, ed. Stephen Greenblatt et al. (New York: W.W. Norton, 2008).

That die unmarried, ere they can behold
Bright Phoebus in his strength—a malady
Most incident to maids; bold oxlips, and
The crown imperial; lilies of all kinds,
The flower-de-luce being one! O, these I lack,
To make you garlands of. (4.4.112–28)

Perdita begins by cataloging actual objects she disperses as gifts, but this list ends with the registration of "lack." It exists as a wish, captured by her words, "I would I had"; within this lies another wish, that she "might" "make [them] garlands." Predicting what she "would" accomplish if the objects were available, she leads her audience into the realm of the potential.[25] Although Perdita imagines the possibilities if these flowers became available, I want to draw out a different conclusion latent in her words: this wish-list rehearses an *impossibility*. If the "flowers o'th' spring" will only "Become [their] time of day" during that season, and if Perdita refuses artificial methods to make them untimely available, her wish expresses an unachievable promise, an act she can never perform.

This catalogue of entities, intimately linked to nature's changes, also gestures to broader issues haunting the play: Perdita, the "lost child" to "be found" (5.1.40), exists as the ultimate yet-unfulfilled wish of the family-romance narrative. As the play echoes the desires that animated natural philosophers to find lost objects (a desire perfectly captured by the title of Pancirolli's work), Perdita's catalogue invites audiences to explore what nature (and particularly the pastoral) might mean in the romance. The pastoral world of *The Winter's Tale*, as in many contemporary works, serves as a space of escape and as a mode of reflection on courtly values.[26] In the narrative logic of the romance, pastoral becomes a necessary but

---

25 At the level of grammar, Perdita delves into the potential mood, known "bi these signes, May, can, might, would, shoulde, or ought." William Lily, *A Short Introduction of Grammar* (London, 1653), *Early English Books Online*, http://eebo.chadwyck.com/.

26 In *The Art of English Poesy*, ed. Frank Whigham and Wayne A. Rebhorn (Ithaca: Cornell University Press, 2007), George Puttenham highlights poetry's reflection on this relation: "the poet devised the eclogue…not of purpose to counterfeit or represent the rustical manner of loves and communication, but under the veil of homely persons and in rude speeches to insinuate and glance at greater matters, and such as perchance had not been safe to have been disclosed in any other sort" (127–28).

temporary detour before redemption at court. But Perdita's list also offers a glimpse of the absolute difference of pastoral from court. The temporality of the play cannot accommodate nature's seasonal creations. Perdita, who will be back in court soon, will never access these flowers. She will be "found," and the issues at court will be resolved, but the list of flowers suspends audiences in a counterfactual instant inaccessible within the theatrical temporality.

While Perdita's words register a *moment* of absence, perhaps no early modern author revels in the continual generative capacity of the list like Ben Jonson. For instance, in *Entertainment at Britain's Burse* (1609), composed to mark the opening of the New Exchange, Jonson repeatedly provokes audiences' desires by cataloguing objects circulating in this socio-commercial space. The following wish-list provides a perfect example of the proliferating significations of the form:

> SHOP-BOY.
> What doe you lacke? what is't you buy? Veary fine China stuffes, of all kindes and quallityes? China Chaynes, China Braceletts, China scarfs, China fannes, China gurdles...Concaue glasses, Triangular glasses, Conuexe glasses, Christall globes,...Estrich Eggs, Birds of Paradise, Muskcads....Beards of all ages, vizards, Spectacles! See what you lack (73–86).[27]

Jonson's list directs audiences from objects of domestic use to marvels that, as James Knowles notes, graced actual cabinets of curiosities.[28] It both quickens our pace (What is the next object we might encounter?) and slows us down (What does each object signify? How do they relate to each other?). The wish-list imagines how people interact in social spaces (and with each other) through their responses to objects they "lacke."

Venturing into the home, Jonson further intertwines one's desire for sociability with the promise of as-yet absent objects. In "Inviting a Friend to Supper," the speaker claims:

---

27 Ben Jonson, *The Entertainment at Britain's Burse*, ed. James Knowles, in *Re-presenting Ben Jonson: Text, History, Performance*, ed. Martin Butler (New York: St. Martin's, 1999).

28 James Knowles, "Jonson's *Entertainment at Britain's Burse*," in *Re-presenting Ben Jonson: Text, History, Performance*, 116.

> Tonight, grave sir, both my poor house, and I
> Do equally desire your company:
> Not that we think us worthy such a guest,
> But that your worth will dignify our feast
> With those that come, whose grace may make that seem
> Something, which, else could hope for no esteem.
> It is the fair acceptance, sir, creates
> The entertainment perfect: not the cates.
> Yet shall you have, to rectify your palate,
> An olive, capers, or some better salad
> Ush'ring the mutton; with a short-legged hen,
> If we can get her, full of eggs, and then,
> Lemons, and wine for sauce: to these, a cony
> Is not to be despaired of, for our money;
> And, though fowl, now, be scarce, yet there are clerks,
> The sky not falling, think we may have larks.
> I'll tell you of more, and lie, so you will come:
> Of partridge, pheasant, woodcock, of which some
> May yet be there, and godwit, if we can:
> Knat, rail, and ruff too. (1–20) [29]

The speaker juxtaposes "desire" and deficiency. Neither the "poor house" nor the "I" is "worthy" of the "guest," and the speaker can only promise an elaborate list of nourishment that might "rectify" these differences. The poem registers fundamental imbalances—in nature, in social status, in knowledge—that trigger the list-making impulse. Yet despite his promises, the speaker cannot guarantee a banquet to "perfect" the setting. Phrases such as "If we can get her," "though fowl be scarce," and "May yet be there, and godwit, if we can," betray the contingency of his remarks. As he sets this table, his wishes hover close to the "lie" he almost acknowledges telling. Lurking beneath this catalogue of potential items exists a question that haunts all poetry: Was it the domain of lies or a form of expression that "nothing affirms"?[30] When the speaker states "I'll tell you of more, and lie, so you will come," he links acts of hospitality to

---

29 Ben Jonson, *The Complete Poems*, ed. George Parfitt (London: Penguin Classics, 1981).
30 Sidney argues in the *Defence* that since the poet "nothing affirms," he "never lieth" (53).

the rhetoric of non-affirmation, and the desire for the friend's company morphs into a wish for "more" objects. The speaker's poetic expression of desires grants his words a different kind of truth-value, one that is distinct from the "bare was" of empirical or historical fact. Like readers of poetry, the guest can wonder but not completely discount that the speaker's "Inviting" will translate into an actual feast.

As these wish-lists use absent objects to invoke different environments, they raise questions crucial to the early modern literary imagination: questions of truth, of artifice, and of authority. But few examples capture the scope of the wish-list as an imaginative thought-experiment as clearly as Edmund Spenser's invocation of travel and projection in the proem to book 2 of *The Faerie Queene*. Spenser embraces the impulse that led to the proliferation of *desiderata*: the possibility of creating complete knowledge systems in the future by recovering lost objects. The narrator laments how critics have dismissed "all this famous antique history" of Faerie Land as "painted forgery, / Rather then matter of iust memory."[31] This is worrisome, "Sith none, that breatheth liuing aire, does know, / Where is that happy land of Faery" (Proem 1). To counter the misperception that Faerie Land does not exist, he catalogs recent discoveries:

> But let that man with better sence aduize,
>   That of the world least part to vs is red:
>   And dayly how through hardy enterprize
>   Many great Regions were discouered,
>   Which to late age were neuer mentioned.
>   Who euer heard of th'Indian *Peru*?
>   Or who in venturous vessel measured
>   The *Amazons* huge riuer now found trew?
>   Or fruitfullest *Virginia* who did euer vew? (Proem 2)

The narrator reinterprets the lack of current proof of Faerie Land's existence as a catalyst for future discovery. Using examples of recent travels (to "Indian *Peru*," "fruitfullest *Virginia*," or "*Amazons* huge riuer"), he imagines an expandable world of potential existence rather than cartographic presence. He lists places that were unknown (and deemed non-existent) but are now found, in the process granting Faerie Land a

---

31 Edmund Spenser, *The Faerie Queene*, ed. A.C. Hamilton et al., 2nd ed. (Harlow: Longman, 2001).

distinct ontological significance. He also implies that this discovery will be made possible not through travel, but by entering the wandering landscape of the epic-romance. This entrance into poetic worlds destabilizes ontological boundaries between reality and fiction: asking readers to embrace Faerie Land's *potentiality*, the narrator suggests that poetry's speculative power—its ability to create worlds that "might best be" ("Letter to Raleigh," 716)—can fulfill the most powerful desires. Poetry, rather than travel, situates, but will also remove, Faerie Land from the realm of *desiderata*. After all, did not "Many great Regions," till recent times, have potential existence? Discovered geographies were once imagined objects, items in his contemporaries' different wish-lists.

Emulsifying Greasy Desire in Shakespeare and John Taylor the Water Poet

Rob Wakeman

A TABLE, A BED, OR A BODY ENCLOSED IN CLEAN LINEN IS SHELTERED from the world. Smocks, shirts, stockings, table cloths, and bed sheets demarcate the discrete boundaries that separate clean objects from unclean environments. The smell of freshly laundered linen is an announcement: "This area has been decontaminated. It has been purified of promiscuous pollutions." But grease has a way of seeping through these borders. Fats and oils indiscriminately and wantonly dribble from the body's pores. They ooze forth from cookware and flatware, sticking to and staining skin, hair, and cloth. In his ribald poem, "The Praise of Cleane Linnen," John Taylor the Water Poet (1578–1653) gives an example of how grease debases a white handkerchief:

> A *Handkerchiefe* may well be cal'd in brief,
> Both a perpetuall leacher, and a thiefe,
> About the lippes it's kissing, good and ill,
> Or else 'tis diuing in the pocket still,
> As farre as from the pocket to the mouth,
> So is it's pilgrimage with age or youth.
> At Christining-banquets and at funerals,
> At weddings (Comfit-makers festiuals)
> A *Handkerchiefe* doth filch most manifold,
> And sharke and steale as much as it can hold.
> 'Tis soft, and gentle, yet this I admire at,
> At sweet meates 'tis a tyrant, and a pyrat.
> Moreouer 'tis a *Handkerchiefes* high place,
> To be a Scauenger vnto the face,

> To clense it cleane from sweat and excrements,
> Which (not auoyded) were vnsauory scents.
> (ll. 217–232, p. 168)[1]

In the execution of its task, the handkerchief rids the lips and face of impurities, but in doing so it becomes a lecher, thief, tyrant and pirate. A simple swatch of linen becomes an unsavory thing as it scavenges for waste and fondles the flesh in the pockets' recesses. The poem goes on to describe the corruptible character of an entire closet full of linens and their daily struggle with undignified pollutions. The sexually stimulating social energy of handkerchiefs and table cloths spills over into the bedroom where a different species of linen wraps the body in sexual caress — an image Taylor describes with mock solemnity:

> Your Dinner and your Supper ouer-past,
> By linnen in your beds, you are imbrac'd,
> Then, 'twixt the sheetes refreshing rest you take,
> And turne from side to side, and sleepe and wake:
> And sure the sheetes in euery Christian Nation
> Are walles or limits of our generation,
> For where desire and loue, combined meets,
> Then there's braue doings 'twixt a paire of sheets:
> But where a Harlots lust doth entertaine,
> There one sheets penance, bides the shames of twaine:
> To all degree my counsaile here is such
> That *of the lower sheet, take not too much.*
> (ll. 81–92, p. 167)

These lines recall how, in the Shakespearean imagination, a mother's "celestial bed" can become "enseamed" and "Stew'd in corruption [with] honeying and making love / Over the nasty sty" (*Hamlet*, 1.5.56, 3.4.92–94); or perhaps these lines might remind the reader of Titania's promise to "purge" Bottom of his "mortal grossness" on her bed of "pressed flowers" (*A Midsummer Night's Dream*, 3.1.159–60); or else, surely, we remember Othello's fiery disgust at the thought of Desdemona's "lust-stained" bed

---

1 All quotations from John Taylor the Water Poet are from *All the Workes of Iohn Taylor the Water Poet* (London: James Boler, 1630). Subsequent references are cited parenthetically in text.

and (*Othello*, 5.1.36).² In Taylor's paean, clean linen is a mark of unsullied sleep, "Christian" sex acts, and a chaste marriage, while a "Harlots lust" stains bed sheets with impure desires.

How then does one rid white linens of a foul stain resulting from sexual corruption? Early modern laundry was a time intensive process involving caustic chemicals that was increasingly outsourced to Dutch and Flemish immigrant women in London and its environs. Leonard Mascall's *A Profitable Booke...to Take Out Spottes and Staines* (1583) describes the process involved in this quotidian labor:

> Firste yee shall laye all your foule clothes to soke in colde water, then driue them as yee doe a bucke of clothes, and when they are well driuen: then shall yee take them all forth of the bucking tubbe, then laye them agayne abroade in the sayd tubbe, without any lye, and e|uer as ye lay them betwixt euery cloth: scrape of chalke thinne all ouer, thus when ye haue all layde them: then put of your lye vnto them, and so chaunge your lye twise or thrise after, then take and wash them forth, and they will be fayre and cleane without greace and very white withall.³

The purity of water alone will not suffice as a cleanser. A fatty body such as grease cannot be dissolved in a polar solvent such as water. Grease can only be dissolved by other grease-like substances; it is only attracted to nonpolar solvents such as oils, fats, and waxes. In order to separate grease from linen dirty laundry requires a soap emulsion. To make soap, Elizabethan laundry workers typically used potash or coal ash dissolved in water. Ash mixed with water creates lye, a caustic alkaline solution rich in potassium salts. The worker then cooks lye with a fat to induce a chemical reaction called saponification—the result is soap.⁴ The newly formed soap molecules each have a head and a tail. At one end of the molecule the

---

2   All quotations from Shakespeare follow *The Riverside Shakespeare*, ed. G. Blakemore Evans, 2nd ed. (Boston: Houghton Mifflin, 1997). Subsequent references are cited parenthetically in text.

3   Leonard Mascall, *A Profitable Booke...to Take Out Spottes and Staines* (London, 1583), 9–10.

4   Alternatively, Mascall includes a recipe for bile soap made using the alkaline gall of an ox instead of rendered fat (*A Profitable Booke*, 4). Mr. Ford calls Falstaff an ox at the play's conclusion, alluding to his cuckold's horns and his symbolic castration (*The Merry Wives of Windsor*, 5.5.120).

triglyceride from fat attracts grime while the strong basicity of the other end of the molecule—the lye created from potash—attracts water from the wash tub. A stain would thus be surrounded and scrubbed by soap molecules that attach both to the stain and to water, but not to the cloth. Surface tension ebbs and grease molecules detach from cloth and slip into the water.

A laundress's washing tub is a cauldron for chemical reactions: the properties of lye soap, bleach, cold water, and dirty laundry are each mediated by some other object in the tub in a calculated and measured process of bucking, scraping, rinsing, and repeating. Each object in the tub acts as the key to some other object's lock; each entity possesses the power to interact with other entities in ways that are unavailable to still other entities. This theory of relations between discrete entities is a crucial aspect of objected-oriented ontologies. As Graham Harman observes, "Any object is a complex and irreducible event; like the moon, one face of the tool is darkened in the silence of its orbit, while another face illuminates and compels us with dazzling surface-effects."[5] Dark to the chemical properties of water, but visible to the lathering suds of a soap emulsion, a grease stain is similarly multifaceted.

Just as the chemical properties of some objects may be withdrawn from the sensitivities of other objects, so too can the potencies of common household objects remain beyond the detection of people. Workers in London's laundries and sculleries, having become attuned to the unique properties of objects over the course of their daily labors, came to possess a knowledge of lye soap's potency that was unknown to English chemists. According to the inventor Hugh Plat in his 1594 book, *The Jewell House of Art and Nature*, cultural prejudices and political tensions between the Dutch and the English inhibited the sharing of knowledge of chemistry. As a result, the effectiveness of lye soap as a cleaning agent was unknown to the English except for its prominent use by Dutch and Flemish immigrant women who were familiar with it through "ancient and common

---

5   Graham Harman, "The Theory of Objects in Heidegger and Whitehead," in *Towards Speculative Realism: Essays and Lectures* (Winchester, UK: Zero Books, 2010), 33. See also, Harman's writings on Latourian Actor-Networks: "the means of linking one thing with another is *translation*...a massive work of mediation." *Prince of Networks: Bruno Latour and Metaphysics* (Melbourne, Australia: re.press, 2009), 15.

experience."⁶ Plat affirms that lye is indeed "better and cheaper then the Masons dust for the scouring of our trenchers, and other wooden vessels, and this can our Dutch liskins and Kitchin maids well approve, whose dressors, shelves, and moldingboards, are much whiter and cleaner kept, then those which are washed, and scalded after the English manner."⁷

As Natasha Korda has noted, these "liskins," Dutch and Flemish women immigrant laborers, were frequently associated with brothels and sexual impropriety in early modern English culture.⁸ The laundress is thus linked with both the sexual pollution of linen and in its ritual purification. John Taylor the Water Poet contests this calumny in his poem, "The Praise of Cleane Linnen":

> All you man-monsters, monstrous Linnen soylers,
> You Shirt polluting tyrants, you sheets spoylers,
> Robustious rude Ruffe-rending *raggamentoyes*
> *Terratritorian tragma Troynouantoyes*
> Remember that your *Lanndresse* paines is great,
> Whose labours onely keepe you sweet and neat:
> Consider this, that here is writ, or said,
> And pay her, (not as was the Sculler paid)
> Call not your *Laundresse* slut or slabb'ring queane,
> It is her slabb'ring that doth keepe thee cleane.
> (ll 319–328, p. 169)⁹

Faced with the menace of greasy man-monsters, Taylor extols the "most mondifying, clarifying, pvrifying, and repvrifying" laundress in London,

---

6   Sir Hugh Plat, *The Iewell House of Art and Nature* (London: Peter Short, 1594), 58, H1v.

7   Plat, *The Iewell House of Art and Nature*, 55, G4r. "Liskin" is a generic name for a Dutch maidservant, equivalent to "Lizzie" in English.

8   Natasha Korda notes that many Dutch widows profitably operated large businesses, including laundries that employed immigrant women, and accusations regarding the sexual impropriety of these business owners is best understood "within the context of their participation in a broader network of unregulated commerce, which included but was certainly not limited to sexual commerce." Natasha Korda, *Labors Lost: Women's Work and the Early Modern English Stage* (Philadelphia: University of Pennsylvania Press, 2011), 115.

9   Undercutting the professed chastity of the laundress, however, is the poem's sexually suggestive descriptions of the laundress's labor as well as bawdy descriptions of the linens they are charged with washing. See Korda, *Labors Lost*, 133.

Martha Legge, as well as the object of her labor. The laundress, exercising a care for humble things, restores integrity to the linen and washes away the indiscretions committed on their surfaces. Taylor says he finds the word laundress, associated as it is with a debauched sexual reputation, "to be both vnfitting and derogatory to your comly, commendable, laudable, neate, sweet and seemely calling; for the Anagram of *Lawndres* is SLAVVNDER" (pp. 164–65). Taylor's use of anagram draws attention to the multifaceted nature of objects, including laundresses, which may appear innocent and pure or, inversely, lusty and sullied.

Soap has the power to dissolve sexual sin, but the gender gap in the knowledge required for laundry-work leaves men frightfully ignorant of how stained sheets and abused women are rehabilitated.[10] In Shakespeare's *The Rape of Lucrece*, after lamenting that "prone lust should stain so pure a bed," the narrator makes a frighteningly dismissive and cruel suggestion—"The spots whereof could weeping purify, / Her tears should drop on them perpetually" (684–86)—as if tears alone could undo the violence. The plays of Shakespeare feature several scenes in which linens, bed sheets, and handkerchiefs are literally, figuratively, or imagined to be tainted by sexual indiscretion, but only the women of *The Merry Wives of Windsor* treat their laundry with soap.[11] When faced with Falstaff's lascivious lusts, Mrs. Page and Mrs. Ford employ a laundry basket to purify the household. But just as oily stains cannot be cleansed with water alone, Mrs. Ford and Mrs. Page know that greasy desires cannot be repelled solely with upstanding moral purity. A slick suitor is best washed away with merry pranks.

In act 3, scene 3, Falstaff, thinking he has nearly been caught *in flagrante delicto*, hides inside a buck-basket in order to escape Mr. Ford's jealous tirade. Mrs. Ford and Mrs. Page conceal Falstaff—his own clothes perhaps already beshitted or soiled from fear, sexual excitement, or other gross secretions—with "foul linen...as if it were going to bucking" (3.3.131–32).[12] He does not realize that he is actually the butt end

---

10 Cf., Roland Barthes's call for a psychoanalytic approach to household cleansers in "Soap-powders and Detergents," *Mythologies*, trans. Annette Lavers (New York: Hill and Wang, 1972 [o.p. in French in 1957]), 36–38.

11 The concluding scene of *A Midsummer Night's Dream*, in which the fairies blessing the beds of betrothed, is also worth noting here. See Wendy Wall, *Staging Domesticity: Household Work and English Identity in Early Modern Drama* (Cambridge, UK: Cambridge University Press, 2002), 94–126.

12 "Bucking" is the sixteenth-century term for bleaching (OED).

of a practical joke. Mrs. Ford and Mrs. Page have plotted to punish the lusty knight for his sexual indiscretions by having two servants carry the buck-basket to the laundresses and whitsters at Datchet Mead. There, Falstaff will be dumped into the Thames along with the Fords' soiled linens. Presumably, Falstaff does not submit to being scraped with chalk and scrubbed with lye soap, as Mascall describes, and only suffers the presoak in Thames. Nevertheless, the buck-basket, like the laundress's washing tub, is a means by which grease is transformed, heated, and broken down. Once he is clean and dry, freshly folded and returned to the Garter Inn in Windsor, Falstaff recounts his humiliation in distinctly chemical-humoral terms that recall the dissolution of a stain through a soap emulsion:

> [I was] stopped in [the buck-basket] like a strong distillation with stinking clothes that fretted in their own grease. Think of that—a man of my kidney. Think of that—that am as subject to heat as butter; a man of continual dissolution and thaw. It was a miracle to scape suffocation. And in the height of this bath (when I was more than half stew'd in grease, like a Dutch dish) to be thrown into the Thames, and cool'd, glowing-hot, in that surge, like a horse-shoe; think of that—hissing-hot—think of that, Master Brook. (3.5.112–22)

The exhortation to "think of that" is an invitation to speculate about what it is like to be composed of such intemperate substances. In her incisive reading of Windsor's domestic economy, Wendy Wall describes Falstaff's body as a disorderly grease ball, "a barely congealed liquid mass of desires subject to dissolution."[13] As a slimy stain that threatens to defile the honor of the Pages and Fords, Falstaff's flesh is variously likened to pudding variously likened to pudding (2.1.32), whale oil (2.2.65), and other cooking fats (2.2.68, 4.5.98). Shakespeare's audience would also be familiar with further descriptions of Falstaff from both parts of *Henry IV* where he is described as a "grease tallow-catch," "fat as butter," and an "oily rascal," (*Henry IV, Part 1* 2.4.228, 511, 526) who leaks sweat all over England (*Henry IV, Part 2* 1.2.206–12, 2.4.216–21, 4.3.11–15, Epilogue 30). His thick, viscous, unctuous body oozes and ingratiates itself into other substances. Glutton and lecher,

---

13 Wendy Wall, *Staging Domesticity: Household Work and English Identity in Early Modern Drama* (Cambridge, UK: Cambridge University Press, 2002), 116.

he adheres to napkins and bedsheets and leaves traces of his corrupting influence from Shrewsbury to Eastcheap. As such, his body is inherently susceptible to the corrective chemical reactions of laundry day. Falstaff prompts us to think about the entailments of reactive substances inside the laundry basket: what is it like to be a stain subjected to a laundress's labor? What is it like to be a spot of grease washed away in the cold water of the Thames? Of course, Falstaff cannot know exactly the answer to the question; he can only translate the experience through the approximation of simile. And yet, the buck-basket enables, even encourages, speculation through the disruption and amplification of the ambient effects of objects. The claustrophobia of this strange environment makes laundry uncomfortably present in a new way. Encased in the basket and layered in grubby, fetid clothing, Falstaff confronts the qualities of substances face to face. The buck-basket represents the inverse of clean linen—whereas linen is meant to repel outside pollutions, the basket keeps the pollutions sealed inside. Confronted with this stew of grease, Falstaff is undone, deterritorialized, "like a barrow of butcher's offal" (3.5.5).[14] Because, as Mrs. Page alleges, Falstaff suffers from a "dissolute disease" (3.3.191), he quickly decomposes amid the greasy substances to which he is joined in the buck-basket. He experiences something approximate to what the foul blots of grease experience: separation, emulsification, and mundification.

The use of stage properties in *The Merry Wives of Windsor*, particularly in the buck-basket scene, allows us to consider how an object-oriented approach to theater can help us understand the mechanics of comedy. Prop comedy finds humor in the split between objects and their qualities, or what Graham Harman defines as "allure." As Harman puts it, "a thing becomes alluring when it…animates those properties from within by means of some ill-defined demonic energy."[15] The comedic prop lies in wait on stage, temporarily withdrawn from our perception, ready-at-hand. The audience is not aware of the comedic prop's power over characters on stage until appropriated for some unexpected purpose. As Harman explains, objects that seem withdrawn to the rest of us are uncomfortably present-at-hand for the "comic dupe" who bumbles about his environment

---

14 I am thinking here of Julian Yates's reading of pie crust in *Titus Andronicus*. "Shakespeare's Kitchen Archives," in *Speculative Medievalisms: Discography*, ed. The Petropunk Collective [Eileen Joy, Anna Klosowska, Nicola Masciandaro, Michael O'Rourke] (Brooklyn, NY: Punctum Books, 2013), 197.

15 Harman, "Physical Nature and the Paradox of Qualities," in *Towards Speculative Realism: Essays and Lectures* (Winchester, UK: Zero Books, 2010), 137.

much to an audience's amusement. The unexpected deployment of a stage prop suddenly erupts as present-at-hand as the audience is forced to consider its presence anew. Props advance from the background to embarrass and ensnare the object of our laughter.[16] Once the stage property is activated by an actor, the "intentional" sensual qualities of objects "*breathe* into their environment" like "open bottles of wine or [befouled!] linen shirts."[17] Clean linen, once ritually purified, demarcates proper boundaries.[18] But when befouled, once stewed together like a greasy "Dutch dish," dirty laundry signifies the collapse of objects into each other. The labor of laundry seeks to undo this collapse, making what is muddled discrete again. Soap and bleach absolve the dirty linen of its worldliness, at least temporarily. As Taylor writes, the laundress's living:

> …is on two extremes relying,
> Shee's euer wetting, or shee's euer drying.
> As all men dye to liue, and liue to dye,
> So doth shee dry to wash, and wash to drye.
> Shee runnes like *Luna* in her circled spheare,
> As a perpetuall motion shee doth steare.
> (ll. 277–82, p. 169)

The laundress is, in Taylor's estimation, "like a horse that labours in a mill" forever circling in "perpetuall motion." The merry wives, too, are not free from their labor after one dowsing of Falstaff in the Thames. His

---

16 Harman, "Physical Nature and the Paradox of Qualities," 137–138.
17 Harman, "Physical Nature and the Paradox of Qualities," 127.
18 Harman would disagree that the pleasant smell of freshly laundered linen is any different ontologically from the odor of befouled smocks, but these odors are valued differently, as evidenced by *Merry Wives* and Taylor's "The Praise of Cleane Linnen." All objects might be said to "breathe into their environment," but not all wafting odors carry the same moral stigma. The perceived threat of grease's foul qualities represents a particularly odious threat that should be avoided. Natasha Korda also notes that "Linen underclothes served the important function of protecting expensive costumes from the sweat of the actor's body and would have needed laundering on a regular basis" and that it is very likely that Shakespeare's acting company relied on the same networks of labor represented in *Merry Wives* and "The Praise of Cleane Linnen." She offers the suggestive possibility that the play's buck-basket is the one the acting company used for their own dirty laundry. *Labors Lost*, 116–17.

greasy desires ooze their way back into Windsor a second and third time only to be subjected to further expurgations. Burdened with an unattainable standard of immaculate purity and under continual threat of greasy corruption, laundresses and housewives are given the impossible task of policing the borders between discrete objects and their environs. Only a soap emulsion can negotiate the narrow line between clean objects and a filthy world. Drawn as it is to both grease and water, the soap emulsion is the chemical equivalent of being "merry, and yet honest too" (*The Merry Wives of Windsor*, 4.2.105).

Lavinia is Philomel
Jennifer Waldron

> If they be two, they are two so
> As stiff twin compasses are two;
> Thy soul, the fix'd foot, makes no show
> To move, but doth, if th'other do.
>   —John Donne, "A Valediction:
>   Forbidding Mourning,"

IN WHAT WAY MIGHT A POEM OR A NARRATIVE SERVE NOT AS A representation but instead as a nonhuman agent? From one perspective, Shakespeare's *Titus Andronicus* seems like an extended meditation on this problem: Ovid's story of Philomel's rape "tampers directly with causality" in Shakespeare's play.[1] Philomel appears first when the villainous Aaron comments, before the rape of Lavinia, "This is the day of doom for Bassianus,/His Philomel must lose her tongue today" (2.2.42–43).[2] After the rape and mutilation, Lavinia is frequently on stage, the mute object towards which many of her male relatives direct their speech: Marcus posits that this is the work of "some Tereus" (2.4.26), or a "craftier Tereus" (46). And Lavinia finally seems to make herself legible only when she gets hold of her nephew's copy of Ovid's *Metamorphoses* and "quotes" (4.1.50) its leaves. Ovid's story takes humans as a kind of "activation device," as

---

1 Timothy Morton, "An Object-Oriented Defense of Poetry," *New Literary History* 43 (2012): 205–24, esp. 215–16.
2 *Titus Andronicus*, ed. Jonathan Bate (London and New York: Routledge, 1995).

Eileen Joy puts it.[3] It seems to preserve a self-replicating power and a certain degree of organizational closure even as it takes its violent effects in the world of the play.[4] What kind of agency is this, exactly?

One approach would be to make a strong distinction between the activities of spoken allusions and those of books as objects. The many verbal comparisons between Lavinia and Philomel are produced by human actors and processed in the minds of human listeners, while the book is a durable object that might seem to have more independent agency. And in Shakespeare's play, Ovidian narrative appears in increasingly concrete forms, moving from the casual mention of "his Philomel" (2.2.43), to the object Lavinia pursues and finally secures: "What book is that she tosseth so?" (4.1.41). Yet as tempting as it is to take the book-as-prop as the crucial example of an object-oriented approach to language or narrative, I want instead to examine the continuities between the initial verbal allusions to Philomel and her later appearance in the leaves of a book. Both kinds of Ovidian artefact activate a metaphorical relation that has violent causal force within the play: Lavinia is Philomel. And both help to suggest the particular capacities of metaphors to generate infrastructures for sensory and affective experience.

One way of thinking about metaphor, broadly construed, is that it serves not as a nonhuman agent but instead as a kind of tool for humans as they attempt to access the nonhuman—to grasp phenomena that are beyond human experience. Mary Thomas Crane takes as a case study the historical circumstances of the new science in the seventeenth-century—the moment when everyday experience of the natural world was increasingly severed from the experimental and mathematical techniques used to model it. She argues that resemblance and analogy did not relinquish their relations with knowledge during this period, as in Foucault's

---

3   Eileen A. Joy, "You Are Here: A Manifesto," in *Animal, Vegetable, and Mineral: Ethics and Objects*, ed. Jeffrey J. Cohen (New York: Punctum, 2012), 165.

4   Mark Hansen helpfully outlines the way in which two systems can maintain a certain degree of organizational closure while still impacting each other indirectly: "Technics and the living impact one another by triggering crises in the organizational closure of the other." See Mark Hansen, "Media Theory," *Theory Culture & Society* 23 (2006), 302. Hansen draws on a line of thinking about autopoietic systems that goes back through Niklas Luhmann to Humberto Maturana and Francisco Varela. For helpful essays on Luhmann, see *Emergence and Embodiment: New Essays on Second-Order Systems Theory*, ed. Bruce Clarke and Mark Hansen (Durham and London: Duke University Press, 2009), 113–42.

well-known account. Instead, Crane proposes that as analogies based on causation and / or the perception of shared qualities lost their explanatory power, they were replaced with structural analogies that conveyed relationships among things that were qualitatively different: the solar system for the atom, for instance.[5]

In the chapter on "Metaphorism" in *Alien Phenomenology*, Ian Bogost describes metaphor in somewhat similar terms (though without suggesting that it serves human ends). If the objective evidence we might use to describe how bats navigate space only leads us farther from the experience of what it's like to "see" as a bat does, the only way to approximate bat experience is by analogy: "The bat, for example, operates like a submarine." Or, in Bogost's later discussion of how metaphor works in Graham Harman's work, "We never understand the alien experience, we only ever reach for it metaphorically."[6] Crane takes John Donne's "stiff twin compasses" to illustrate metaphor's capacity to give humans this kind of access to things invisible to see. Yet Donne's poem also illustrates the strange agency of metaphor as a technical device—its capacity to give the alien access to the human as much as the other way around. Here we might take Bogost's use of the term "metamorphosis" not only to characterize metaphor as a transfer or translation of one object into another but also to signal the two-way capacities of this pathway.

In "A Valediction: Forbidding Mourning," the speaker famously dismisses those lovers whose "soul is sense" (14) and whose love is tied to concrete body parts such as "eyes, lips, and hands" (20). He then offers the compass metaphor to his beloved in its capacity to offer special access to things invisible to the common eye. Most obviously, the "stiff twin compasses" afford a concrete model for the higher connection between the lovers. The feet of the compass only appear to be separated from a ground-level perspective, but they are in fact joined on a higher plane,

---

5 "Analogy, Metaphor, and the New Science: Cognitive Science and Early Modern Epistemology," in Lisa Zunshine, ed. *Introduction to Cognitive Cultural Studies* (Baltimore, MD: Johns Hopkins University Press, 2010), 103–14, esp. 104–5.

6 Ian Bogost, *Alien Phenomenology: or What It's Like to Be a Thing* (Minneapolis, MN: University of Minnesota Press, 2012), 64, 66. Bogost, unlike Crane, does not take metaphor as a representational tool that humans use to model alien phenomena. Instead, metaphorical operations are understood to underpin object relations themselves (including human perception). On metaphor, see Morton, "Poetry," 206; Bogost, *Alien Phenomenology*, 66; and Graham Harman, *Guerilla Metaphysics: Phenomenology and the Carpentry of Things* (Chicago: Open Court, 2005).

where the hinge links the two feet. At the second level, however, the metaphor's power derives not from the physical shape of the compass but from its status a technical instrument that models space and time mathematically, joining human and nonhuman scales. A relatively new invention in Donne's time, the geometric compass was used for the disposition of military troops as well as for making circles "just." As such, the compass figures the technical capacities of structural analogies themselves — including the poem's own metaphors — as they reconfigure the human sensorium. My broader point is that even with the rise of the "new" science, when these kinds of analogies came to be understood primarily as an epistemological tool, they continued (like the compass itself) to serve as technical interventions in sensory perception.

To offer a contemporary analogy, Google Street View offers a set of images of streets, buildings, and landscapes that are keyed approximately to human scales — or at least to human-automobile scales. But this densely rendered perspective is also coupled with several layers of abstraction that operate above ground level, like the hinge of Donne's compass. The screen includes a small inset map on which an iconic figure stands, facing the direction that is visible in the larger street view. Clicking on an area of the two-dimensional map causes the figure to turn, and the view of the street changes accordingly — as if the character's eyes were turning in space. At another level of abstraction, a small schematic image of a magnetic compass appears superimposed on the street-level image. It indicates cardinal directions, but it does so in a way that makes sense only when looking at the bird's-eye map. When you click on the compass to rotate it, the iconic figure on the map turns and the street view swings around with it. It shows, for instance, the view looking north when the compass points upward toward the sky at the top of the screen. What I want to point to here is the tight bond between human and nonhuman scales, as well as between street-level sensory data that seem immediate and technologically mediated navigational systems that do not. As with Donne's compass metaphor, which seeks to structure the beloved's perspective, the Google compass need not be entirely concrete in order to swing our vision towards magnetic north. It requires only the algorithmic joint that connects this floating digital circle to the iconic foot that turns in place.

This look at compasses of various kinds helps illuminate the workings of metaphor as a nonhuman agent in the world, a technical device that structures human experience but is not reducible to it. As Mike Witmore has argued of narratives, metaphors put humans in touch with "forms of reduction or compression that are every bit as diagrammatic and so (potentially) inhuman as...compression algorithms."[7] These linguistic structures are nonhuman agents that have been co-evolving with the human since long before the advent of the computer, the compass, or even the written word.[8] And metaphor is a particularly potent kind of algorithm because it often enacts a transfer between the concrete and the abstract, between phenomenological experience that seems directly available to humans (e.g., the onstage character "Lavinia") and compressed concepts or inaccessible worlds that may be less so (e.g., the ancient story of "Philomel"). In other words, the potency of metaphor relies in part on its capacity to structure relations between the "human" and "nonhuman"—to generate spaces and times for transfer between two domains. One tendency is to take the direction of metaphorical transfer as being from the concrete (which is often understood as readily available) toward the abstract or alien, as with the language of "source" and "target" in cognitive linguistics. A related assumption is that the abstract/figurative components of metaphor are merely representations of a more concrete and pre-existing reality—that they are parasitical upon their source domains, as the language of concrete "vehicle" and abstract "tenor" also suggests to some extent.[9] Yet metaphor also gives the alien access to the human, with metamorphic metaphor serving as a prime illustration of this phenomenon. In other words, it's not only that humans might turn to metaphor when they lack direct experience, but also that the alien components of metaphor inflect so-called primary or direct experience, even

---

7 Michael Witmore, "We Have Never Not Been Inhuman," in "When Did We Become Post/human?" ed. Eileen A. Joy and Craig Dionne, special issue, *postmedieval: a journal of medieval cultural studies* 1.1–2 (2010): 208–14.

8 For an account of the co-constitution of humans and technics, see Bernard Stiegler, *Technics and Time*, trans. Richard Beardsworth and George Collins, 3 Vols. (Stanford: Stanford University Press, 1998), esp. 1.142. My work on technics and media theory also informs this piece: Jennifer Waldron, "Dead Likenesses and Sex Machines: Shakespearean Media Theory," forthcoming in *A Handbook of Shakespeare, Gender, and Embodiment*, ed. Valerie Traub (Oxford, 2016).

9 This is a tendency in cognitive metaphor theory and theories of "embodied mind." See, e.g., Andy Clark's critique of "strong sensorimotor models" in *Supersizing the Mind: Embodiment, Action, and Cognitive Extension* (Oxford: Oxford University Press, 2008), 169.

sensation itself. This volatility seems to be the point of the "Lavinia is Philomel" plot of *Titus Andronicus*.

Ovid's narrative comes to have the kind of causal force in Shakespeare's play that metaphoric/metamorphic descriptions have in Ovid. In the passage describing the severed tongue of Philomel, for example, the description of the snake's tail takes on a certain kind of agency:

> The tip fell downe and quivering on the ground
> As though that it had murmured it made a certaine sound.
> And as an Adders tayle cut off doth skip a while: even so
> The tip of Philomelaas tongue did wriggle to and fro,
> And nearer to hir mistresseward in dying still did go.[10]

Before the "as" conjoins it with the Adder's tail, the tip of the tongue lies on the soil, "quivering" on the ground. After the comparison, the tongue wiggles "to and fro" as it moves toward its mistress. Perhaps the tongue and the snake's tail simply share the essential quality of convulsive movement. However, as elsewhere in Ovid, the comparison itself becomes part of an emergent structure: words seem to participate in or even to cause physical transformations (e.g., Lycaon as wolf, Daphne as tree, etc.).[11] In this case, once tongue and snake are joined by the structure of comparison it is as if snake's capacity for self-movement were transferred to the severed tongue: "And nearer to hir mistresseward in dying still did go." What is this entity that moves toward Philomel in the act of dying? A tongue-snake? A snake-tongue? The metamorphic coupling of "tongue" and "snake" emerges through and as convulsive movement.

It's worth noting that Shakespeare takes more than one leaf from Ovid in this sense: Lavinia is described as "Philomel" before the rape and mutilation, so that the comparison seems to take on an instrumental role in the action. In subsequent scenes, when her mutilation becomes visible, she becomes a kind of Lavinia-Philomel, a theatrical palimpsest of the Ovidian narrative and the actions of the character visible onstage. To emphasize the metamorphic capacities of metaphor thus signals its potentially non-representational functions — its causal force.

---

10 Ovid, *Metamorphoses*, trans. Arthur Golding (London, 1567), 6.557–60.

11 On Ovid's interest in metamorphosis as an attempt to turn words into things, see Leonard Barkan, *Mute Poetry, Speaking Pictures* (Princeton: Princeton University Press, 2013), 51.

The world of *Titus* not only replays and redoubles features of Ovidian myth (two rapists, two sons in the pie, etc.) but in some sense seems to coexist with it, with the temporal, spatial, and ontological boundaries between the two rendered highly unstable: Did Chiron and Demetrius learn the lesson of Tereus in Gothic grammar school? Why is it that despite Marcus's immediate identification of Lavinia with Philomel (2.3.43), it is only in conjunction with the proof-text of the *Metamorphoses* in act four that Lavinia becomes impelled to reveal the names of her rapists, writing them with a staff in a "sandy plot" (4.1.69)? One response would be to say that Marcus's initial reference to Lavinia's Ovidian prototype requires conceptual work only, while the mode of transfer becomes more concrete when Lavinia finally gets hold of a copy of Ovid. Yet in the end, each version of the metaphorical relation offers a two-way passage between the alien compressions of narrative and the sensorimotor world of human actors.

When the actor playing Lavinia encounters the prop playing the *Metamorphoses*, Titus and Marcus narrate as Lavinia turns the pages of the book:

> TITUS
> What would she find? Lavinia, shall I read?
> This is the tragic tale of Philomel,
> And treats of Tereus' treason and his rape —
> And rape, I fear, was root of thy annoy.
>
> MARCUS
> See, brother, see: note how she quotes the leaves. (4.1.46–50)

While this interaction might seem finally to ground the Lavinia / Philomel metaphor in material objects, my sense is that the phrase, "quotes the leaves" (Q1 "coats"), offers a particularly powerful example of a metamorphic transfer that works against any firm grounding in time or space.[12] From a temporal perspective, the belatedness of any act of quoting serves as a reminder of the strange agency by which these Ovidian leaves seem

---

12 On problems surrounding the term "materiality," see Bill Brown, "Materiality," in *Critical Terms for Media Studies*, ed. W.J.T. Mitchell and Mark B.N. Hansen (Chicago: Chicago University Press, 2010). See also Timothy Morton, "Here Comes Everything: The Promise of Object-Oriented Ontology," *Qui Parle* 19 (2011): 163–90, esp. 177–85.

to have caused the existence of the Lavinian branches that turn them.[13] The phrase similarly serves to intermodulate the various sensory and conceptual pathways through which an Ovidian text might be "quoted."[14] Since she has no tongue, Lavinia cannot quote Ovid's book by repeating a passage aloud; nor can she quote it by writing out the words. The lopped branches of her arms instead quote these leaves by touch. The coupling of these more learned dimensions of the word "quotes" with Lavinia's actions thus introduces unresolvable conflicts in the sensory/conceptual modes through which audiences might apprehend this event. Written word, spoken voice, and bodily gesture remain in tension with one another, underlining both the strange temporality and the nonlocalized agency of Ovidian narrative in *Titus Andronicus*. The process of transfer is itself the point—the two-way traffic between Lavinia and Philomel, body and book, gesture and written word. When the book's pages finally become leaves for Lavinia's bare branches, this is not a grotesque literalization of relations that should properly remain metaphorical. It is instead a moment that lays bare the nonhuman agency of metaphor itself, its compass of the body as much as the soul.

---

13 For a compelling account of how Lavinia represents "a relay between the Latin eloquence of Ovid's poem" and the eloquence of Shakespeare's own *Titus Andronicus*, see Sean Keilen, *Vulgar Eloquence: On the Renaissance Invention of English Literature* (New Haven: Yale University Press, 2006), 130.

14 On competitive mutilation, Shakespeare's sense of rivalry with Ovid, and the importance of this scene of "quoting," see Leonard Barkan, *The Gods Made Flesh: Metamorphosis and the Pursuit of Paganism* (New Haven: Yale University Press, 1986), esp. 243–47.

The Fate of the Second Bird
Luke Wilson

AN ASPERGILLUM SOMETIMES LOOKS something like this:

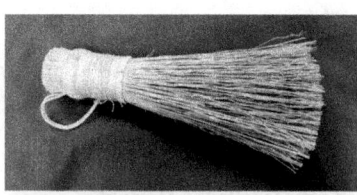

And sometimes something like this:

Here is one being used by a ram in a late thirteenth-century book of hours:

From top to bottom:

Figure 1. Aspergillum. Author photo.

Figure 2. Aspergillum. Author photo.

Figure 3. Walters Art Museum. "Book of Hours, Ram, with situla, sprinkling holy water with an aspergillum, Walters Manuscript W. 102, fol. 8or detail" (CC BY-NC-SA 3.0).

Mostly, though, the aspergillum was used by Catholic priests to sprinkle holy water on the congregation. After the use of holy water was written out of the English liturgy in the 1549 Prayer Book, the aspergillum (or "holy water sprinkle," as it was more commonly called) didn't get used so much, in England, at least not as an element in the official liturgy.[1] But it was still good for a few laughs, as in the following jest from the popular joke book, *Nugae venales* (1642):

> *Mulier Hugenota & Papistica quaenam?*
> Hugenota est, quae omni tempore desiderat carnem; papistica quae saepe voluit & tractat aspergillum.
>
> [Which is a Huguenot woman, and which a Papist? A Huguenot woman is one who at all times longs for meat; a papist woman is one who often craves, and handles, the aspergillum.][2]

Or consider Henri Estienne, who in mocking fake learning and papist practices tells the story of

> An other [divine] (of more learning but of lesse wit) [who] being asked in Latine, *Quot sunt septem Sacramenta,* answered, *Tres, Aspergillum, Thuribulum, & Magnum Altare:* which is in English, *How many be the seuen Sacramentes,* the answere, *Three, the Holye water Sprinckle, the Sensar, and the highe Altar.*[3]

These jokes rely on the idea of an inordinate interest in liturgical tools on the part of lascivious Catholic women and dimwitted Catholic priests alike (leaving aside the Huguenot women, who evidently have their own issues); both kinds of Catholic err in investing these tools with excessive importance by way of an improper substitution. Or rather, importance at all: underlying the joke that the women find the aspergillum so useful as a dildo is the scandal that, from the Protestant English perspective, that instrument is all too useless: no holy water, no need for an aspergillum.

---

1 Eamon Duffy, *The Stripping of the Altars: Traditional Religion in England c. 1400– c. 1580* (New Haven: Yale University Press, 1992), 465–466.

2 *Nugae venales, sive, Thesaurus ridendi & jocandi* (1642), 16, sig. A8v.

3 Henry Estienne, *The stage of popish toyes conteining both tragicall and comicall partes: played by the Romishe roysters of former age* (1581), 13–14, sig. B3-B3v.

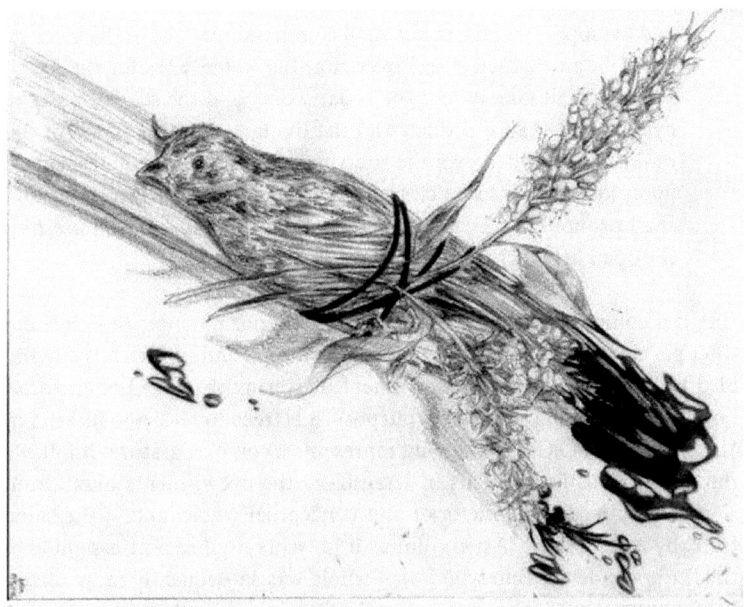

Figure 4. Julia O'Gara, "Aspergillum."

This uselessness makes the priest's error, for the Protestant, a metonymy (though for the Catholic, in contrast, it is a synecdoche). And since the association on which the metonymy is based is in error—since the aspergillum has no part at all in the Protestant liturgy—the materialization it represents imports the violence of sacrilege (abuse of the tool) only for the Catholic. It's as if Protestant women are free to use aspergilla as dildos if they like: doing so is simply finding a use for something useless, rather than abusing that which ought to be used otherwise.

What is interesting here, however, is that the aspergillum itself is, archaeologically speaking, built on a foundation of repurposed elements. This fact emerges clearly if we look at the aspergillum's original, which came to me as I present it here, by way of Julia O'Gara's recent drawing, entitled "Aspergillum" (Figure 4). The reference is to Leviticus 14, which presents "the law of the leper," including the process by which the leper, having been healed, is to be cleansed:

> 4 Then shall the priest command to take for him that is to be cleansed two birds alive *and* clean, and cedar wood, and scarlet,

and hyssop; 5 And the priest shall command that one of the birds be killed in an earthen vessel over running water: 6 As for the living bird, he shall take it, and the cedar wood, and the scarlet, and the hyssop, and shall dip them and the living bird in the blood of the bird *that was* killed over the running water: 7 And he shall sprinkle upon him that is to be cleansed from the leprosy seven times and shall pronounce him clean, and shall let the living bird loose into the open field. (KJV)

This is a complicated, hybrid device, consisting of no fewer than five distinct parts (two birds, wood, thread and hyssop), and in which the living bird becomes a part of the instrument delivering the blood of the dead bird, though, having served this purpose, it is freed to return to its kind in "the open field." O'Gara's drawing represents a complex gesture. It follows the instructions in Leviticus in assembling the five elements into a functional and functioning pictorial and conceptual whole; and at the same time, by calling itself "Aspergillum," it presents itself as a disassembly of the liturgical device into which that whole was subsequently rationalized. It makes us ask: in what sense does Leviticus 14 describe *a thing* (rather than, say, a bunch of things)? And, in what sense is this original of the aspergillum already a device or instrument? What the passage tells us how to construct seems to me to stand just at the edge of being a thing, a device, tool, or instrument. The functional nexus it represents is both structurally loose (susceptible of disassembly) and destined, in the fulfillment of its function, *to* disassembly. The release of the living bird represents the completion of the process the priest performs with its help; and if a tool must be useful, must be used, to be a tool, this one becomes a tool only in the moment of its disintegration. This is not the only tool that is used up in being used; you could call such tools devices or contraptions, but better perhaps to call them *contrivances* in order to show that they are jerry-rigged and precarious, and to remind us that their assembly always has disassembly and disintegration in mind.[4]

---

4   Despite not appearing until the early nineteenth century, "contraption" would also work well here, in emphasizing "ingenuity rather than effectiveness" (OED), and thus assembly rather than utility. "Contrivance" has the advantage, however, of appearing in English as early as 1599 (with its verb form much earlier), and also of suggesting etymologically an ingenuity that expresses itself in working with found objects, and beyond that with stirring things up (< It. *con*, with + Fr. *trouver*, to find < L. *turbare*, to disturb, stir up, wake up), as it were by repurposing them (OED). The

Figure 5. *Blade Tool for Easter* by Sarah Stengle. Photo: Cie Stroud, 2011.

Another way to approach the contrivance that becomes the aspergillum is to ask what's it good for? And when's it good for it? The answers—not much, and not for long—point toward two indices: usefulness and durability. As we have seen, when it becomes rationalized as an aspergillum it scores higher on both indices, both until and, in an altered sense, after the Reformation. But rationalization itself buries rather than eliminates its beginnings as a hybrid contrivance composed of disparate parts that have an unsettled relation to one another. It is as if these parts are not used to one another, and, as a result, they will talk. Here, for one thing, the dead bird, in its blood, is in conversation with the living bird, even if it's hard to tell what they're saying. (As we will see, Christian commentators were sure they knew what the conversation was about; but we can afford to understand less.) Consider in this connection Sarah Stengle's *Blade Tool for Easter* (Figure 5).[5] This is a very different tool, but the communicative

---

    air of fraudulence with which its use was associated is also relevant. But really the choice is not very important. As we'll see, for the aspergillum as an achieved form the best word is probably "utensil."

5 Sarah Katherine Stengle and Michael Joseph, *Useless Tools For Every Anxious Occasion* ([Clinton, NJ]: Hunterdon Art Museum, 2011), 9. I thank Stengle for generously permitting me to reproduce the *Blade Tool* here, and for many stimulating conversations about it.

ratio of end to end is similar: the knife-like end is in a formal *and functional* conversation with the tail-like end that it has already, or might even still, cut off.[6] In both it is as if it is the very idea of the tool to unsettle a separation of instrumentality and organic form. And, notwithstanding the sense, whatever it might be, in which it is "for Easter"—there is plenty of wit in just this "for"[7]—this tool wears on its sleeve its own uselessness in a way that the rationalized aspergillum managed to escape, though only until it took its place in the imagination of Protestant Englishmen, where if in one sense it remains very useful as a dildo, as in the joke from *Nugae venales*, in another it is the very essence of the criminal pointlessness of Catholic ritual.

In the *Blade Tool*, the wheel-set that provides the pivot on which the tool balances cites the expectation of both functionality and coherence, of which it is almost a burlesque: surely something with *wheels* can *do* something, and surely it must have a center, an armature around which its parts are organized into a meaningful whole. The *Blade Tool* is, in this sense, a meditation on the process exemplified in the conceptual assembly of the contraption of Leviticus 14 into a proper instrument in the form of the aspergillum. This process is reflected materially in two developments: first, reusability; and second, that *sine qua non* of the hand-tool, the emergence, unambiguously, of a handle end and a business end. This appears to have been complete very early on, and indeed, given the presence of the aspergillum (in its brush form) in religious ritual among the gentiles (it is to be seen on coins produced in first-century BC Rome, and surely it originated much earlier), one may ask whether, rather than constituting the original of the aspergillum, the contraption of Leviticus 14 is designed to *represent*, as it were to partially *reassemble*, something that already

---

6   In fact the end opposite the knife blade is Eastern European sambar antler, and specifically the tip of the antler discarded in the manufacturing of knife blanks (personal communication with Stengle). Horn-handled knives are in the best of circumstances bizarre things; but here, communication between the two ends of the tool is complicated by the fact that the horn end is and is not a handle to serve the blade end, as if each end is saying "fuck you" to the other.

7   The relation between the *Blade Tool* and Easter is actually intelligible, and in fact brings it even closer to the contraption of Leviticus as it is read typologically as figuring sacrifice and resurrection. But it would make more sense, if that's what we're after, to speak of Easter as being "for" the *Blade Tool*, rather than the other way round.

existed. In any case, Leviticus 14 participates in a network of scriptural passages with which the aspergillum, as an element of Christian liturgical practice, was directly connected. These are united by their mention of the hyssop plant, and in a sermon on Psalm 51.7 ("Purge me with Hyssope, and I shall be cleane; wash me, and I shall be whiter then snow"), Donne summons together Exodus 12.22 (hyssop used to mark the doors of the Israelites on the first Passover), John 19.29 (Jesus on the cross reached a sponge soaked in vinegar "*upon Hyssop*," possibly, Donne speculates, at the end of a stick of cedar), and Leviticus 14.[8] He calls the plant itself "that *Aspergillum*, that Blood-sprinckler"; and he is so preoccupied with the hyssop that he leaves the living bird out of Leviticus 14 entirely, even though it is his primary example: "In the cleansing of the Leper, there was to be the blood of a sparrow, and then Cedar wood, and scarlet lace, and Hyssop: And about that Cedar stick, they bound this Hyssop with this lace, and so made this instrument to sprinkle blood. And so the name of the *Hyssop*, because it did the principall office, was after given to the whole Instrument; all the sprinkler was called an *Hyssop*."[9]

Although Donne's reading is inevitably typological in a broad sense, his omission of the second bird in Leviticus 14 forecloses the typological account that was preferred almost universally by Protestant commentators. Predictably, and at least since Origen, the passage had been read as figuring the sacrifice and resurrection of Christ. As Henry Ainsworth, analogizing the scapegoat of Leviticus 16 to the birds of Leviticus 14, explains, "Because these two things [viz., Christ dead, Christ resurrected] could not be shadowed by any one Beast, which the Priest having killed could not make alive again and it was not fit that God should work miracles about Types; therefore he appointed two, that in the slain Beast his death might be represented; in the Live Beast his immortality. The like mystery was represented also in the two birds for the cleansing of the Leper."[10] Although there is no contradiction between the typological

---

8   John Donne, *LXXX Sermons* (1640), 645–46, sig. Iii6-Iii6v.

9   *LXXX Sermons*, sig. Iii6v. This appears to have been true, though the OED's only instance dates from 1838.

10 Henry Ainsworth, *Annotations upon the five books of Moses* (1627), 139, sig. Mm3. The tradition of reading the procedure and all elements of the contraption described in Leviticus 14 allegorically and typologically is already in place in Origen (early third century CE); see *Homilies on Leviticus*, trans. Gary Wayne Barkley (Washington, DC: Catholic University Press of America, 2010), Homily 8, esp. 168.

account of the contraption of Leviticus 14 and the idea that that contraption is a prototype of the aspergillum, the two may be said to represent parallel, rationalizing abstractions, and it is almost as if Donne has chosen one path rather than the other. The other path predominated among Protestant commentators, to the near total exclusion of the latter, and to the extent that the passage could be read as supplying a scriptural warrant for a liturgical instrument that had been rendered useless by the elimination of holy water, it's no surprise that this was the case. Perhaps it was owing to his Catholic background and complicated relation to Catholic theology that Donne is able to talk about the aspergillum without the contempt that was usual among Protestant commentators and poets alike.

Una's father "sprinkled" "holy water" in preparation for her marriage to the Red Crosse Knight (*The Faerie Queene* 1.12.37), and that seems to be a good thing; but it is otherwise with Hope, who comes between Fear and Dissemblance in the masque of Cupid in book 3: "She always smyld, and in her hand did hold / An holy water sprinkle, dipt in deowe, / With which she sprinckled fauours manifold, / On whom she list, and did great liking sheowe, / Great liking unto many, but true loue to feowe" (3.12.31).[11] Significantly, Una's father does not use a brush (that we hear of) to do his sprinkling. As in the dildo joke, it's the woman who is associated with the instrument. Hope does not *abuse* the aspergillum, because as we know, aspergilla are useless; she abuses those who trust in her. And her appropriation of the aspergillum for this new, useless purpose reminds us that it always *was* useless, and / or that it was in itself never more than an instrument *of* abuse.

Useful in being useless, or useless in being useful. The aspergillum exemplifies, in short, the "idle utensils" Marvell invokes in order to dismiss at a key moment in "Upon Appleton House": "But now away my hooks, my quills, / And angles, idle utensils. / The young Maria walks tonight: / Hide trifling youth thy pleasures slight" (649–652).[12] The phrase

---

11 Compare the emblem titled *"Aula"* (the court) in Henry Peacham's *Minerva Britanna* (1612), which depicts "Favour" holding aloft a holy water brush, "Where with her bountie round about she throwes, Faire promises, good words, and gallant shows," and dangling from the handle end of which is a "knot of guilded hookes," which Favour presumably uses to ensnare those who seek their fortunes at court (sig. Ff1–1v); the brush and hooks are assembled pictorially into a two-ended weapon of entrapment that also materializes the familiar contrast between fair appearance and concealed threat.

12 *The Poems of Andrew Marvell*, ed. Nigel Smith (London: Pearson, 2007).

has several distinct but related meanings: things useful in some useless pursuit (fishing or poetry, for example); things that have no use; things (utensils) found ineffectual in the performance of some task; and things (temporarily) not being used ("sitting idle"). It brings the useful and the useless together to produce a maximally evocative contradiction: a thing-fit-for-use (from Latin *utensilis*, useful) that is useless, a useful/useless thing. This paradox, hardly particular to the practice of literature, is nevertheless apt in relation to it, though, unexamined, the idea that literature's use lies in its uselessness takes us nowhere interesting; and it is perhaps central to Marvell's poetics specifically, a compact expression — coming as it does at the moment the speaker professes to stand aside when Maria Fairfax sweeps onto the scene — of the dialectic of pastoral retirement and political engagement encountered so often in his poems.

But the phrase "idle utensils" also looks back to the devotional and liturgical implements, including their "*Wooden Saints*" and "*Beads*" (250–254), with which the nuns make war against Isabel Thwaites' supposed rescuer, William Fairfax. In the seventeenth century, "utensil" was frequently used to refer to just such objects, particularly in the conventional pairing of "ornaments and utensils" to describe church furnishings. In particular, one nun "bolder" than the others, "stands at push / With their old holy-water brush," performing a repurposing I have elsewhere described as "tool abuse."[13] (One wonders about "old": is the brush old because it *will have been* old, that is, is old at the time the story is told? Has Marvell made it obsolete anticipatorily?) If they repurpose their holy water brush as if in resistance to its, and their own, imminent transformation into idle utensils, these particular nuns seem likely, in view of the eroticization of their attempts to ensnare Isabel Thwaites (lines 97–196), to have also had other uses for the aspergillum along the lines suggested in the *Nugae venales*; so that Marvell's poem is consistent with the latent anti-Catholicism of the representation of the holy water brush as an instrument of female seduction, as in Spenser and Peacham.

The nuns can only remobilize their idle utensils in a narrow and as it were strictly defensive context, but "bloody Thestylis" (lines 401–408) is equipped to undertake a more radical reactivation of the elements of the aspergillum. She is associated with the only death in the poem (that of a

---

13 Luke Wilson, "Renaissance Tool Abuse and the Legal History of the Sudden," in *Literature, Politics and Law in Renaissance England*, ed. Erica Sheen and Lorna Hutson (New York: Palgrave, 2005), 121–145.

rail killed by a mower), and her epithet marks her, despite her pastoral getup, as a disguised representation of Bellona, the goddess of war — so that, in a poem in which images of ablution are everywhere, it is reasonable enough to say that she represents the baptism in blood that was the civil wars. There's much, much more to Thestylis.[14] I propose to explain here only one thing, and that is the *structure* of Thestylis's encounter with the rails — of which there are *two*. Despite her reputation in the criticism as bloodthirsty, Thestylis herself, oddly enough, kills nothing. That she does not kill the first rail makes sense enough; that death is caused by the mower just because that's the kind of thing Marvell's mowers do. But that there is a second bird at all, that Thestylis comes upon it herself, and that it remains for the time being alive (though the poet mourns both birds, anticipatorily, at line 409) — all this is surely more mysterious. It puts her in the position of the Priest in Leviticus, bringing together the dead bird and the live one, which, though destined it would seem to end up in a stew with the first one, is alive when last we see it.

What this suggests, I think, is that Leviticus 14 is rattling around somewhere in Marvell's head. In weaponizing their holy water brush the nuns repurpose the aspergillum as if in anticipation of its obsolescence-to-come; they work forward, as it were, from its achieved structure.[15] Thestylis starts from the other end, beginning to reassemble the aspergillum out of the surrounding environment as if returning to Leviticus and working forward from there. She herself occupies a complicated position: she hails

---

14 Almost every critic who talks about "Upon Appleton House" talks about Thestylis, mostly in connection with her ostentatious breaking of the frame: "He called us Israelites" (406), she says of the poet, who has just described the mowers in that way. And of course she derives from Virgil's second *Eclogue* — her epithet "bloody" coming in, I propose, by way of Martial's epigram "Of Flaccus" (8.56), which supplies the novel expression "Thestylis rubris" (ruddy or sunburnt Thestylis); Marvell's apparent conversion of ruddy to bloody has not, as I far as I know, been noticed before.

15 Whether the nuns had a precedent for their idea that the aspergillum might be used as a weapon is unclear. At least from the late seventeenth century medieval weapons of certain designs were called "holy water sprinklers"; see for example John Guillim, *A Display of Heraldry* (1679), describing heraldic emblems that look like spiked balls: some think them "the heads of clubs called Holy-Water sprinkles; other suppose them to be balls of wild fire; I rather think them to be some murdering chain shot" (245). But how early this usage began, and whether it was strictly post-Reformation, or even later, I don't know. Many examples of these weapons are to been seen at http://pixgood.com/holy-water-sprinkler-weapon.html. For what it's worth, aspergilla themselves (not as weapons) seem to have been frequently depicted in heraldry.

from Virgil, she is among the crew of mowers Marvell calls Israelites, and she appears in a setting that is not only Christian but post-Catholic; one might say that she is idled and reactivated, at several levels, several times over. And her work of reassembly is and is destined to be radically incomplete: frozen, in the poem, at the moment at which assembly is about to cross paths with disintegration, that work reminds us that for the assembled elements (which are of course themselves incomplete) to become an aspergillum, even in its original, disassembled assembly, the second bird would have to fly free. And we can't have much confidence about that. If the two birds are to end up in the pot, as is certainly what Thestylis appears to have in mind, then the aspergillum that was to be, never was. Is there in this the dark suggestion that cleansing cannot, will not, never was going to, happen here? Not quite, though it's true that it doesn't look good. Perhaps it is closer to the small uncertainty that comes with the indefinite suspension of the soul of the narrator in "The Garden," which sits "like a bird" among the boughs, "till prepared for longer flight" (lines 52–55), a flight we don't see happen. There just isn't that much to go on. All we have is the living bird and the dead bird placed in conversation with one another across the person of Thestylis, who would be more like the priest of Leviticus 14, but also more like the wheel around which the ends of the *Blade Tool* organize themselves, if only she weren't about to dine on the second bird. And yet it makes a difference that she hasn't done so *yet*.

In 1642, John Shaw, pastor at Rotherham, preached at Selby, in Yorkshire, a few miles from Appleton House, on Leviticus 14. As we learn from the sermon's publication two years later, his audience included "Ferdinando, Lord Fairfax, General of the Northern Forces"—the father of the Thomas Fairfax who was Marvell's employer at Appleton House six years later.[16] His sermon, entitled *Two Clean Birds, or, The cleansing of the Leper*, did approximately the same typological work with Leviticus as others of his kind had done before. Even so the connection to Marvell, indirect as it is, is suggestive—though here all I suggest is that if what Marvell did with two clean birds was strange and mysterious in itself, the greater mystery is the scarlet threads that tied his birds to Shaw's.

---

16 John Shaw, *Two Clean Birds, or, the cleansing of the Leper* (1644), t.p.

Walking Tours
(Three Tracks)

Show and Tell
Drew Daniel

IT STARTED OUT WITH AN EXEMPLARY PEDAGOGICAL EXERCISE: "SHOW and tell." As a way to commence our seminar, we were all asked to bring objects to the SAA seminar room. Those writing essays were put to the challenge of somehow bringing their chosen object into the conference room, a task which proved quite simple for those who had selected tiny and compact objects and rather daunting, or loosely followed, in the case of those hunting larger, more elusive, legally touchy, or medically toxic objects. For the respondents, the task was far more open-ended: we could bring any object we wanted that might exemplify our own response to the open rubric of "objects and environs," itself an already capacious formulation.

Thinking ahead, I hatched a plan, did some internet sleuthing and, after some eBay auction combat, secured a truly unusual object which I duly placed on my shelf in preparation for the conference. But this plan foundered upon the rocks of my own distraction and professorial absent-mindedness, when the morning of the seminar dawned, and I reached into my bag in St. Louis and discovered, to my horror, that I had left my object behind in Baltimore at the exact location where it had rested since I pulled it out of its envelope: on my desk, beside the stereo. We are told by Graham Harman that objects are, at a fundamental metaphysical level, "withdrawn" (an assertion in Harman's work that seems to be more axiom than argument), but this was a more pressing and homely case of mere, but decisive, absence. Adjusting my necktie and hustling through the hotel corridor, I quickly came up with a Plan B. Since transcripts are not available, what follows is an inevitably unreliable and no doubt romanticized paraphrase of my remarks when the fatal hour struck and I was called upon to present my object for inspection.

I am holding in my fist a bezoar harvested from the innards of a Peruvian llama, which I have purchased on eBay. This is a gastrolith, a stone composed of hair, and as such it is an object, that is, a discrete, nameable entity that can be ostensibly indicated, shown, described, and, in this case, held in my hand. At another level, this object is an assemblage, insofar as it has a singular, expressive consistency but is composed out of sub-components: individual strands of hair pulled off the surface of a llama's body by its tongue and then swallowed and congealed by mysterious bonding agents in the stomach via a process I don't honestly know that much about, being neither a medical doctor nor a llama. Bezoars were thought in the medieval and early modern period to have powerful medicinal properties, and show up in medical receipts as part of the treatment for a variety of ailments, though by the time of Sir Thomas Browne's "Pseudodoxia Epidemica" they were beginning to come under increasingly skeptical scrutiny. Were I to show it to you, it would look small, and oddly nobbled on its shiny, mineral-esque surface. But I'm not showing it to you. You'll have to trust that I'm holding it in my hand, right here.

[brief pause, and then the hand is opened to reveal...nothing.]

In fact, my object was not a bezoar, a thing, an object in the material sense, but an epistemological object: namely, my object was a lie. I wasn't holding anything at all. Thus, my "object" was actually an epistemological relationship of trust and faith and deception, the bezoar-in-your-mind which I articulated through language and which you, if you did in fact believe me, ascribed to a location in space, but which I, in the very process of my articulating it, knew to be false. Insofar as the flat ontologies that have generated so much recent discussion pro and con seem to insist upon, at the level of the object, the equality of real mountains and imaginary mountains, it seemed apt that I avow and then undo the assertion of the ontic particularity of a particular bezoar. I did so in favor of a demonstration of the epistemological problems that attend encounters with language as it posits, and thus "realizes" at the level of linguistic objects, all manner of entities which both are and are not there (they are there as objects of reference, but not there as actually existing material things, other than the air vibrations moved when I falsely utter the sentence "I am holding a bezoar in my hand").

I did this not to be a jerk, and not because I enjoy tricking or deceiving people, but instead to instantiate the basic methodological problem that I regard as essential to the current state of discussion with regards to flat ontologies, object-oriented ontologies, speculative realist ontologies, and the ongoing critique of so-called "correlationism": ontology in these discussions tends to become valorized as a way of escaping or avoiding epistemological questions, which are regarded as passé or outmoded indications of an attachment to mind / world distinctions, but many of the claims about that ontology seem themselves to have unfinished business with the processes of criteria, verification, evidence and appearance that we associate with epistemology.

Or words to that effect. I don't have a transcript of my remarks, and they were probably far more digressive and rambling than that. Having confessed to this Stalinist revision of history, a few further caveats are worth pointing out: this everyday bit of deception does not in some way demonstrate that there is no way out of correllationism, nor does it show that attempting to undo the primacy of correllationism is not a worthy goal, nor does it demonstrate that there is no way out of language, nor does it demonstrate that there is no way out of the phenomenological encounter, nor does it invalidate the desire to re-situate discussion in terms of the robust reality of observer-independent physical realities that have preceded human beings and will survive them (i.e. the primordial arche-fossils of Quentin Meillassoux, or the futural zones of planetary extinction posited by astrophysics and theorized in their existential ramifications by Ray Brassier). I'm not kicking a stone (or imputing a gastrolith) and "refuting thus" a particular dogma, doctrine, or metaphysical stance.

In telling a lie about a bezoar, in crafting a bezoar-of-the-mind, I was simply practicing what we had gathered at the SAA to discuss in the first place: theater, a human practice of pretending, a practice at once enmeshed in material and physical realities and productively distorted by epistemologically fraught abysses between what we can see and hear and what we cannot access, verify or resolve about the capacity of language to exceed or distort those material and physical realities. To talk about "objects and environs" in a metaphysical seminar is to assess the systematic construction of claims about what has being, substance, or materiality. To talk about "objects and environs" in a literary critical setting is to consider and evaluate the borders of access and intelligibility posited by the templates of texts and the history of theatrical practices. But perhaps the latter can't fully proceed without drawing upon, learning from, but also perhaps productively distorting and betraying, the terms defined and set by the systems that are the purview of the former. That is, assessments of early modern drama have both a historical archive (say, Renaissance lore about bezoars as it shows up in particular texts) and an epistemological horizon which opens onto the virtual, the unreal, the hypothetical, the possibly false, the partly true, simply insofar as they are about literary language and its fictional constructions.

On to the nitty gritty of response. Reading these papers as a group under the organizing stance of object orientation, I am tempted to simply list in sequence the Latour Litany they already constitute: channels, ditches, waste-water, planks, bushes, a corpse, trick chairs, coral, hives, plague, a tomb. The litany gesture in ooo tends to function as a theoretical welcome mat, an inherently incongruous catalog whose self-differential open-ness constitutes itself a juicy demonstration of ooo as an inclusive metaphysical "come as you are" party that is rather similar to the ritual of "show and tell" with which we began. But this list, and by extension the network of smart, poised papers it compresses, also prompts me to consider the spectre that haunts object oriented approaches: relationality. Quite simply, the designation of an object as such is always in dialectical tension with the interactions, relations, processes, and practices that frame and surround it and, from at least some perspectives, merge with, create or support its existence.

So there's always a question of how one focuses and defines what counts as the object in the first place, and not one question but accordingly a litany of questions: Is the "channel" the object under discussion, or the water and sewage mixture it conveys, or the Marlovian dramatic re-use of that mixture? If a plank-form is just part of the shape-space of the body, then how many objects does the body contain in its mimetic repertoire? Are we talking about plants, genitals, or a literary effect of metaphorical linkage and coy interchangeability at the level of the signifier? Is coral a singular or plural entity? Are glass hives an object unto themselves or just one variant of hives? (and from the perspective of which species?) Are trick-chairs still chairs or are they actually something else? Are they traps? Can the plague function as a singular object in the first place, free of a complex historical back-projection? Rather than an object at all, might the plague not be an exemplary case of what Timothy Morton terms a "hyperobject," insofar as it is radically extended in space and time and thus non-localizable? If a Norwich tomb occasions a dense web of social relations, are we still discussing the tomb as an object or the affective webs and textual trails it induces as a topos in all senses of the term?

In all cases, the point is that the singularity or "withheld" ipseity of the object as a separable unit stands in danger of dissolving into, or merging with, the busy field of other actors, other things/agents/environs/factors upon the scene. This, to me, is A Good Thing. To some within ooo, such surroundings and co-stars are a wrapper to be ripped off as we rush to assert the core of "withholding" at the dark center of all objects as such. For others (and I am of this party), it's just a part of how assemblages get stacked inside other assemblages. The object/environ grounding loop is, in a sense, a version of the The One and The Many. To take us to a quotidian grocery level, consider the following question: is a carrot a single object? Yes, but. Without the environmental surround of the water/ground/air/nutrients/plant assemblage as a system, all of which must be in place for "carrotness" to happen, the singularity of a carrot as separable object can't, as it were, get off the ground.

The same could be said, of course, for Shakespeare as a disciplinary object, whose author-function is at present defined by the pedagogically guarded brightline of a canon that supposedly designates a distinct textual corpus. But Shakespeare is not an object we can profitably dislocate from his environs: the historical, political, textual, philosophical, religious, sexual surroundings that condition and co-create his own standing forth. Yet if ever there were a candidate for an object that withholds, that remains knottily withdrawn from our full comprehension, it's Shakespeare. For all of us who hope to work with objects, whether we are intrusively attempting to crack open their secrets or demurely ceding their withdrawal and recalcitrance, a basic question remains and pressurizes our work: where are the limits of an object? Does your object have temporal limits? When a corpse or a carrot rots? When a coral dies? When a joke or a trick chair has "sprung" upon its listeners and viewers? When you just can't hold yourself in a plank pose anymore? Does your object have conceptual limits, and if so, what are they? What did you have to leave out in order to sharpen your object's separateness, and what are the costs and benefits of those choices? These are the productive questions that linger when the fist unclenches and exposes the airy nothing that it once held fast.

OOO + HHH =
Zany, Interesting, and Cute

Julia Reinhard Lupton

MY FIRST VENTURE WITH PUNCTUM BOOKS AND THE DYNAMIC CIRCLE OF scholars associated with it began in March 2011, at the conference on "Animal, Vegetable, Mineral: Ethics and Objects in the Early Modern and Medieval Periods" hosted at George Washington University. The conference led to a volume of the same name, and my article "The Renaissance *Res Publica* of Furniture," remains one of my favorite pieces, in part because of the company it keeps with such an innovative group of collaborators. I am thrilled to rejoin the conversation in this volume, which brings together some of the same authors with other scholars investigating Shakespearean thing worlds.

My response scans these papers through the scrim of two triads of terms: the aesthetic categories *zany, interesting,* and *cute,* as established for our time by Sianne Ngai; and the methodological categories of *historicism, humanism,* and *hermeneutics*. At stake in the relation between OOO and HHH are the vectors of usage and forms of significance that bind objects to worlds, to actions, and to language, and the extent to which Shakespearean drama and its criticism accommodates, exhibits, and reflects upon the traffic patterns that constitute the real and theatrical life of persons and things.

POINTS OF ENTRY: ZANY, INTERESTING, AND CUTE?

I began my 2011 furniture essay with a consideration of Sianne Ngai's contemporary aesthetic categories, the zany, the interesting, and the cute. Ngai associates the *zany* with production and performance; the *interesting* with networks of information and exchange; and the *cute* with the allure of the object in relation to its consumption, which might also include its curation, exhibition or display.[1] Ngai's typology felt newly relevant to me as I read through the engaging essays assembled for this volume.

Ngai associates zaniness with the "politically ambiguous intersection between cultural and occupational performance, acting and service, playing and laboring."[2] It is the only category of the three that she explicitly derives from early modern theater, where the *zanni* of *commedia dell'arte* was "an itinerant servant, modeled after peasants forced by droughts, wars, or other crises to emigrate from the hills near Milan to Venice in search of temporary work."[3] In this volume, the zaniest essays are those that take up the kinetic assemblages formed by actors and objects in theatrical environments. Joanna Hoffman's delightful "Much Ado About Planking" uses a recent internet performance meme as a frame for considering the way in which "prop humor" forces actors to readjust their bodies in relation to the shifting affordances of the stage and the changing narrative conceits of the action. Patricia Cahill's trick chair is also zany in its emphasis on the mechanical and distributed nature of affect on stage. Karen Raber's "performing meats" are zany in their unexpected animism and uncanny entertainment value on the stage of the Renaissance banqueting table. Finally, Lindsey Row-Heyvald's reflections on disability and Tripthi Pillai's essay on shoes are zany in their analysis of action as both supported and diverted by prostheses that extend, configure, and contort the human body.

After the manic energy of the zany, the judgment that something is "merely interesting" may seem like a comedown, yet its link to conceptual seriousness, disciplinary knowledge, and the exchange of ideas makes it an apt category for understanding more antiquarian and scientific approaches to objects and environments in our period. "Interesting" as an aesthetic judgment is for Ngai "underpinned by a calm, it not necessarily weak, affective intensity whose minimalism is somehow understood to secure its link to ratiocinative cognition and to lubricate the formation of social ties."[4] Building on Isabelle Stengers, Ngai notes that in science,

---

1 Sianne Ngai, *Our Aesthetic Categories: Zany, Cute, Interesting* (Cambridge, MA: Harvard University Press, 2012).
2 Ngai, *Our Aesthetic Categories*, 183.
3 Ngai, *Our Aesthetic Categories*, 192.
4 Ngai, *Our Aesthetic Categories*, 113.

"'interesting' is what links or reticulates actors; it is not just an adjective but a verb for the action of associating."[5] Keith Botelho's hive is "interesting" in its systems-theory approach to the political life of bees and their role in early-modern gift economies. Neal Klomp's plague-object is also "interesting," insofar as pestilence is bound up with the life of the city, the economics of the theater, and the emergence of public health as the cornerstone of biopolitics.

Finally, the papers that home in on an object in its ontic mystery and affective allure are allied with what Ngai calls "the cute." Ngai associates the cute primarily with the modern commodity. Although the commodity is certainly emergent in Shakespeare's age, its mass-market smirk is still very far on the horizon. Sea-changes in religious affect, however, are perhaps more immediately relevant to the charm of small things in the period. The modern cute may be the late progeny of the "coy," "tender," and "delicate" remnants of political theology as they toddle, blush, flirt, and purr towards their disenchanted future. The paper that traces these processes most precisely is Luke Wilson's essay on the aspergillum, a liturgical instrument that changes purposes from Hebrew to Catholic to Protestant object regimes. Lizz Angello's bushes are "cute" in their low-lying, bunny-harboring, fur-evoking haptic halo. Sallie Anglin's corpses just might be said to be cute in their insistence that we "acknowledge the object as object." Sallie writes that the corpse makes me "acknowledge that my life is dependent on the body, but that the body is not dependent on the life." The allusion here is to Hamlet's enigmatic phrase, "the body is with the King, but the King is not with the body," and thus opens onto an immense political-theological region of sacral symbology on its way to miniaturization, satirization, and auratic repackaging, of which the modern cute is one instance.

Ngai's triad provides one way of mapping the territory of the early modern object and its environs implied by this rich collection of essays, which address theatrical settings for action (zany), environments as systems (very interesting indeed!), and objects caught in post-enchantment rehab (cute, in an uncanny, Early Modern kind of way). To deploy Ngai in this way risks anachronism, yet what distinguishes object-oriented criticism from the study of material culture is the willingness of these scholars to handle Renaissance things as portals between periods and not only as antiquarian traces of a lost age. Ngai's compelling consideration

---

5   Ngai, *Our Aesthetic Categories*, 114.

of hyper-contemporary aesthetic categories is itself exquisitely attuned to the origins of these affective lures in mixed sources and impulses that include early modern theater, science and domestic arts. Ngai's work combines descriptive liveliness and analytic acuity, integrating surface reading, close reading, and causal analysis—and so do the essays collected in this volume.

QUESTIONS THAT REMAIN: OOO VS. HHH

When I responded to these papers at the SAA, I asked some questions of the contributors that I had also been asking of myself. These concern OOO's relationship to *historicism*; to *humanism*; and to *hermeneutics*.

In the case of historicism, I'd suggest that although OOO appears to offer an alternative to historicism, in fact its impact has been to open new archives—texts and artefacts dealing with objects, animals, and locations—for literary investigation. As with prior forms of historicism, OOO essays sometimes build out the secret life of objects in the plays that are fascinating in their own right, but do not necessarily touch what remains most urgent, compelling, moving, or challenging for readers, audiences, and theater makers in their primary encounters with these works. In 2009, Christopher Warley characterized *Shakespeare Quarterly* as "country fair meets yard sale."[6] Has OOO intensified the clutter, or rather helped to organize it, providing new shelving systems that help connect objects to worlds in a manner that opens up questions that are not simply archival? In this regard, the challenge for OOO as I see it is to integrate the academic need to produce new knowledge with the aesthetic and philosophical imperative to encounter the truth of art.

A variant of the same question involves humanism. Drama concerns significant action and interaction among persons. Although drama may also use props, and always occurs within some kind of setting, even a minimal or virtual one, the centrality of significant speech and action is hard to dislodge from the core of Shakespearean theatrical experience. Post-dramatic experiments have taught us to reencounter the non-linguistic

---

6 Christopher Warley, "Michael Jackson: Never Can Say Goodbye," *Arcade*, August 27, 2009, accessed January 12, 2015, http://arcade.stanford.edu/blogs/michael-jackson-never-can-say-good-bye.

and non-human dimensions of all theater, but the Shakespearean corpus nonetheless harbors an investment in human action, consciousness, and experience at its core. (Just go to any rehearsal and see where the efforts collect.) Tzachi Zamir's *Acts: Theater, Philosophy, and the Performing Self*, Hannah Arendt's derivation of drama from *drān*, to act, and Alain Badiou's *Rhapsody for the Theater* are testaments to the role of human subjects in drama as an art form.[7] How do we balance our interest in objects and environments with our readings of plays as dramatic works that draw their life from the incorporate ensemble work of kingship, kinship, courtship, diplomacy, and statecraft as well as the ambivalent partnerships between truth and lie that constitute the inadvertent disclosures of person in life and art?

Finally, there is the question of hermeneutics. As professors of English, we are exegetes. What happens when we interpret objects and places instead of, or through, or with, words? The *objective turn* is a response to the *linguistic turn*, and as such an important corrective to the desire to textualize everything. At the same time, dramatic texts—above all the poetically demanding and compelling works of Shakespeare—are composed out of language, admittedly in tandem with the resources of embodiment, gesture, props, and architecture. Jennifer Waldron's reflections on metaphor for this volume have been highly helpful to me. Rather than opposing metaphors and things, she considers metaphor as a kind of a thing, a nonhuman tool that establishes "spaces and times for transfer between two domains." To describe metaphor as nonhuman may sound odd (don't human beings make metaphors? aren't we metaphor-making animals?), but Waldron's point is that by comparing unlike things, the metaphor is revealed as itself a thing, a tool for instituting alliances among unlikes that can alter how we perceive, understand, and act in and on a world that itself consists of the planned and unplanned networks of meaning and use among the items in it. She argues that metaphor's two poles interact bilaterally, not simply moving from the concrete plane of immediate experience to higher abstractions, but delivering new instances of ideation, attention and connectivity into the realm of the concrete from the alien plane of the tenor. Metaphor can be a cause of action, and not

---

7 Tzachi Zamir, *Acts: Theater, Philosophy, and the Performing Self* (Cambridge: Harvard: 2014); Alain Badiou, *Rhapsody for the Theate*, ed. and trans. Bruno Bosteels (London: Verso: 2013); Hannah Arendt, *The Human Condition* (Chicago: University of Chicago, 1957).

simply a means of representation, when it introduces new scenarios into a play, as is the case with Ovidian imagery in *Titus Andronicus*: "The process of transfer is itself the point—the two-way traffic between Lavinia and Philomel, body and book, gesture and written word."

A similar claim might be made for the traffic between the human and the nonhuman, language and the non-linguistic, and the historical and the phenomenological in Shakespearean drama—between OOO and HHH. In my evaluation, what object-oriented Shakespeare bids us attend to is a setting in which the fluid exchanges among persons (in their language-wielding, thought-provoking, memory-haunted, acknowledgment-hungry co-presence) and environments (in their object-rich, action-inviting, systems-sensitive vitality) is made to appear and resonate. Shakespeare's characters act in what theater theorist Temu Paaovlainen calls a "causal milieu" in which cognition, intentionality, and agency are shared by human and non-human actors on the stage, a stage whose craft consists of mediating between objects and settings on the one hand and the central actions and affective dynamics of the texts before us on the other.[8] This causal milieu of accidental affordances yields a humanism that is vulnerable and creaturely rather than triumphalist, pointing outwards towards the environment and upwards towards divinity as sources and reminders of human incompleteness. This creaturely humanism involves acknowledging our dependencies and exposures, which include not only our need for shelter and sustenance, but also for sociability and expression. In my current book project, I associate this creaturely humanism with dwelling, a bio-theo-architectural hybrid that combine domestic arts with linguistic and poetic ones in managing the myriad forms of making by which we find our way in the world. Combining OOO and HHH, Shakespeare's dramas of dwelling acknowledge human beings as creatures who depend on things (including divine things and last things) for their sense of duration as well as their survival, and who express those reliances by facing each other in intersubjective acts of avowal, care and benediction as well as conflict, curse, betrayal, and revolt.

---

8 Teemu Paavolainen, "From Props to Affordances," *Theatre Symposium* 18 (2010): 127. See also his book, *Theatre/Ecology/Cognition: Theorizing Performer-Object Interaction in Grotowski, Kantor, and Meyerhold* (Palgrave MacMillan 2012).

Remembering Premodern Environs

Vin Nardizzi

IN THE EARLY 1990S, ACTIVIST AND POET WENDELL BERRY CHARACTERized the popular use of the term "environment" as "utterly preposterous." The word, he says, "means that which surrounds, or encircles us; it means a world separate from ourselves, outside ourselves." In outlining how the "real state of things," which "is far more complex and intimate and interesting" than an anthropocentric term like "environment" allows, Berry generates a list: "The real names of the environment," he itemizes, "are the names of rivers and river valleys; creeks, ridges, and mountains; towns and cities; lakes, woodland, lanes, roads, creatures, and people."[1] Nearly contemporaneously, the philosopher Michel Serres also exhorted us to "forget the word *environment*." "If the soiled" and endangered "world" is what we mean when we employ the term, then we have it all wrong, Serres says: this use of the term "assumes that we humans are at the center of a system of nature." He instead proposes that "we...place things in the center and us at the periphery, or better still, things all around and us within them like parasites."[2] Like Timothy Morton's "Nature" (with a capital "N"), "environment," Berry and Serres indicate, seems to be "getting in the way" of environmental work and theory.[3] We would do well, then, to unlearn the term.

---

1   Wendell Berry, *Sex, Economy, Freedom, & Community* (New York: Pantheon Books, 1993), 34–35. I thank Jeffrey Jerome Cohen and Julian Yates for their insightful feedback on this response essay.
2   Michel Serres, *The Natural Contract*, trans. Elizabeth MacArthur and William Paulson (Ann Arbor: The University of Michigan Press, 2001), 33; emphasis in original.
3   Timothy Morton, *Ecology Without Nature: Rethinking Environmental Aesthetics* (Cambridge, MA: Harvard University Press, 2007), 1.

The leaders of the Shakespeare Association of America (SAA) seminar for which the essays gathered in this collection were first shared asked us to do no such thing. As the seminar description indicates, participants were prompted to query the making of false boundaries that create "a world separate from ourselves, outside ourselves" (Berry) and, of course, the necessary anthropocentrism of such endeavors (Serres). In "Object-Oriented Environs," Jeffrey Jerome Cohen and Julian Yates invited us to join a seminar that "stages a confluence of two important trends in critical theory: the environmental turn and object-oriented ontology (vibrant materialism, new materialism, speculative realism). These modes of inquiry move beyond anthropocentrism to examine nonhumans at every scale, their relations to each other, and the ethics of human enmeshment with a material world that possesses its own agency. How does our apprehension of the inhuman change when texts become laboratories for probing the liveliness, mystery, and autonomy of objects, in their alliances and in performance?"[4] In articulating these objectives, Cohen and Yates provocatively charged us to remember and to figure out what our "environs" were. One way that they did so was by asking us to get up on our feet and move around the venue. Our seminar leaders built into the schedule a perambulation of the conference space in an effort, I presume, to interrupt normal proceedings and to enact a quirky form of scholarly disobedience. What would happen to us — as individuals and as a collective — if we opened the closed doors of the room and put our seminar into motion? How would apprehending the "environs" of the SAA hotel, when most all other participants were tucked inside meeting rooms, inflect our conversations about "the liveliness, mystery, and autonomy of objects" when we returned to our seats?

As with most such experiments, people were game, although the result was a mixed bag. Eileen A. Joy and I decided in advance that we would lead the perambulation around the larger conference space, effectively tracing out the squared structure of the floor plan. In a fit of theatricality, I borrowed an object from a fellow seminar participant — a mask of Angelina Jolie — and, after affixing it to my face, led the group out of the seminar room and into the conference hallway. Our perambulation, of course, was halted by a door, the entrance to the kitchens that formed one full side of the square we were walking out. The impediment was enough to give some participants pause. Would we get into trouble with hotel security for

---

4   I quote the seminar description from the SAA *Bulletin* (June 2013), 6.

having crossed this threshold? Undeterred, a handful of participants followed Jolie into the kitchen area, and we had a pleasant encounter with an amused hotel worker who helped us find our way out of the labyrinthine space. Once we returned to the seminar room, after sharing a good laugh, we sat down and reinitiated scholarly conversation.

Was there a pedagogical point to the partial success—because partial buy-in—of the seminar participants' full perambulation? I hope so. I attempted to link our act of walking to one of the seminar's keywords, "environs." As its earliest recorded use in the *Oxford English Dictionary* witnesses, "perambulation" named in the early fifteenth century "the action or ceremony of officially walking round a territory (as a forest, manor, parish, etc.) to determine and record its boundaries, to preserve rights of possession, etc., or to confer a blessing." By the sixteenth century, it could describe "the action of walking through or around a place or space; a walk, a journey on foot."[5] Then as now, I emphasize the "round" and "around" associated with and enacted by "perambulation," since both are words that, again according to the OED, would have had a close relation to the prepositional use of "environ" ("Round; about") from the fourteenth to the sixteenth centuries.[6] In our goofy, possibly risky, walkabout at the SAA, then, we were literally circumscribing—that is, writing—with our feet an environment. This is an idea that I thought we needed to feel with our bodies because, on the basis of reviewing the seminar papers, it became clear to me that our collective employment of "environs" and "environment" was under-theorized in a way that "object-oriented" and that the objects themselves were not.

I focus my response on this topic because, although I think that, as a group, we have made great strides in remembering what "environment" and "environs" are in this collection, we could still theorize and historicize (and theorize by historicizing) the concept with more rigor. Let me be clear: I am challenging us all, and in no way is my challenge meant to be a critique of any individual associated with this publication, from chapter-writer to editor to respondent. The seminars at the SAA were enlightening, and the essays submitted for this volume open new vistas for research and teaching. The contributions gathered here are insightful and searching about the objects that they discuss, from shoes, to poisoned books, to tiny and invisible aids for seeing, to crutches, to stage corpses, to

---

5 "Perambulation, *n.*, 1.a, 3.a," OED.
6 "Environ, *prep.*," OED.

instruments of torture and ritual purification and sacrilegious bawdiness, to meat, to grease stains, to wish-lists, to beehives, to dogs, to be-plagued and planked human bodies, and so on. But still left unaddressed for me are these questions: What are the contours of a premodern environment, and how might the range of objects on display in these essays help us to describe them in a preliminary fashion?

One curious fact about the early history of the word "environment" is that, according to the OED, it enters the English language at the turn of the seventeenth century. Before then, the noun form in print circulation was "environ," which referred to the "range or extent within limits; compass."[7] The second curious fact about the word is *not* that it first appears in Philemon Holland's translation of Plutarch's *Morals* (1603) — "environ" enters English through French and so through an earlier act of translation — but that it appears in the plural form, "environments."[8] The third curious fact about the word is that, in the OED's definition, it means "the action of circumnavigating, encompassing, or surrounding something; the state of being encompassed or surrounded." The fourth curious fact in this story is that "environment" seems to disappear in print after 1603 and resurfaces again in 1727.

This concatenation of philological curiosities reminds me in some measure of Debapriya Sarkar's fabulous essay on early modern wish-lists. In her hands, "the wish-list [i]s a 'thing' that enabled early modern thinkers to curate new ways of interacting with their environs, both real and imagined. Wish-lists became instruments through which writers attempted to make intelligible a world that was fundamentally in flux, one in which new geographies were being discovered through travels and a new cosmology was displacing both earth and man from the center of the universe" (123). Fulfilling these wishes, as Sarkar observes in the context of Baconian science, required "factors and merchants [who went] everywhere in search of [the materials on which the intellect has to work]" (126). These "factors and merchants" could also be said to be participants in acts of environing, in creating environments, in its earliest circumnavigational sense, all in an effort to facilitate the accumulation and possession of the world's "things" — knowledge, objects, peoples, and properties. There is, I am suggesting, a philological relation between early European colonialism and *environment*alism that we could elaborate more fully.

---

7   "Environ, *n.*," OED.
8   "Environment, *n.*, 1," OED.

If it is the case, as Sarkar explains, that the wish-list was an "[attempt] to make intelligible a world that was fundamentally in flux" and that they are best understood, following Ian Bogost, as open-ended "provocations" to the production of knowledge (125), then I also wonder about the relation between such wished-for intelligibility and environment. More precisely, I wonder if an environment ever entirely circumscribes or surrounds, if it is, as a concept, inadequate to the task of describing what Wendell Berry calls the "real state of things." Is an "environment" in today's common parlance a distortion, a convenient un-truth that helps human beings cope with the disorientations of environmental reality, of Serres's mind-bending recasting of the environment as comprised of "things all around and us within them like parasites"? In this connection, Tara E. Pedersen's fantastic essay about Sir John Oglander, who testified to the "Blood that rained in the Isle of Wight" itemized in the catalogue for the cabinet of wonders established by the Tradescants, is illuminating (61). From Oglander's account books, Pedersen highlights one entry in which Oglander imagines his "Carracter" as a ghost (62) and another in which, "next to a listing of the cattle slaughtered on his estate in 1643," he remarks, "'I only knowe this, that I knowe nothing I cannot read eythor my selve, or other men, this world is Changed, and our Antipodes possesseth owr places'" (63). For Pedersen, these episodes are evidence of "the profound disorientation of a being who is uncertain about how to interpret the objects (including himself) that inhabit the world" (63). Does Oglander's autobiographical, nearly surrealist writings record an insight about the "real state of things" that acts of environing aim to stabilize?

In our own changing times, perhaps there is merit in embracing such disorientation. The geometrical impossibility (preposterousness?) of environing—that is, circling—the square floor plan of the SAA conference hotel might have been a collective step in the right direction. The experiment certainly reminded us that environments are unequally shared spaces: had we remained in the seminar room, ruminating together, the staff whose labour and work area were designed to remain invisible to us would have remained just so. The amused and helpful response we received is the most generous way to react to the weird encounter we—including Angelina Jolie—all shared in the kitchens, where our environments met.

About the Contributors

LIZZ ANGELLO responds to the call of things doing stuff in medieval poetry and early modern drama and is particularly interested in transcribing conversations between textual objects across the pleats in time and space. She teaches literature at the University of South Florida, St. Petersburg and is currently revising her dissertation, "Paradise Always Already Lost: Myth, Memory, and Matter in English Literature," for publication.

SALLIE ANGLIN is an Assistant Professor at Penn State Altoona. She has a PhD from the University of Mississippi and studied at the School of Criticism and Theory at Cornell. She has published essays on Thomas Middleton, Philip Sidney, queer ecology in popular culture, and alternative ecologies in early modern Romance. She is currently working on a book manuscript, *The Ecology of the Stage: Environment and Embodiment in Early Modern English Drama*.

KEITH M. BOTELHO is an Associate Professor of English at Kennesaw State University. His book, *Renaissance Earwitnesses: Rumor and Early Modern Masculinity* (Palgrave Macmillan), was published in 2009, and he is currently completing his second book, entitled *Little Beasts: Cultures of the Hive in Renaissance England*. He is also co-editing (with Joseph Campana) a book on insects in the early modern world, entitled *Lesser Living Creatures of the Renaissance*.

PATRICIA A. CAHILL is Associate Professor of English at Emory University. She is the author of *Unto the Breach: Martial Formations, Historical Trauma, and the Early Modern Stage* (Oxford University Press, 2008) and is currently completing *Shakespeare's Skins: Surface Encounters in Early Modern Playhouses*, a study of the eco-material valences of skin-related language, costumes, and stage properties.

ABOUT THE CONTRIBUTORS

JEFFREY JEROME COHEN is Professor of English and Director of Institute for Medieval & Early Modern Studies at George Washington University. He blogs at www.inthemedievalmiddle.com and his most recent book is *Stone: An Ecology of the Inhuman* (University of Minnesota Press, 2015). A full bio may be found at jeffreyjeromecohen.net. His other punctum projects include *Animal, Vegetable, Mineral: Ethics and Objects*; *Inhuman Nature*; and *Burn After Reading*.

DREW DANIEL is Associate Professor in the Department of English at Johns Hopkins University. In addition to numerous articles on Renaissance literature, political philosophy, contemporary aesthetics, sexuality studies, and musical subcultures, he is the author of *20 Jazz Funk Greats* (Continuum, 2008) and *The Melancholy Assemblage: Affect and Epistemology in the English Renaissance* (Fordham, 2013). He is currently working on a book on suicide and politics. He is also one half of the electronic duo Matmos, whose forthcoming album *Ultimate Care II* is made entirely out of the sounds of a washing machine.

CHRISTINE HOFFMANN is an Assistant Professor in the English department at West Virginia University, where she specializes in early modern English literature and the rhetoric and ethics of social media. Drawing comparisons between the Renaissance period and the twenty-first century has allowed her to write and publish essays that put together Milton and memes, queerness and copia, Spenserian allegory and humble-bragging, Shakespearean comedy and negative campaigning, early modern melancholy and twenty-first-century public shaming. She is at work on a book that examines copia as a posthumanist project.

NEAL ROBERT KLOMP is a PhD Candidate in the Department of English at Michigan State University. His dissertation, "Plagued Subjects: Political Culture in Crisis in Early Modern English Drama," attempts to plague the political culture found within the literature of the period. Neal's interest in zombies began with a general curiosity about the relationship between the historical plague and this popular fictional genre dealing with the catastrophic outbreak of some strange disease—this is the "classic" zombie narrative. As represented in this essay, he has found the connection of plague and zombie to be quite fruitful intellectually as well as a popular pedagogical tool for rethinking some of the courses he teaches.

ABOUT THE CONTRIBUTORS

JULIA REINHARD LUPTON is professor of English and Comparative Literature at the University of California, Irvine and the author or co-author of four books on Shakespeare. She is a former Guggenheim Fellow and a Trustee of the Shakespeare Association of America. She is finishing a book entitled *Shakespeare Dwelling: Habitation, Hospitality, Design.*

VIN NARDIZZI is Associate Professor of English at the University of British Columbia. He has published *Wooden Os: Shakespeare's Theatres and England's Trees* (University of Toronto Press, 2013), which was shortlisted for the 2013 Theatre Book Prize. He is working on a new book project called *Vaster Than Empires: Growth, Vegetables, and Poetry*. With Stephen Guy-Bray and Will Stockton, he co-edited *Queer Renaissance Historiography: Backward Gaze* (Ashgate, 2009) and, with Jean E. Feerick, *The Indistinct Human in Renaissance Literature* (Palgrave Macmillan, 2012).

TARA E. PEDERSEN is Assistant Professor of English at the University of Wisconsin-Parkside. Her research focuses on how literature participates in constructing categories of knowledge, with a special emphasis on categories related to sexuality, gender, and the boundaries of the human. She has published in *Early Modern Women: An Interdisciplinary Journal* and is a contributor in *Mapping Gendered Routes and Spaces in the Early Modern World*. Her book, *Mermaids and the Production of Knowledge in Early Modern England* (Ashgate), examines epistemological questions about embodiment and perception in early modern theatrical culture.

TRIPTHI PILLAI is an Assistant Professor of Renaissance literature at Coastal Carolina University. Her recent work includes an essay on violent cuteness in Marlowe's drama and Bollywood cinema, a co-authored book chapter on autopoietic and allopoietic remediations of *Macbeth* in *Serena*, and a co-authored screenplay on queer migrant identity. Pillai is working on a monograph on Renaissance temporalities and also on a collaborative media installation project on "item" songs.

KAREN RABER is Professor of English at the University of Mississippi. She has published numerous essays on early modern women writers, gender, animals, and ecology, and is series editor for Routledge's "Perspectives on the Non-Human in Literature and Culture." Her most recent monograph is *Animal Bodies, Renaissance Culture* (University of Pennsylvania Press,

2013) and she is currently working on a monograph to be called *Animals at the Table: Making Meat in the Early Modern World.*

PAULINE REID works as an Assistant Teaching Professor at the University of Denver's Writing Program. Her research focuses on early modern literature and rhetorical history, and she has published and forthcoming articles in *LIT: Literature Interpretation Theory, Word and Image,* and *Rhetorica.* She is revising a larger project, *A Dark Glass: Vision, Rhetoric, and the Problem of Perception in the English Renaissance Book,* which is under advanced contract at the University of Toronto Press. This study explores the relationship between visual phenomenology and early modern print.

EMILY RENDEK is a PhD Candidate at the University of South Carolina. Her dissertation, "Bound Bodies: Book Use and the Early Modern Reader, 1450–1660," investigates early modern reading practices and argues that books are a form of prosthesis — use demonstrates that readers viewed printed texts as extensions of their own bodies. Her research interests include book history, bibliography, and early modern drama. She has taught courses such as Writing about Children's Fantasy Literature, Writing about Shakespearean Adaptations, Monsters in British Literature, and Revenge in British Literature. Before beginning her PhD at USC, Emily received her master's from Florida State University and her bachelor's from the University of West Florida.

LINDSEY ROW-HEYVELD specializes in early modern drama and disability studies. Her work has appeared in *Disability Studies Quarterly, Allegorica,* PEDAGOGY, and the first major collection on early modern disability, *Disabling the Renaissance: Recovering Early Modern Disability* (Ohio State University Press, 2013). She is currently at work on a monograph, *Dissembling Disability in Early Modern England,* which explores fraudulent disability on and off the stage. She is Assistant Professor of English at Luther College in Decorah, Iowa.

DEBAPRIYA SARKAR is an Assistant Professor of English at Hendrix College. Her work appears in *Exemplaria: A Journal of Theory in Medieval & Renaissance Studies* and in *Macbeth: The State of Play* (Bloomsbury Arden Shakespeare, 2014). She is currently working on a book project that investigates the intersections between literary and scientific thought in early modern England; it argues that ideas of possibility shaped new methods of knowing both natural and imaginative worlds. Her research and teaching interests include sixteenth- and seventeenth-century literature, poetry and poetics, theories of genre, medieval and early modern women writers, and the history and philosophy of science.

A recent graduate of the University of Georgia, PAULINE REID works as a lecturer at the University of Denver's Writing Program, where she teaches first-year writing courses on topics such as this quarter's "Visual and Material Rhetoric" and next quarter's "Cultures of Collection." She researches early modern literature, as well as rhetorical history and theory. Her book project in progress, tentatively titled *A Dark Glass: Vision, Rhetoric, and the Problem of Perception in the English Renaissance Book*, explores the intersection of visual phenomenology and book history in early modern print.

ROB WAKEMAN is a PhD Candidate at the University of Maryland. His research focuses on the changing status of animals from farm to fork in English drama of the long sixteenth century. His dissertation is a literary history of four meals: city comedy's representation of London's festival fast food, pastoral dramas shepherds' meals, Shakespeare's hunting luncheons, and Noah's banquet on Mount Ararat.

JENNIFER WALDRON is Associate Professor of English and Director of the Program in Medieval and Renaissance Studies at the University of Pittsburgh. She has published articles on early modern embodiment, post-Reformation theatre, and Shakespeare. She is the author of *Reformations of the Body: Idolatry, Sacrifice, and Early Modern Theatre* (2013). Her current book project, titled "Shakespeare, Language, and Sensation," makes a case for the importance of cross-modal sensory and linguistic effects in Shakespearean theatre.

LUKE WILSON is Associate Professor of English at Ohio State University. He is author of *Theaters of Intention: Drama and the Law in Early Modern England*, and has published articles on a variety of topics in *Representations*, *ELH*, *Renaissance Drama*, and elsewhere.

ABOUT THE CONTRIBUTORS

JULIAN YATES is Professor of English and Material Culture Studies at University of Delaware. He is the author of *Error, Misuse, Failure: Object Lessons from the English Renaissance* (University of Minnesota Press, 2003), which was a finalist for the MLA Best First Book Prize; *What's the Worst Thing You Can Do to Shakespeare?* (Palgrave Macmillan, 2013), co-authored with Richard Burt; and *The Multispecies Impression*, forthcoming from the University of Minnesota Press.

www.ingramcontent.com/pod-product-compliance
Lightning Source LLC
Chambersburg PA
CBHW071741150426
43191CB00010B/1650